About Island Press

Since 1984, the nonprofit Island Press has been stimulating, shaping, and communicating the ideas that are essential for solving environmental problems worldwide. With more than 800 titles in print and some 40 new releases each year, we are the nation's leading publisher on environmental issues. We identify innovative thinkers and emerging trends in the environmental field. We work with world-renowned experts and authors to develop cross-disciplinary solutions to environmental challenges.

Island Press designs and implements coordinated book publication campaigns in order to communicate our critical messages in print, in person, and online using the latest technologies, programs, and the media. Our goal: to reach targeted audiences—scientists, policymakers, environmental advocates, the media, and concerned citizens—who can and will take action to protect the plants and animals that enrich our world, the ecosystems we need to survive, the water we drink, and the air we breathe.

Island Press gratefully acknowledges the support of its work by the Agua Fund, Inc., The Margaret A. Cargill Foundation, Betsy and Jesse Fink Foundation, The William and Flora Hewlett Foundation, The Kresge Foundation, The Forrest and Frances Lattner Foundation, The Andrew W. Mellon Foundation, The Curtis and Edith Munson Foundation, The Overbrook Foundation, The David and Lucile Packard Foundation, The Summit Foundation, Trust for Architectural Easements, The Winslow Foundation, and other generous donors.

The opinions expressed in this book are those of the author(s) and do not necessarily reflect the views of our donors.

Seven Rules for Sustainable Communities

Seven Rules for Sustainable Communities

Design Strategies for the Post-Carbon World

◆

Patrick M. Condon

ISLANDPRESS

Washington | Covelo | London

ISLAND PRESS is a trademark of the Center for Resource Economics.

Library of Congress Cataloging-in-Publication Data

Condon, Patrick M.
  Seven rules for sustainable communities : design strategies for the post-carbon world / Patrick Condon.
    p. cm.
  Includes bibliographical references and index.
  ISBN-13: 978-1-59726-650-5 (cloth : alk. paper)
  ISBN-10: 1-59726-650-7 (cloth : alk. paper)
  ISBN-13: 978-1-59726-665-9 (pbk. : alk. paper)
  ISBN-10: 1-59726-665-5 (pbk. : alk. paper) 1. Sustainable living. 2. Sustainable development. I. Title.
  GF78.C66 2010
  307—dc22

                                                                                          2009034920

Printed on recycled, acid-free paper

✹

Manufactured in the United States of America
10 9 8 7 6 5 4 3 2 1

Keywords: Climate change; Sustainable communities; transit-oriented development; urban policy and planning; walkable communities; urban design

Design and typesetting: Karen Wenk
Font: Dante

This book is dedicated to my son, William, whose childhood concerns about global warming launched this effort, and to my daughter, Kate, who—now in her twenties—knows that climate change matters to her too. To both of you I dedicate this book.

Contents

Foreword

It is now official government policy in both Washington, D.C., and Ottawa that the United States and Canada must reduce greenhouse gas production by 80 percent by 2050. Until now, public debate on strategies to achieve this goal has focused on cap and trade programs to reduce power plant emissions. Others are promoting alternative energy technologies: just build windmills, or vast photovoltaic arrays, or new energy-efficient cars, say the promoters of these technologies, and everything will be fine. But in the face of an expected 150 million North Americans by 2050—a third more than the current population—even these innovations will merely slow the rate of growth in greenhouse gas production.

For this reason, an equally important contribution must come from transforming North America's cities and metropolitan regions into places that strike a new balance between their human inhabitants and the planet's air and water systems. This will mean building more compact, energy-efficient, and pedestrian- and transit-friendly regions, with green infrastructure systems that reduce resource consumption and pollution of all kinds.

Eighty percent of Americans and Canadians live in metropolitan areas, and these places produce an equal amount of the continent's greenhouse gases. Current decentralized, automobile-based patterns of development helped make North Americans the biggest generators of greenhouse gases in the world per capita. For this reason, transitioning to less land- and energy-consuming patterns of development will be crucial to reducing overall carbon production. Cities and regions, not national governments, will play the leading role in achieving these goals. This book shows how changes in the design of our cities and metropolitan areas can achieve dramatic reductions in carbon emissions while improving livability and competitiveness and at the same time reducing the cost of building and maintaining infrastructure systems.

For more than a decade, Professor Condon has used his own hometown, Vancouver, as a virtual laboratory to demonstrate the new green designs of buildings, neighborhoods, infrastructure, and transportation networks that will become the building blocks for achieving national and global climate goals. In this book, he describes these demonstrations and similar interventions in other North American cities, and how these experiments can be brought to scale.

Condon's plans have demonstrated a renewed understanding of the city and how it can operate more efficiently. Not since the time of the streetcar have we gotten this right. This generation of designers, planners, elected officials and, most importantly, citizens must act—and soon—to turn our urban regions away from ever greater per capita demands for materials and energy and toward something closer to what the earth can handle.

This book attempts to clarify in simple language what such a world might look like and how it might emerge organically from the one we have. It is an attempt to comprehend the basic architecture of our cities and to suggest a simple set of rules aimed at preparing them for a low-carbon future. It sets forth seven simple rules that operate at all scales, from the parcel to the region. In this important book, Professor Condon offers a vision of a green and sustainable future for our cities and regions, and indeed the whole planet, and details the steps needed to take us there.

Robert D. Yaro
President, Regional Plan Association, and Professor of Practice, University of Pennsylvania

CHAPTER 1

Introduction

Figure 1.1. Icebergs floating in Jokulsarlon Lagoon, Iceland. One hundred years ago, this lagoon did not' exist; it was under one hundred feet of glacial ice. (Credit: Deborah Benbrook, iStock)

In 2002, scientists sounded the alarm about the loss of ice on the Arctic Ocean. Global warming was affecting the arctic climate more rapidly than anyone had previously thought possible. They predicted that if nothing was done to curb the level of greenhouse gas (GHG) pouring into the atmosphere there might be no summer ice covering the North Pole by 2050. Early in 2009, they updated their projection. Given the rate of ice loss, the new date by which the Arctic Circle will be ice free could be as soon as 2012. The loss of ice triggers other effects, none of them good. The white ice that once reflected warming sun rays no longer does so. The deep blue ocean water that takes its place absorbs those rays, warming the water and further accelerating the warming of the planet. Bad things happen in threes. The added heat also releases methane gas that was previously trapped under polar ice. Methane gas, like carbon dioxide (CO_2), traps heat in the atmosphere, but molecule per molecule it is many times more damaging. The cascading effects of climate change, previously predicted for the distant future, are already here.

Experts at the United Nations–sponsored Intergovernmental Panel on Climate Change (IPCC) all agree that the two-degree-Celsius rise in global temperature, the so-called "safe" level of warming that we will still get even if we cut GHG emissions by 80 percent, is a rise that is unavoidable. The IPCC predicts that, even at this "safe" temperature increase, up to 50 percent of the planet's species will become extinct. But we are on a path where GHG produced from the burning of fossil fuels is not dropping but increasing rapidly. With a five-degree rise, much more would be lost. Former U.S. vice president Al Gore, when seated before a U.S. Senate hearing on climate change held in January 2009, was asked if a five-degree rise in global temperature would "end life as we know it". "No, Senator," he replied, "people will survive in some form, but likely all of our institutions would collapse and billions would die."

What have all of these gloomy scenarios to do with a book on city design? Everything. If we change the way cities are built and retrofitted, we can prevent the blackest of the nightmare scenarios from becoming real and can create the conditions for a livable life for our children and grandchildren. It is not apocalyptic to say we can save their lives.

Normally, GHG production is described by sector. We often read that buildings account for about half of all GHG production; transportation, for about 25 percent; and industry, for most of the rest.[1] But this division obscures a fundamental point: cities are responsible for 80 percent of all GHG—caused by the way we build and arrange our buildings, by all the stuff we put in them, and by how we move from one building to the next. Since the problem is caused by cities, the solution should be there too.[2]

Citizens and their elected officials have been slow to acknowledge the connection between GHG and urban form. This book may help change that. It is written for designers, policy makers, developers, regulators, and ordinary citizens in the hope that it will arm them with an understanding of the ways our cities are failing and offer them very specific actions to cure them.

Figure 1.2. Sprawl outside of Calgary, Alberta. (Credit: Micycle, Flickr.com)

HOW DID CITIES GET THIS SICK?

In any journey, it helps to start with a look back from where we once came. Various historical starting points could be studied, but the end of World War II marks the time after which cities changed the most. Many compelling reasons drove the crucial choices we made at that time; foremost among these was the need for a place to live.

After World War II, a variety of policy inducements provoked a massive redistribution of population across metropolitan landscapes. In the United States, the mortgage interest income tax deduction, low interest GI loans, restricting new mortgages through bank "red lining" of older residential areas, and the 1956 National Interstate and Defense Highways Act,

[1]U.S. Environmental Protection Agency, "U.S. Greenhouse Gas Inventory Report (1990–2007)" (2009), http://epa.gov/climatechange/emissions/usinventoryreport.html (accessed July 20, 2009).

[2]Kevin R. Gurney, Daniel L. Mendoza, YuYu Zhou, Marc L. Fischer, Chris C. Miller, Sarath Geethakumar, and Stephane De La Rue Du Can, "High Resolution Fossil Fuel Combustion CO2 Emission Fluxes for the United States," *Environmental Science and Technology* (forthcoming).

[3]As U.S. and Canadian populations moved outward from the central cities, urbanized population density dropped dramatically. In the United States, population density in urbanized areas fell from 3,175 persons per square mile in 1960 to 2,900 persons per square mile in 2006 (Demographia, 2006). A similar pattern can be seen in Canada, where the urbanized population density dropped from 6,803 persons per square mile in 1960 to 4,000 persons per square mile in 2006 (Demographia, 2006).

[4]Historically, the rate of decentralization in Canada was most pronounced between 1941 and 1961 and again between 1966 and 1971, coinciding with major expansions of highway construction in metropolitan Canada (Edmonston, Goldberg, and Mercer, 1985). Clearly, a number of factors are influencing growth and development patterns in cities (see Burchfield et al., 2006; Ellis, 2001); however, there is little doubt of the significant role highway construction has on expanding boundaries and decreasing density in metropolitan areas (Handy, 1993). Interstate highways transformed urban America by opening up the peripheries of cities for development and facilitating the blending of communities along their corridors (Milner, 2007).

[5]Transit ridership is lowest in the suburbs, where low population densities make reliable service difficult. This is illustrated by the difference between auto-oriented areas of the Vancouver, British Columbia, metropolitan region, such as Surrey and Langley, where the transit ridership is 4.4 percent and 1.2 percent of all trips, respectively, and streetcar neighborhoods of Vancouver, where the transit ridership is 20.1 percent (GVTA, 2005).

[6]In the United States, families spent an average of 3.1 percent of their household expenditures on transportation in 1918; by 1950, this number had risen to 13.8 percent (Johnson and Tan, 2001). In 2001, households spent 21 percent of all household expenditures on transportation (U.S. Department of Transportation, 2003). Personal expenditures (meaning all pretax dollars made) on transportation climbed as high as 12.7 percent in 2000 but have since dropped, to 11.3 percent in 2008 (Research and Innovative Technology Administration, 2009). Between 1995 and 2006, average household transportation expenditures rose from $6,361 to $8,508 (in 2006 dollars) (U.S. Department of Transportation, 2008). Bernstein, Makarewicz, and McCarty (2005) found that lower-income households generally spend proportionally more than the national average on transportation; however, regions that have invested in public transportation are not being hit as hard, even as gasoline prices are rising. Lipman (2006) found that when many working families move far from work to find affordable housing, they end up spending their savings on transportation; by moving twelve to fifteen miles, the increase in transportation costs outweighs the savings on housing.

[7]In both U.S. and Canadian cities, commuting distance is increasing. Between 1969 and 2001, commuting distance in the United States increased from 9.4 miles (15.12 km) to 12.11 miles (19.48 km), while in Canada the commuting distance increased from 4.34 miles (7.0 km) to 4.47 miles (7.2 km) between 1996 and 2001 (Statistics Canada, 2003). In the United States, this increase in commuting distance was greatest between 1983 and 1990, with a jump from 8.54 miles (13.75km) to 10.65 miles (17.15 km) (Hu, 2004). The average commuting time in the United States increased from 22.4 minutes in 1990 to 25.1 minutes in 2007 (McGurkin and Srinivasan, 2003; U.S. Census Bureau, 2007). In Canada, travel time increased from 27 minutes in 1992 to 31.5 minutes in 2005 (Statistics Canada, 2005).

which funded the construction of the interstate highway system, were most significant.[3] Provoked by these inducements, middle-class and working-class families who had traditionally occupied higher density walkable and transit-served neighborhoods fled to much lower density and car-dependent suburbs.[4] Average densities began to fall in every North American metropolitan area, while transit ridership as a percentage of all trips began to fall with it. Older, prewar parts of the metropolitan landscape still maintained healthy transit ridership, but transit use in newer areas was near zero.[5]

As North Americans moved from transit to cars, their per capita GHG amounts began to rise too. Of course, no one worried. GHG production was not important at that time, as the implications of this increase were not widely known and were even less widely accepted. Buying fuel for the family car was also not a concern, as prices were low.[6] The brand-new high-speed freeways provided previously unimaginable freedom of motion, allowing workers to hold jobs twenty-five or more miles from home.[7] This was a massive change that fundamentally altered the reach of cities. In 1950, the Boston metropolitan urbanized area was only 345 square miles. In 2000, it sprawled over 1,736 square miles, a quintupling in only five decades (U.S. Census Bureau, 2000a).

During this period of dramatic metropolitan expansion, land was generally less expensive on the peripheries. This made it profitable to build residential developments ever farther away from the metropolitan center, with single-family homes generally dropping in price as one moved farther out. This concentric reduction in house prices gave rise to the saying "drive till you qualify," a widely used phrase meaning that home buyers were induced to push a home search farther and farther from the center of the region until their income matched the qualification requirements for the mortgage.

With so much unprecedented freedom of movement in this new urban landscape, house price became much more important than location. A distant job was easy to reach, and shopping centers catering to millions of auto nomads were soon to come. Eventually, vast stretches of the metropolitan landscape become completely car dependent, forcing individuals and families to spend more and more time behind the wheel and to rack up ever increasing vehicle-miles traveled (VMT).

The new single-family homes were not only auto dependent but, because of their shape and exposure to the elements, also inherently hard to heat. We now know that the GHG production of this style of home is up to four times greater per capita than that of home types common to older center cities.[8]

Not only price but school quality strongly influenced location decision. Here, newer communities had a distinct advantage over older ones. Newly developing areas had new schools, whereas older areas had older schools that were populated by children from families without the economic resources to follow the migration and that were located in cities hampered by declining property values to fund them adequately. Of course, the new schools were sprawling one-story buildings that were impossible to reach on foot, requiring expensive fleets of carbon-producing buses to ferry children back and forth.[9]

Unquestionably, this new low-density and car-dependent development pattern successfully supplied millions of new housing units at prices that North Americans could afford. This success has led many to claim that sprawling urban areas are more affordable than those with metropolitan growth controls. For example, for decades well-financed lobbying groups have attacked Oregon's growth controls, in force since 1974, on this ground, even though Portland's housing costs are lower than other similar-sized western U.S. communities, such as San Diego, Seattle, San Francisco, and Sacramento—all metropolitan areas with no such laws.[10] Thus, the claim that low density is more affordable than higher density cannot be credible.[11] This is especially true when transportation costs are considered. The more sprawling the metropolitan area is, the higher the percentage of family budget devoted to auto use. When these additional costs are factored in, the "affordable" house in a third-ring suburb is not nearly so affordable, a fact made sadly obvious when in 2008 the combination of sky-high gas prices and the mortgage meltdown led to the virtual abandonment of many subdivisions in third ring suburbs.

Low-density sprawl also costs much more per dwelling unit to service than does higher density development. A subdivision of single-family and duplex units on 2,800- to 3,300-square-foot lots can be serviced for 75 percent less per dwelling unit than can single-family homes on larger lots of 8,000 to 9,000 square feet. The cost of providing streets and utilities to a new

Figure 1.3. An aerial view of Levittown, New York, in 1948, shortly after completion. (Credit: Associated Press)

[8]Jonathan Norman, Heather L. McLean, and Christopher A Kennedy, "Comparing High and Low Residential Density: Life-cycle Analysis of Energy Use and Greenhouse Gas Emissions," *Journal of Urban Planning and Development* (March 2006): 10–21.

[9]In 2005–2006, more than 25 million children enrolled in public school K–12 were bused to school at public expense. During the same period, the United States spent $18.9 billion on school bus transportation at an average cost of $746 per student transported. This is up from $198 per student transported in 1980-81 (National Center for Education Statistics, 2009).

[10]In 1973, the Oregon legislature enacted landmark state planning legislation called Senate Bill 100, under which cities and counties implement zoning at the local level subject to state oversight. The central policy of Oregon's land use planning program is curbing urban sprawl (Oregon Coastal Zone Management Association, 2008). A copy of the bill can be accessed online at http://www.oregon.gov/LCD/docs/bills/sb100.pdf.

[11]Patrick Condon and Jacqueline M. Teed, *Alternative Development Standards for Sustainable Communities: Design Workbook*, James Taylor Chair in Landscape and Livable Environments (1998), http://www.jtc.sala.ubc.ca/projects/ADS.html.

home can be substantial. Each home requires a certain amount of paved street, storm drains, and utilities before it can be occupied. At lower densities, the cost of providing required streets and services can be over $100,000 per dwelling unit.[12] Home buyers are seldom aware of this cost, which is always buried in the cost of the home purchase, and thus do not know that streets and pipes can account for over 20 percent of the purchase price. This cost can make the difference between a home that is affordable and one that is not. When houses are built at higher densities, they are closer together. Thus, the length of roadway and utilities required to get from one house to the next is reduced as lot sizes shrink. If a lot holds two dwelling units, then the cost for servicing each dwelling unit is cut by half again. The land component of the house cost will also be proportionately less as density increases, since the cost of an acre of land can be recouped on the sale of more houses.[13]

SEPARATION BY CLASS AND INCOME

The "drive till you qualify" concentric rings of increasing affordability discussed above do not capture the whole story. After World War II, a second, finer-grain distinction emerged, particularly noticeable in metropolitan landscapes made up of dozens of quite small, formerly rural communities, such as Boston's. Whether by accident or intent, formerly rural towns now part of Boston's suburban ring adopted zoning policies that narrowed the income range of new residents.[14] Towns that allowed subdivisions made up of lots of one eighth, one quarter, or one half acre attracted middle-class and lower-middle-class home buyers. Towns that allowed only large lots of two, four, or five acres per dwelling unit attracted only upper-income earners. Land in towns with the large lots was quickly used up (it only takes 122 houses at 1 house per five acres to consume a square mile of land). Exclusive zoning increased the average number of VMT as home buyers, unable to afford homes in the low-density communities near where they worked, could only buy homes in distant communities and make long daily commutes. In many cases, these low-density communities went so far as to exclude any new commercial development to serve new residents, leaving it to neighboring

[12]Homes built at one dwelling unit per five acres would require more than two hundred feet of roadway to serve each one. Assuming standard suburban infrastructure of underground services for all utilities, curb and gutter road designs, and storm systems designed to deliver the one-hundred-year storm, the cost per lot could easily exceed this amount.

[13]Housing prices are determined by a host of interacting factors, such as the price of land, the supply and types of housing, the demand for housing, and the amount of residential choice and mobility in the area (Nelson et al., 2002). Urban growth boundaries can affect land values, but their effects on housing affordability remain in dispute. Research done in Portland shows that growth in housing prices can be attributed more to increased housing demand, increased employment, and rising incomes than urban growth boundaries (Phillips, 2000). Traditional zoning and land use regulations often place greater limits on the supply and accessibility of affordable housing (for example, low-density-only designations, minimum housing size, and bans against attached or cluster homes) (Nelson et al., 2002).

[14]Davidoff (2005) found that the Boston metropolitan statistical area is heavily income sorted by jurisdiction and that housing quality and extra-governmental amenities play a large part in this process. Boston's suburbs show a large range in both median home price and household income. Newton has the highest median home price, at $438,400 (in 1999 dollars), compared with Lawrence at $114,100. The highest median household income, at $141,818, is found in Dover, while the lowest, at $27,983, is found in Lawrence (U.S. Census Bureau, 2000a).

Figure 1.4. Boston area context map.

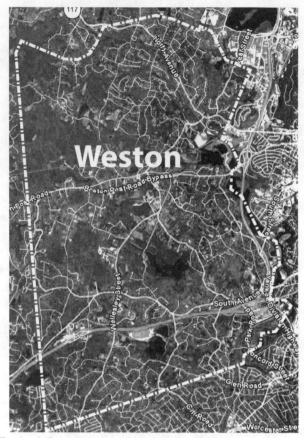

Figure 1.5. Weston, Massachusetts, has excellent access to free-ways and commuter rail, but the population density remains low.

communities to supply supermarkets and other shops, further increasing the need to drive.

THE PROBLEM EMERGES

The cracks in the system began to emerge after the 1974 "oil shock," a supply constraint caused when the OPEC (Organization of the Petroleum Exporting Countries) nations cut off the flow of oil to the West. Spending long hours in line for gas exposed the weakness of the economy to interruptions in the flow of imported oil, by now a clearly vital resource. At first the response was significant, provoking a shift away from larger cars and a lowering of speed limits to save fuel. But over the longer term, the lesson went unlearned. Dependence on imported oil has increased dramatically in the intervening decades, and average fuel consumption per capita has risen sharply and steadily, only reaching a plateau in 2007. Also unfortunate: scientists who began loudly sounding the alarm about global warming at this time were largely ignored, and with the election in the United States of Ronald Reagan, a man who had no interest in energy conservation, the moment was lost. During the 1980s and 1990s, suburban low-density development moved the United States from being a country where most of its residents lived in former streetcar-served districts, where alternatives to the car were possible, to one where the majority of residents lived in districts that were completely auto dependent.[15]

Rather than put in place national, state, and regional poli-

[15]According to the U.S. Census Bureau (2000a), 21 percent of the total U.S. population lived in central cities in 1910 while only 7 percent lived in suburbs. From 1910 to 1930, population increased rapidly in both central cities and suburbs; however, after 1940, suburbs accounted for more population growth than did central cities, and by 1960 the proportion of total U.S. population living in the suburbs (31 percent) almost equaled the proportion living in central cities (32 percent). From 1940 to 2000, the proportion of the total U.S. population (urban, suburban, and rural) living in central cities remained relatively stable (ranging from 30 to 32.8 percent) while the proportion living in suburbs continued to grow steadily, finally reaching the 50 percent mark in 2000.

Figure 1.6. Leapfrog sprawl at the exurban fringe north of Atlanta transforms former rural roads into dangerous arterials.

cies to reverse or at least mitigate an ever rising per capita use of fuel for the single passenger automobile, the reverse occurred. U.S. transportation bills from the 1970s through the 1990s favored expanding the interstates and feeder highways over transit; no policy proposals to require walking-distance access to transit and commercial services in new districts were ever seriously considered. Canada fared somewhat better. The Canadian federal government was happy to collect a substantial gas tax but, unlike the U.S. government, was under no obligation to return it to the provinces in the form of highway funds. Thus, Canadian cities have far fewer freeway miles per capita than do U.S. cities.[16]

Absent any national, state, and provincial policies, average densities in metropolitan regions continued to drop until at least the year 2000. Exceptions were few, with Vancouver, British Columbia, and Portland, Oregon, notable among them. More numerous were the extreme examples of centrifugal forces pushing population to peripheries, impelled by vast new highway expenditures, even where regional population was stable. Detroit and St. Louis are two instructive examples. Unabated freeway construction even absent significant population increase has left many neighborhoods in older center cities of St. Louis and Detroit virtually abandoned; both cities lost two thirds of their population to the suburbs during that period.[17]

Current aerial photos of a once-attractive single-family-home neighborhood in Detroit show urban blocks with all but one or two houses razed (figure 1.7). The same population that

Figure 1.7. These urban blocks in Detroit were once filled with homes. More than two thirds have been demolished.

[16]Transportation plans from the 1920s and 1930s show simpler designs with less capacity and lower speeds than those eventually built; they were meant to facilitate a multimodal system, were often connected to adjacent land uses, and were tied closely to existing roads. Ambitious planning goals in the 1920s and 1930s—including rejuvenating communities, reducing congestion, preserving central business districts, and improving public transit—suffered dramatically when the depression brought a severe drop in property tax revenue and, with it, urban road and highway finance (Taylor, 2000). After WWII, state departments and federal transportation boards took control from cities and implemented their own agendas focused around moving people long distances quickly rather than supporting local communities (Taylor, 2000; Brown, 2005).

[17]Birch (2005) found that between 1970 and 2000 the cities with the largest decreases in central city populations were St. Louis, Missouri (52 percent decrease); Columbus, Ohio (52 percent decrease); Columbus, Georgia (46 percent decrease); and Detroit, Michigan (46 percent decrease). Many experts attribute growth away from central cities in part to the building of the highway system in the United States (Berry and Dahmann, 1977; Chi, 2006; Goldberg and Mercer,1980). In Canada, Saskatoon and Regina exemplify this "doughnut hole effect," but in a less extreme way. According to the 2001 Canadian census, Saskatoon's core population grew by 1.6 percent while its surrounding area grew by 14.6 percent; Regina's core declined by 1.2 percent while its surrounding area increased by 10 percent (Statistics Canada, 2001).

once lived there has since spread out over a landscape four times its original size. Now an urban population that prior to World War II lived almost entirely in walkable, transit-served communities mostly lives in auto-dependent, low-density districts.

Infinitely Increasing Car Dependence

All of these forces combined to create an entirely new U.S. and Canadian urban landscape. Many thoughtful voices argue that this is a good landscape where families can find a house they can afford with a yard for the kids in a community of their own choosing. This is a strong argument, but one that can be sustained only if we are willing to forever increase the percentage of national treasures we commit to highway construction, the amount of personal wealth we pour into the gas pump, and the amount of carbon we pour into the atmosphere.

The trends are not hopeful. Per capita driving has increased alarmingly for decades, and until 2008, when fuel costs leapt briefly to over four dollars per gallon, was increasingly inelastic (meaning not responsive to market signals, such as increased fuel price).[18] For most people, driving is no longer a discretionary expense. They cannot just shift to walking or taking mass transit in auto-dependent landscapes; there are no sidewalks to walk on, there are no walkable destinations to walk to, and for all intents and purposes there are no buses to catch. Absent a practical way to shift to alternative modes, residents in auto-dependent landscapes can economize only by cutting discretionary car trips, forcing families to give up the leisure or social activities they once enjoyed to preserve precious fuel for trips to work. Much of the 2008 drop in VMT seems a consequence of such sad choices.

Auto-dominated landscapes have forced families to devote ever larger shares of their income to transportation, a share that now, for the first time in history, approaches the share consigned to paying for a home. Whereas in 1965 most families owned one car, now two cars is the norm.[19] The increase in two-income households has contributed strongly to this trend. The two incomes needed to pay off the mortgage on the home can be maintained only if both workers have a car

[18]Turcotte (2008) shows that the proportion of people age 18 and older who went everywhere by car rose from 68 percent in 1992 to 74 percent in 2005 while the proportion of Canadians who made at least one trip by bicycle or on foot declined from 26 percent in 1992 to 19 percent in 2005. In low-density neighborhoods, more than 80 percent of residents made at least one trip by car per day while less than half of the people living in very high-density neighborhoods did so (Turcotte, 2008). Dependence on automobiles differs considerably among census metropolitan areas, especially because of housing density (Turcotte, 2008). In Canada, the Montreal metropolitan region has the lowest percentage of people making all their trips by car (65 percent), and only 4 percent of dwellings in Montreal's central neighborhoods were single-family detached homes (Turcotte, 2008). In the United States, the number of miles driven every year per capita rose by 151 percent between 1977 and 2001 (Polzin, 2006).

[19]In both Canada and the United States, the number of vehicles per capita has been steadily increasing since the 1950s (Schimek, 1996). By 2007, there were 247 million motor vehicles in the United States, 42 million more than the number of drivers (Federal Highway Administration, 2007).

Figure 1.8. Sprawl pattern at Interstate 285 and Georgia Route 400 north of Atlanta. All trips include at least one arterial, and walking is by the longest possible routes.

[20]For many people, the suburban home is little more than a place to sleep, eat a meal or two, and store personal belongings; most of their waking hours are spent elsewhere, at work or school or in recreation (Gurstein, 2001). This leaves people who work from home, especially those with young children, particularly isolated. Because the majority of people in their age group work outside of the community, the streets and other public spaces where passive social interaction would normally occur are empty and therefore ineffective places for socializing (Gurstein, 2001). Similarly, suburban teenagers suffer from the lack of active and passive participation in street life. Neighborhoods separated from their main streets and from one another in highly disconnected street networks deter walking (Barnett, 1995) and create a street environment often devoid of life. As depicted in a *New York Times* article, a growing number of suburbanites are suffering from the isolation and lack of social contact in suburban communities (Rogers, 2006).

[21]Ewing et al. (2003) found that residents of sprawling counties were likely to walk less during leisure time, to weigh more, and to exhibit more hypertension than residents of compact communities. Frank et al. (2004) found that land use mix had the strongest association with obesity and that each quartile increase was associated with a 12.2 percent reduction in the likelihood of obesity. Their study also found that each additional hour spent in a car per day was associated with a 6 percent increase in the likelihood of obesity, while each additional kilometer walked per day was associated with a 4.8 percent reduction in the likelihood of obesity. Papas et al. (2007) reviewed the literature on built environment and obesity between 1966 and 2007 and found that 84 percent of the sources reported a statistically significant positive association between some aspect of the built environment and obesity.

to get to work. Dropping children at daycare and driving older children to otherwise inaccessible schools makes a car even more indispensable.

But it's not just "bread winners" who need a car. Everyone of driving age needs one. To be without a car in these landscapes imprisons one in the home, leading to a craving for escape with a car as the means. But in this case, escape does not mean freedom.[20]

Health Effects

A landscape where walking is impossible is a landscape where our legs are used only to get from the couch to the refrigerator and from the front door to the driveway. Residents of auto-oriented suburbs walk less and weigh more than people in walkable areas. While direct causation is difficult to definitively ascribe, the evidence is highly suggestive. The body is designed primarily for walking. If walking is systematically denied by one's environment, this cannot be a good thing. Many studies suggest that the epidemic increase in teenage obesity and alarming rise in juvenile-onset diabetes can be at least partly ascribed to the physically paralyzing influence of auto-oriented landscapes.[21]

Spending and Spending to Stay in One Place

For all of these reasons, a system that had the capacity to accommodate the family car trips of thirty years ago, when these trips were half their current level, now utterly fails. The limited-access highway system and its corollary, the development of auto-dependent sprawl, generate ever greater demand for travel. Families are driving twice as much not because they like to but because they have to. All of this "induced demand" (the cause-and-effect- relationship between adding highway capacity and changes in driver behavior and land uses that quickly eat up that capacity) leads inevitably to paralyzing congestion. We should have seen this failure coming. To get the system back, even temporarily, to the efficiencies of thirty years ago would require a doubling of highway lanes per square mile in most metropolitan areas a proposition that most metropolitan regions have understandably resisted.[22]

But even if we could double the amount of national treasure committed to such an enterprise, the dream cannot become real.[23] The space demands of the car are such that in many sprawling metropolitan areas there are ten parking spaces scattered around the region for every car. That's an acre of land for every fifteen cars, not counting the roads, garages, driveways, and freeways they also demand. In the city of Sacramento, California, for example, more than 35 percent of all city land is paved for car use.[24] As auto dependence increases, the percentage of land required to keep the system flowing smoothly increases steadily even beyond 35 percent to absurd heights. Many metropolitan areas are in danger of being consumed by roadways and parking lots while worthy destinations to drive to and from become increasingly rare.

Climate Change

Thirty percent of the world's carbon dioxide production comes from the United States and Canada, where only about 6 percent of the world's people live. Of this amount, about a quarter comes directly from transportation—and the bulk of that from single-passenger automobiles. This number does not include the CO_2 consequences of the immense infrastructure of car manufacturing and support or the CO_2 production from building the roads and highways all those cars need (concrete production is the largest single industrial producer of climate change gas, with most concrete in North America used for highway and bridge construction).[25] Factoring in those amounts brings the CO_2 share for transportation closer to 40 percent (Gagnon, 2006).

The community of nations is finally agreeing that planetary meltdown can be avoided only if we cut climate change gases by 80 percent by 2050. The United States and Canada, who have heretofore been the most reluctant of the G8 nations to acknowledge the crisis, have now agreed. During a period when the United States alone will add 130 million more people, it is madness to assume an 85 to 90 percent per capita reduction can

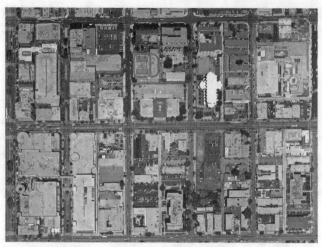

Figure 1.9. This photograph shows the extent of paved area typical in Los Angeles, California.

[22]Between 1989 and 2003, Houston invested around a billion dollars annually in highway improvements, resulting in significant progress in relieving traffic congestion, far above that of most other metropolitan areas in the United States (Cervero, 2003, p. 159).

[23]The national funds dedicated to transportation are already significant. In 2007, the total value of transportation-related goods and services purchased by consumers, businesses, and government (including vehicles, fuel, and the construction, maintenance, and administration of infrastructures) in the United States reached $1.469 trillion and accounted for 10.6 percent of the national gross domestic product (U.S. Department of Transportation).

[24]Litman (2008) found that given two to three off-street parking spaces per capita there would be approximately one thousand square feet of parking pavement per capita and two thousand square feet of urban land devoted to paved roads and parking per capita. In Canada, this is about three times the amount of land devoted to home rooftops (Litman, 2008). Another study, led by Bryan Pijanowski from Purdue University, surveyed the total area devoted to parking in a midsize midwestern county and found that parking spaces outnumbered resident drivers three to one and outnumbered resident families eleven to one (Main, 2007). In 2005, freeway lane-miles per square mile in London was 0.58; Paris and New York were similar, with 1.52 and 1.50, respectively; and Los Angeles had 2.57 (Demographia, 2005).

[25]In 2006, the U.S. transportation sector's GHG emissions from fossil fuel combustion totaled 1,856 teragrams of carbon dioxide equivalents (TgCO2 Eq.), accounting for 26.3 percent of the total GHG emissions in the United States (U.S. Environmental Protection Agency (EPA), 2008). This estimate did not include vehicle, fuel, or infrastructure life-cycle emissions, such as the extraction and processing of raw materials, the production of fuel, and infrastructure construction and maintenance. The total life-cycle emissions for the transportation sector (not including emissions from the construction and maintenance of transportation infrastructure) are estimated to be 27 to 34 percent higher than direct fuel

be achieved unless we reverse the trend toward ever greater auto dependence. Misplaced faith in such technological quick fixes as hydrogen cars, electric cars, or switching to ethanol will not help us. Changing to alternative energy sources will do nothing to change the fundamental entropy of our transportation choices; many other sources require huge energy inputs in their creation, lead to food scarcity in developing countries, and in the case of corn-based ethanol require more petroleum to make the fertilizer, drive the farm equipment, and truck the raw materials here and there than they give back in fuel.[26]

REASONS FOR HOPE

At this point, the problem may seem too big to solve. But all is not lost. As Robert Yaro, president of the Regional Plan Association of New York, says: "The bad news is that we have massively overbuilt the freeway system. The good news is that we have massively overbuilt the freeway system." By the first part of this sardonic aphorism, he means that America has overinvested in a system that has, in the absence of any other land use planning controls, made a sprawling and highly inefficient urban landscape inevitable, as the excessive transportation demands that this infrastructure unleashes became impossible to satisfy. By the second part, he means that the exact system that unleashed these forces is large and extensive enough to accommodate through infill the expected massive increases in population. If a way could be found to increase the land use intensity of all of the districts within the freeway service area to double or triple their present level (and surely, given the low coverage by buildings, such a thing should be easily possible), then per capita demand for long-distance travel should gradually drop as well. When land use intensity increases, alternatives to the car become possible, allowing a gradual mode shift to transit, walking, and biking. What this suggests is that the retrofit and intensification of the North American suburb is both a strong possibility and a means to address the three linked sustainability problems of the city: our damaging cycle of ever increasing car use, our increasingly unaffordable infrastructure maintenance costs, and the larger global crisis of climate change (Nelson, 2004).

---

combustion emissions (EPA, 2003). Emissions associated with the construction and maintenance of transportation infrastructure have yet to be studied in depth, but CO_2 emissions from the chemical process of cement production are the second-largest source of industrial CO_2 emissions in the United States, at 45.7 TgCO2 Eq. (EPA 2008). According to the World Business Council for Sustainable Development (2002), only 50 percent of the CO_2 emissions resulting from the production of cement come from this chemical process; 40 percent are from the combustion of fossil fuel for energy and are not included in the GHG inventory for the cement industry. Taking the chemical, combustion, and energy emissions into account, Worrel et al. (2001) estimate that the cement industry is responsible for 5 percent of global anthropomorphic CO_2 emissions.

[26]Ethanol has higher total energy use than gasoline primarily because of the large amount of process energy consumed in ethanol plants and the significant energy loses accrued during the conversion of corn or cellulosic biomass to ethanol (Wang, Wu, and Huo, 2007). Searchinger et al. (2008), found that "corn-based ethanol, instead of producing a 20 percent savings [in greenhouse gas emissions], nearly doubles greenhouse gas emissions over 30 years and increases greenhouse gases for 167 years" (p. 1238). In addition, as global energy prices jumped in 2007, the value of corn as an energy source skyrocketed (Blythe, 2007). This in turn had impacts on the price of corn for the food industry and for feeding livestock, such as pigs and chickens. Any diversion of land from food or feed production to production of energy biomass will influence food prices from the start, as both compete for the same inputs (Doornbosch and Steenblik, 2007).

Fortunately, in many areas this infill is already under way. According to the U.S. Census Bureau, the year 2000 marked the first time in fifty years that the average density of metropolitan areas increased. This is not just because young professionals are flocking to high-density warehouse districts; the shift is much more systemic than that. The five-room ranch house of the 1950s, a 1,200-square-foot home on a 20,000-square-foot lot is now a thing of the past. Now, the 3,500-square-foot home on the 5,000-square-foot lot is much more the norm.[27] While these puffed-up houses on smaller lots are decried by many, they represent a huge shift in the market to a density that is at least conceivably compatible with walkable and transit-served communities. This trend is most advanced in the greater Vancouver region, where between 1986 and 2001 the percentage of residents living in compact, transit-friendly neighborhoods increased from 46 percent to 62 percent.[28] Also, the city of Vancouver is now North America's most successful example of center city densification. In the ten years between 1990 and 2000, the population of the downtown peninsula increased from forty thousand to eighty thousand. During that same time, the total number of car trips into and out of the downtown actually decreased, while average commute times in the region dropped by six minutes (Vancouver was the only Canadian city where commute times went down during this period, a period where no additional freeway miles were added but during which population increased by over 20 percent).[29]

And there is more. Center city urban infill projects have been very successful in this decade, notably in Portland's "Pearl District." Three decades spent maintaining Portland's compact metropolitan region, often against the weight of tremendous political and industry opposition, have helped the city avoid the crippling shift of property value from center city to sprawling suburbs, a shift that has killed other cities, including Detroit and St. Louis. By controlling the amount of suburban land available for development and by limiting freeway construction, Portland has successfully protected inner-city property values, making reinvestment in that city's former warehouse district possible. What, sadly, is now inconceivable in Detroit or St Louis is an accepted fact in Portland: there is a strong market for center city high-density housing even in relatively small cities. Young professionals are willing to invest up to $500 per square foot for an

[27]Looking at neighborhoods of varying age in five study areas (Maricopa County, Arizona; Orange County, Florida; Minneapolis–St. Paul, Minnesota; Montgomery County, Maryland; and Portland, Oregon), Knaap and Song. (2004) found that lot sizes rose between 1940 and 1970 and then fell continuously, reaching an all-time low in 2000. Smith (2003) found similar trends in Las Vegas, where the average lot size for a new home fell 500 square feet in the previous two years. In 2001, only 13 percent of new residential lots in Las Vegas were smaller than 4,000 square feet; however, in 2003 this number had doubled to 26 percent (Smith, 2003). In 1976, the median lot size of new one-family American houses was 10,125 square feet but fell to 8,854 in 2008 (U.S. Census Bureau, 2008). The U.S. census shows a decrease in the density of urbanized areas in the United States from 3,052 people per square mile in 1990 to 2,300 in 2009 (Demographia, 2009).

[28]Sightline Institute and Smart Growth BC, "Sprawl and Smart Growth in Greater Vancouver: A Comparison of Vancouver, British Columbia, with Seattle, Washington," http://www.sightline.org/research/sprawl/res_pubs/sprawl_smart_van.

[29]Nationally, the average time spent commuting to and from work in Canada increased between 1992 and 2005 from 54 minutes to 63 minutes. In contrast, residents of the Vancouver region spent less time on average getting to work in 2005 than they did in 1992 (Turcotte, 2008).

Figure 1.10. The Pearl District, in Portland, Oregon.

urban lifestyle, if past decisions have left any urban life to enjoy. Significantly, these values have stayed relatively strong despite the 2008 global market meltdown when compared with the more precipitous declines experienced in newer second- and third-ring suburbs in more sprawling metropolitan areas.[30]

The success of Vancouver, echoed later by Portland and increasingly in other cities, including San Francisco, Washington, D.C., and Toronto, give reason for hope. Efforts to infill, complete, and re-urbanize the metropolitan landscape are possible and indeed seem to be compatible with current market demand.

So while the symptoms of the disease are most certainly debilitating, and while the disease is itself life threatening, there are signs that the patient is capable of responding. As in so many other things, there first has to be a desire for change, and this desire is now apparent. The first step in recovery is always admitting that there is a problem and then taking responsibility for change. But proven therapies for restoring the health of a region are required. Citizens are justifiably insecure about how and what to change. Changing the way we build regions is like changing any habitual behavior. Habitual behaviors, such as drinking, smoking, or taking drugs, anesthetize us in the near term but lead to larger problems in the long term. Building sustainable regions is the same. NIMBYism in the face of higher density development proposals is tremendously satisfying for citizens who understandably feel they have protected their community through their opposition. But the long-term effect of these actions, multiplied by many thousands of other equally habitual actions, is to worsen the disease. A set of principles—

[30]Cities are reviving at the end of the twenty-first century and surviving a recession that has been much harsher for other parts of the landscape (Dougherty, 2009). In many parts of the United States, suburban developments are decaying quickly. In Charlotte, North Carolina, the ten areas with the highest number of foreclosures are suburban areas filled with starter-home subdivisions (Chandler and Mellnik, 2007). House prices in the urban sprawl of Ashburn, Virginia, fell 50 percent between August 2005 and April 2008, while inside the city of Washington, D.C., the median home prices rose 3.5% between 2007 and 2008 (Schalch, 2008). According to David Goldberg of Smart Growth America: "Philadelphia was losing downtown housing and in-town housing until very recently. And now that's the hottest part of their market" (Schalch, 2008). In general, neighborhoods with the shortest commutes are faring better than places with long drives into the city (Schalch, 2008). The evidence suggests that cities are big enough and diverse enough that they are able to survive these ups and downs in the economy much better than their suburban counterparts (Dougherty, 2009).

(a)

(b)

Figure 1.11. These two photographs show the dramatic change in the skyline of Vancouver,' British Columbia, between (a) 1978 and (b) 2003.

call them rules for healing cities, if you will—is a necessary tool for recovery.

Over the years, many others have recognized this same thing. The list of simple rules, or "steps to recovery," that forms the core of this book is not original. What is unique to this book is the attempt to simplify and order them clearly as a set of integrated urban design therapies for healing the urban landscape. The hope is to provide citizens and leaders in the public and private sector with a simple but credible framework for action. What follows then is a listing of the rules, followed by a short explanation that introduces and anticipates the seven additional chapters, which explain them in much greater detail.

SEVEN RULES FOR SUSTAINABLE, LOW-CARBON COMMUNITIES

1. Restore the streetcar city.

   The North American city was and is a streetcar city. Streetcar cities are characterized by easy access to transit, a wide variety of house types, and services and job sites very close at hand—the exact elements of a sustainable city. We have largely ignored this fact. It needs rediscovering.

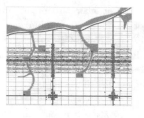

2. Design an interconnected street system.

   Fine-grain interconnected street networks ensure that all trips are as short as possible, disperse congestion, and are compatible with walking, biking, and transit.

3. Locate commercial services, frequent transit, and schools within a five-minute walk.

   People will walk if there is something to walk to. The most important walking destinations are the corner store and a transit stop. A minimum gross density of ten dwelling units per acre is required for this to work.

4. Locate good jobs close to affordable homes.

   The trend toward ever larger commute distances for workers must be reversed. "Good jobs close to home" is a fundamental requirement. The vast major-

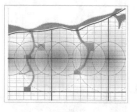

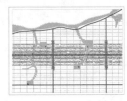

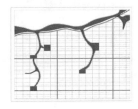

ity of new jobs in the United States and Canada are compatible with complete community districts.

5. Provide a diversity of housing types.

Zoning laws have tended to segregate communities by income. Communities designed for only one income cannot be complete, and when repeated throughout the region, they add to transportation problems.

6. Create a linked system of natural areas and parks.

Keeping our waters clean and our streams and rivers healthy requires a rethinking of urban drainage systems and stream protection policies. Maintaining the integrity of these systems must be a first design move when planning new communities. Far from protecting these systems through restriction, these systems must form the public space armature of new and restored communities.

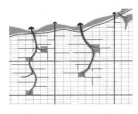

7. Invest in lighter, greener, cheaper, and smarter infrastructure.

Suburban homes have at least four times more infrastructure per dwelling unit than do walkable streetcar neighborhoods. Exaggerated municipal standards for roads and utilities cost too much to build and maintain, and they destroy watershed function. Smarter, cheaper, and greener strategies are required.

The Final Rule: Love One Rule, Love Them All

These principles represent the elements of a whole. Achieving one without the others—particularly if it is at the expense of the others—will be of limited value and could be counterproductive.

2 | *Restore the Streetcar City*

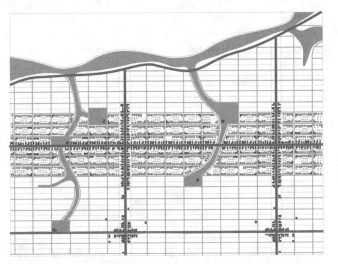

Figure 2.1. This diagram shows how the many components of a sustainable urban landscape work together in the streetcar city.

U.S. and Canadian cities built between 1880 and 1945 were streetcar cities.[1] It was a time, very brief in retrospect, when people walked a lot but could get great distances by hopping on streetcars. By 1950, this system was utterly overthrown, rendered obsolete by the market penetration of the private automobile. Both walking and transit use dropped dramatically afterward, all but disappearing by 1990 in many fast-growing metropolitan areas.

The collapse of that world constitutes a great loss, because the streetcar city form of urban development was a pattern that allowed the emerging middle class to live in single-family homes and was sustainable at the same time. Streetcar cities were walkable, transit accessible, and virtually pollution free while still dramatically extending the distance citizens could cover during the day.

The planning literature occasionally refers to the streetcar city pattern, but seldom is the streetcar city mentioned for enhancing human well-being or lauded as a time when energy use per capita for transportation was a tiny fraction of what it is today. This is tragic, because the streetcar established the form of most U.S. and Canadian cities. That pattern still constitutes the very bones of our cities—even now, when most of the streetcars are gone. To ignore the fundamental architecture when retrofitting our urban regions for a more sustainable future will fail. It is like expecting pigs to fly or bad soil to grow rich crops. Accepting this premise, it may help to examine the forces that spawned this distinctive urban pattern and to understand which of these forces still persist. A "day in the life" story will start to reveal this genesis and help us read more clearly what remains of this urban armature.

---

[1] Between 1850 and 1900, horse-drawn and then electric streetcars enabled large numbers of upper- and middle-class commuters to move farther out of the city, eventually giving rise to residential enclaves organized around streetcar lines that were referred to as "streetcar suburbs" (Warner, 1962). By 1910, almost every American city with more than ten thousand people had one or more streetcar lines, and per capita transit ridership peaked in 1920 at about 287 annual rides per urban resident (American Transit Association, 2006). In 1917, there were 72,911 streetcars in service in the United States, but for several reasons that number had dropped to 17,911 by 1948 (Toronto Star, 1999).

A DAY IN THE LIFE

The year is 1922, and Mr. Campbell is house shopping. He has taken a job with Western Britannia Shipping Company in Vancouver, and his family must relocate from Liverpool, England. He plans to take the new streetcar from his downtown hotel to explore a couple of new neighborhoods under development. A quick look at the map tells him that the new district of Kitsilano, southwest of the city center, might be a good bet. It is only a fifteen-minute ride from his new office on the Fourth Avenue streetcar line and is very close to the seashore, a plus for his young family. When he enters Kitsilano, he finds construction everywhere. Carpenters are busy erecting one-story commercial structures next to the streetcar line as well as very similar bungalow buildings on the blocks immediately behind. As Mr. Campbell rides the streetcar farther into the district, the buildings and active construction sites begin to be replaced by forest; the paved road gives way to gravel. Soon the only construction seems to be the streetcar tracks themselves, which are placed directly on the raw gravel. The streetcar line seems out of place in what appears to be raw wilderness. Taken aback by the wildness of the landscape, Mr. Campbell steps off the streetcar where a sign advertises the new Collingwood street development. Here, things are more encouraging, as workers are laying new concrete sidewalks and asphalt roads. Stepping into the project's show home, he is immediately surrounded by activity.

Carpenters and job supervisors waste no time inviting Mr. Campbell in, offering coffee and dropping him in a seat before the printed display of new homes. All the homes fit on the same size parcel or "lot", with the bungalow detached, single-family home the predominating style.

Mr. Campbell has many questions, but getting to and from work every day is his most important concern.

"Well then, sir, how do I know I can get downtown to my job from here dependably?" asks Mr. Campbell.

The salesman smiles and says, "Because we own the streetcar line, of course![2] Naturally, we had to put the streetcar in before we built the houses, and a pretty penny it cost too. But nobody will buy a house they can't get to, will they? The streetcar lines have to be within a five-minute walk of the house lots or we can't sell them. But we make enough on the houses to pay

Figure 2.2. Vancouver's Fourth Avenue streetcar line freshly installed. Streetcars were provided before roads were improved or land subdivided for homes, as a necessary precondition for development. Here is the scene a few years before these other urban features were built. (Source: Michael Kluckner, *Vancouver, The Way It Was*. North Vancouver: Whitecap Books, 1984).

Figure 2.3. Streetcars going over the Kitsilano trestle in 1909, west of the Granville trestle, which is now Granville Street Bridge. (Source: Vancouver Public Library)

[2]Early in the twentieth century, "streetcar lines and their adjacent residential communities were typically developed by a single owner who built transit to add value to the residential development by providing a link between jobs in an urban center and housing at the periphery." Private developers built transit to serve their developments, and as part of this formula small retail outlets were often built in clusters around streetcar stops, to serve both commuters and local residents (Belzer and Autler, 2002, p. 4).

Figure 2.4. Shown on Arbutus Street in Vancouver (1952), this streetcar is an example of the interurban type of vehicle that was used for longer trips and between rural communities in the Lower Mainland.

Figure 2.5. One-story commercial buildings in the early 1900s on Fourth Avenue, Vancouver.

off the cost. If we didn't, we'd be out of business! But there have to be enough houses to sell per acre to make it all work out financially. We have it down to a formula, sir: eight houses to the acre give us enough profit to pay off the streetcar and enough customers close to the line to make the streetcar profitable too. That's why all of the lots are the same size even when the houses look different. You're a business man, Mr. Campbell. I'm sure you understand, eh?" he says with a smile.

"But what of commercial establishments, sir?" asks Mr. Campbell with reserved formality. "Where will we buy our food, tools, and clothing?"

"Oh, all along Fourth Avenue, sir. Don't worry! By this time next year it will be wall-to-wall shops. One-story ones at first, to be sure, but when this neighborhood is fully developed we expect Fourth Avenue to be lined with substantial four- and five-story buildings to be proud of.[3] Liverpool will have nothing on us! You'll always be just a couple of minutes from the corner pub. Anything else you need, you can just hop on and off the streetcar to get it in a tic."

Mr. Campbell was sold. He was overjoyed to be able to buy a freestanding home for his family, something only the very rich of Liverpool could afford. All of the promises the salesman made came true more quickly than Mr. Campbell imagined possible, with the single exception of the four-story buildings on

Figure 2.6. Four-story mixed-use buildings now line block after block on Fourth Avenue in the Kitsilano District of Vancouver. Buildings of this scale were originally anticipated in the 1920s, when this area was built, but economic circumstances only became favorable for this type of building in the 1990s. All of the four-story buildings shown here were built after 1990.

---

[3]This is what is called "tax lots" or "taxpayer blocks," which refers to developers who built for low-density interim land uses, believing the land would eventually gain value and thus making more permanent commercial buildings worth their while. The low-density buildings produced enough revenue to pay taxes and essentially held the land for future development (Rowe, 1991).

the main commercial street. Rather than ten years, it would take another eighty. First, the Great Depression froze economic activity; then World War II redirected economic activity to the war effort. By the 1950s, the economic pendulum had swung toward suburban development fueled by increasing car ownership. Not until the 1990s, during the decade of Vancouver's most intense densification, would the vision of four-storey buildings lining both sides of Kitsilano's Fourth Avenue be realized.

THE STREETCAR CITY AS A UNIFYING PRINCIPLE

The streetcar city principle is not about the streetcar itself; it is about the system of which that the streetcar is a part. It is about the sustainable relationship between land use, walking, and transportation that streetcar cities embody. The streetcar city principle combines at least four of the design rules discussed in the following chapters: (1) an interconnected street system, (2) a diversity of housing types, (3) a five-minute walking distance to commercial services and transit, and (4) good jobs close to affordable homes.[4] For this reason, it is offered as the first of the rules and as a "meta rule" for sustainable, low-carbon community development.

Basic Structure of the Streetcar City

Streetcar cities in North America have unique characteristics not found in European cities or even in older parts of North American cities, such as Boston and Montreal. Classic streetcar cities, such as Dayton, Minneapolis, Seattle, Los Angeles, Edmonton, and Vancouver, are all laid out in a gridiron, with streets generally orienting to the cardinal axes. The typical urban grid is formed by subdividing the original, perfectly square 40-acre quarter rural parcels of the Land Ordinance Survey of 1795 into urban blocks. Both U.S. and Canadian officials divided entire states and provinces into perfect one-mile squares of 640 acres during this time. These mile squares were most commonly subdivided further into sixteen equal quarter-mile-square, 40-acre parcels. When nineteenth- and early-twentieth-century cities were cut from this 40-acre rural quilt, each 40-acre

[4]Vernez Moudon et al. (2006) found that environments associated with more walking were denser, had activities closer together, and had more sidewalks and smaller blocks. Handy (1993) found that residents living in traditional neighborhoods made two to four more walk or bike trips per week to neighborhood stores than those living in nearby areas that were served mainly by auto-oriented, strip retail establishments. Ewing, Haliyur, and Page (1994) found that sprawling suburban communities generated almost two thirds more per capita vehicle hours of travel than did the "traditional city." Neighborhoods that have gridded streets, convenient transit access, and destinations such as stores and services within walking distance result in shorter trips, many of which can be achieved by walking or biking. Streetcar city districts tend to have these attributes, thereby reducing vehicular travel and allowing for higher than normal public transit service (Hess and Ong, 2002).

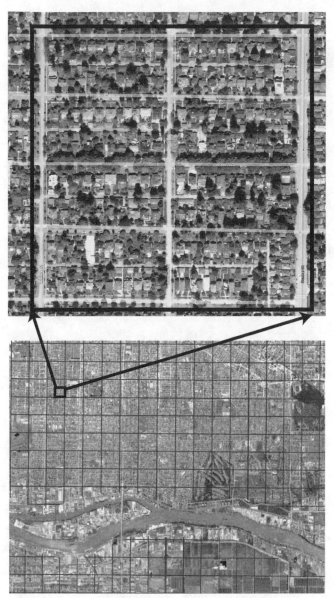

Figure 2.7. The grid overlay makes it clear that urban blocks were cut from the original agricultural pattern. The unaltered agricultural pattern in Richmond, British Columbia, shown near the bottom of photo, still retains this original pattern.

square was typically divided into eight equal 5-acre rectangles called "blocks," each block roughly 660 feet by 330 feet.

The Land Ordinance Survey had both political and practical goals. Thomas Jefferson, its author, believed that rendering the vast American continent into uniform squares would provide the ideal setting for the rural democracy he believed in so passionately.[5] Unlike the European feudal villages organized around manor houses, or the early New England towns organized around churches, no position in the rural grid is elevated above any other. At the same time, all lands are equally available for character-building husbandry and individual effort. The grid was, therefore, the ideal expression of the anti-aristocratic, personally entrepreneurial, and religiously neutral democracy idealized by Jefferson. This same lack of hierarchy adheres to urban districts that are cut from this democratic rural tapestry. In the urban gridiron, no streets terminate at palaces, churches, courthouses, or the homes of the august. All views are into the infinite distance of the public landscape—into the country itself. Streetcar cities are organized around the main threads of this grid, and their nonhierarchical structure still bespeaks this democratic intention.

In conformance with the practical economics exposited in the "day in the life" story earlier, streetcar cities were built out at consistent densities of between seven and fourteen residential dwelling units per gross acre (gross acre meaning inclusive of street space). In streetcar city districts, most homes are located within a five-minute walk (or a quarter mile) of the nearest streetcar stop. These stops line "streetcar arterials." If most residents are to live within a five-minute walk of a streetcar arterial, they must be no more than a half mile apart (with a maximum quarter-mile distance to the nearest arterial). Typically, commercial services occupy the ground floor of most street-fronting buildings along both sides of the streetcar arterial.

In European or early American cities, civic life happened in nodes around key crossroads, such as the various five-corner "squares" of Boston, or around designated civic centers, such as the colonial commons of New England. In contrast, the civic life of the streetcar city extends along the entire line of the arterial and thus constitutes a uniquely American and Canadian social milieu. This begs the question: is this kind of linear space socially impoverished when compared to nodal urban spaces—

[5]Jefferson even went so far as to sketch a pure grid plan for the District of Columbia. How seriously his plan was considered is not known. George Washington hired Charles L'Enfant, who produced the complex multi-axis plan that was ultimately built. Jefferson was not supportive of L'Enfant's plan but was overruled by Washington (Linklater, 2002; Kite, 1970; Malone, 1948).

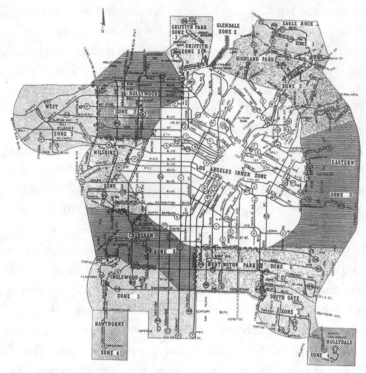

Figure 2.8. Historic streetcar routes in Los Angeles.

Figure 2.9. A typical Sunday afternoon on Broadway in Vancouver's Kitsilano District. The residential density on the surrounding streets is roughly fifteen dwelling units per gross acre.

spaces like Rockefeller Plaza in New York City and Boston Common in Boston.

No, it does not. Streetcar arterials can be amazingly rich in sense of place and civic life. Virtually all of the city of Vancouver's richest social settings are on streetcar arterials. While the high-rise neighborhoods of Vancouver are justifiably famous, almost all of the rich street life of the downtown core still occurs on the streetcar arterials of Granville, Robson, Denman, and Davey Streets. Beyond the core lie miles and miles of very active streetcar arterials. These streets are typically thronged with pedestrians, in numbers that rival the much higher density areas of New York City.

URBAN FORM AND THE PATTERN OF WALKING AND RIDING

Much has been made of the American Dream (or, in Canada, the Canadian Dream) of owning one's own home on its own lot. The dream was presumably realized after World War II

Figure 2.10. Original "town houses" in Boston, Massachusetts, a type typical of walking-distance cities built prior to the widespread use of the streetcar. (Credit: Gaither Limehouse Pratt)

[6]In the 1990s, the average commute time began to increase and is now up 18 percent from its historic norm, with almost 10 million Americans driving more than an hour to work, an increase of 50 percent between 1990 and 2000 (Siegel, 2006). In 2007, the average time Americans spent driving to work was 25.1 minutes (U.S. Census Bureau, 2007).

[7]Historically, walk-up tenements allowed for compact, high-density, walkable cities. Ancient Rome reached urban densities of 95,000 people per square mile of built-up land, while Manhattan reached a peak of 130,000 around 1910 (Pushkarev and Zupan, 1977). In 1880, 45 percent of all adult male workers employed in Philadelphia lived within one mile of the central business district, and 96 percent lived within six miles (Gin and Sonstelie, 1992). Historically, people had much less indoor housing space than they do today, so higher average population densities could exist while the density of structures remained relatively low (Pushkarev and Zupan, 1977). However, allowing for modern space requirements (dwelling units ranging from one thousand to two thousand square feet with one parking space and one hundred square feet of open space per dwelling), Ellis (2004) found that four-story walk-up townhouses could still reach densities of 30 to 40 dwelling units per acre or 19,200 to 25,600 units per square mile. The benefits of this type of development have been studied by Cervero and Kockelman (1997), who found that compact, mixed-use, pedestrian-friendly designs can "degenerate" vehicle trips, reduce VMT per capita, and encourage nonmotorized travel.

[8]Even today, the built form of the Beacon Hill neighborhood supports almost ten thousand people within one half square mile (Beacon Hill Online, 2003). In comparison, streetcar suburbs in Cleveland historically supported population densities of around 500 to 1,200 people per half mile square, demonstrating the up to sixteenfold drop in density permitted by the streetcar access (Borchert, 1998).

when the auto-oriented suburb was born. But the dream was actually realized two generations earlier in the streetcar city. With the emergence of the streetcar, the radius within which urban residents in the United States and Canada could operate expanded dramatically. Prior to the streetcar, the radius of the average person's activities was proscribed by reasonable walking distance.

Despite great changes in transportation technology between 1800 and 2000, it appears that Americans always spent about twenty minutes on average getting to work—whether by foot, on streetcar, or in modern automobiles.[6] Residents of pre-transit Boston, for example, lived in a city that could be easily crossed on foot in less than a half hour, with most of the city confined within a one-mile-radius, twenty-minute-walk circle. The need to keep everything within a one-mile walking distance in the more populous pre-streetcar walking cities required that the cities be quite dense by modern standards, with populations per square mile more than ten times higher than in later streetcar cities, and scores of times higher than in later, auto-dominated residential districts.[7] Beacon Hill in Boston is a good example of the very high density, four- and five-story walk-up neighborhoods characteristic of this time. These neighborhoods strongly resemble even earlier cities, including ancient Rome, itself dominated by house types and densities not unlike Beacon Hill.[8]

With the advent of the streetcar, the distance traveled in twenty minutes increased from one mile to four miles (assuming an average speed of ten miles per hour inclusive of stops and intersection waits). This fourfold increase is actually much greater than it seems when you consider that this increases by sixteen times the area one can cover in twenty minutes. Thus, the same sixty thousand people who were compressed into one square mile could now be spread over sixteen square miles (lowering the density to four thousand people per square mile), allowing much lower density housing while still maintaining easy access for workers across the service area. With the intense pressure to concentrate development partly relieved, houses could spread out and the urban middle class could afford to buy detached homes. Thus, most new streetcar city residential districts were composed mostly of single-family homes on relatively small lots, with the bungalow house style predominating.

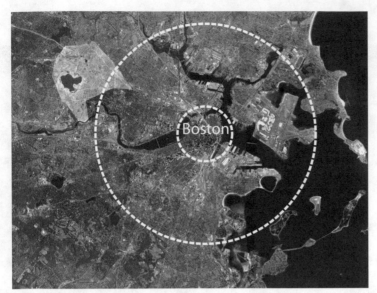

Figure 2.11. The smaller circle around downtown Boston represents the distance a person could walk in twenty minutes. The larger circle shows the distance a person could travel by taking a streetcar.

This pattern of density and land use, knitted together over large areas by the streetcar, could extend great distances. Thus, the streetcar city form allows detached housing within walking distance and short transit distance of jobs and services over very large metropolitan-scale areas, all at very low energy demand while preserving traditional residential home types. If our challenge is to make North American cities more sustainable by dramatically reducing their energy requirements and greenhouse gas (GHG) production, while not ignoring the desirability in the minds of most home buyers for ground-oriented, detached dwellings, then the streetcar city is a proven prototype, uniquely suited to U.S. and Canadian cultural circumstances.

FORTY PERCENT STILL LIVE THERE

Close to half of urban residents in the United States and Canada live in districts once served by the streetcar.[9] In these neighborhoods, alternatives to the car are still available and buildings are inherently more energy efficient (due to shared walls, wind protection, and smaller average unit sizes).[10] Most of these districts are still pedestrian and transit friendly, although with rare exception the streetcar and interurban rail lines that once served them

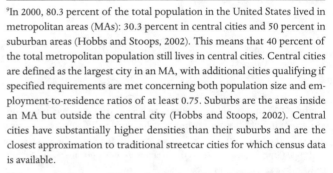

[9]In 2000, 80.3 percent of the total population in the United States lived in metropolitan areas (MAs): 30.3 percent in central cities and 50 percent in suburban areas (Hobbs and Stoops, 2002). This means that 40 percent of the total metropolitan population still lives in central cities. Central cities are defined as the largest city in an MA, with additional cities qualifying if specified requirements are met concerning both population size and employment-to-residence ratios of at least 0.75. Suburbs are the areas inside an MA but outside the central city (Hobbs and Stoops, 2002). Central cities have substantially higher densities than their suburbs and are the closest approximation to traditional streetcar cities for which census data is available.

[10]Norman, McLean, and Kennedy (2006) conducted a life-cycle analysis of energy use and GHG emissions for high and low residential density that included the construction materials for infrastructure, building operations, and transportation. They found that low-density suburban development was more energy and greenhouse gas intensive, by a factor of 2.0 to 2.5, than was high-density urban core development. Ewing et al. (2007, pp.20) looked at the relationship among urban development, travel, and CO_2 emitted by motor vehicles. They found that "the evidence on land use and driving shows that compact development will reduce the need to drive between 20 and 40 percent, as compared with development on the outer suburban edge with isolated homes, workplaces, and other destinations . . . smart growth could, by itself, reduce total transportation-related CO_2 emissions from current trends by 7 to 10 percent as of 2050." Ten percent may seem small until one considers this 10 percent drop against what would most certainly be a large *increase* in GHG production if current trends continue. More dramatic differences are revealed in the work of the Center for Neighborhood Technology (CNT) in Minneapolis, where total per capita costs for transportation in former streetcar neighborhoods were less than half of what they were in third-ring suburbs, even when income disparities had been equalized. More recent analysis by the CNT in the New York metropolitan area has shown that overall GHG production per capita is roughly 200 percent less in Queens streetcar neighborhoods like Jackson Heights when compared to lower-density, auto-oriented areas such as Great Neck, New York, a community that is less than ten miles away (Center for Neighborhood Technology, 2009).

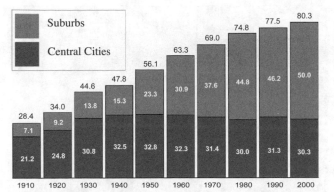

	1910	1920	1930	1940	1950	1960	1970	1980	1990	2000
Total	28.4	34.0	44.6	47.8	56.1	63.3	69.0	74.8	77.5	80.3
Suburbs	7.1	9.2	13.8	15.3	23.3	30.9	37.6	44.8	46.2	50.0
Central Cities	21.2	24.8	30.8	32.5	32.8	32.3	31.4	30.0	31.3	30.3

Figure 2.12. This table shows the percent of total population living in metropolitan areas and in their central cities and suburbs, 1910 to 2000. (Source: U.S. Census Bureau, dicennial census of population 1910 to 2000)

Figure 2.13. James Trowley presents a check to Twin City Rapid Transit company chief Fred Ossana as a streetcar burns behind them. National City Lines negotiated scores of contracts with transit agencies across the continent, requiring them to scrap their rail infrastructure as a precondition for attractive financial considerations. In 1960, Fred Ossana was convicted of fraud for activities associated with the conversion of Minneapolis streetcars to GM buses. (Source: Minneapolis collection, M3857)

---

[11]National City Lines (NCL) was organized in 1936 "for the purposes of taking over the controlling interest in certain operating companies engaged in city bus transportation and overland bus transportation" (Bianco, 1998, p. 10). In 1939, when NCL needed additional funds to expand their enterprise, they approached General Motors for financing. GM agreed to buy stock from NCL at prices in excess of the prevailing market price under the condition that NCL would refrain from purchasing equipment not using gasoline or diesel fuel (Bianco, 1998).

have been removed (Toronto is a rare example of a city where the streetcar lines remain largely intact). While there is much debate about what precipitated the demise of North America's streetcar and interurban systems, one thing is certain. In 1949, the U.S. courts convicted National City Lines—a "transit" company owned outright by General Motors (GM), Firestone, and Phillips Petroleum—for conspiring to intentionally destroy streetcar systems in order to eliminate competition with the buses and cars GM produced. While it may seem impossible to envision today, Los Angeles once had the largest and most extensive system of streetcars and interurban lines in the world. In a few short years, this system was completely dismantled by National City Lines, at the same time that an enormous effort to lace the LA region with freeways was launched. Today, no hint of this original streetcar fabric remains. Only by perusing old photos can one sense the extent of the destruction.[11] Now, some sixty years later, elements of this system are being painfully replaced at great cost. The LA area Metrolink system has restored some of the historic interurban lines, while inner-city surface light rail lines have replaced a small fraction of the former streetcar system.

CONTINUOUS LINEAR CORRIDORS, NOT STAND-ALONE NODES

Linear public space is the defining social and spatial characteristic of the streetcar city. This obvious fact has been ignored at best and derided at worst. Most planning, urban design, and economic development experts favor strategies that ignore corridors in favor of discrete and identifiable places, key urban "nodes" in planning terms. Their plans focus most often on an identified "downtown" or a key transportation locus, while the thousands of miles of early-twentieth-century streetcar arterials are either allowed to languish or blithely sacrificed for parking lots. Yet, very few of us live within walking distance of a "node," whereas most of us live within a reasonable walk of a corridor, however gruesome it may now be. The Vancouver region, for all of its notable successes, has not been immune to this planning habit. The Vancouver region's consensus vision, the Livable Region Strategic Plan (LRSP), adopted in 1995, has several

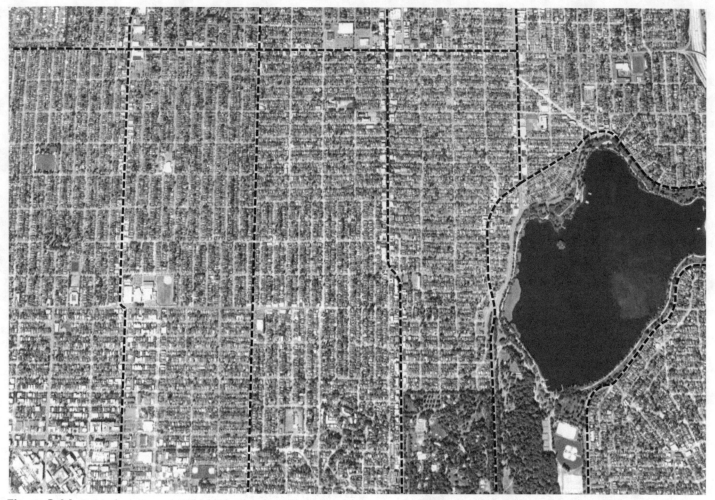

Figure 2.14. Original streetcar routes highlighted in the Whittier Heights District of Seattle show the linear nature of a streetcar city.

key objectives, all laudable and pathbreaking. Two of the most important objectives are to create complete communities through "regional town center" nodes where people can live, recreate, and work close to home, and to link these complete communities by high-speed transit.

The regional town center nodes were identified on the LRSP map as relatively small nodes and were defined in the text as locations where jobs, homes, and commercial services were to be found at densities and intensities tens of times higher than surrounding districts. The plan was mute on the role of districts between the regional town centers, which constituted more than 80 percent of the urban landscape. These other areas were, and still are, the areas where most transit trips originate, where most jobs are located, and where most commercial services are

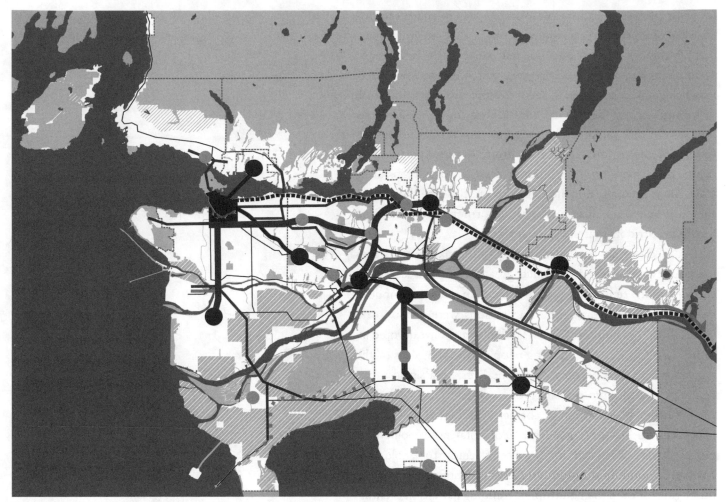

Figure 2.15. The Greater Vancouver Liveable Region Strategic Plan: Transportation and Town Centres.

to be found. The overemphasis on nodes led naturally to choosing a transit technology, the grade-separated "Skytrain" system (actually a scaled-down subway system), that was great for connecting the designated town center nodes but very poor at serving the streetcar city districts in between. Now, twenty-five years after the plan was first discussed, and fifteen years after it was officially adopted, certain results are clear. While high-density high-rise housing has been attracted to some of the regional town center nodes, attracting jobs has proven much more difficult. The plan is thus considered a failure in this key respect by many of the region's authorities.

The province is now investing in controversial freeway expansion to, in the words of former British Columbia minister of transportation Kenneth Falcon, "fix the failed plan." The minister justified the project, in part, by noting that job targets for the regional town center nodes were not met, that job growth was outside the centers and thus not reachable by the new transit system. Consequently, more freeway lane-miles and more freeway bridges were required to serve this presumably random job distribution. Now, the region finds itself having invested billions in a system that cannot fully integrate with the underlying armature of the region, its streetcar arterials; nor do these town center nodes have the gravitational strength to pull jobs away from these arterials. But these jobs did not escape the region; they just ended up close to the same former streetcar and interurban corridors that the plan ignored.[12]

Vancouver has been damaged by its mistake, but mistakes made elsewhere have done much greater harm. At least Vancouver had the sense to designate more than one center node in the region. Other North American regions were not so fortunate. Officials in most other metropolitan areas have devoted infinite transit resources to getting people from the edges of the region, where they presume everyone lives, to a single urban center, where they presume everyone works.

Neither presumption is correct. Traditional downtowns have been losing percentage share of total metropolitan regional jobs for over a century. Since the streetcar took hold, jobs have been migrating out of traditional center city nodes to other parts of the urban metroplex, trending toward an eventual balance between jobs located in the center of the region and jobs located in its outer districts (see chapter 4). But an urge to support the traditional downtown locus, and a not always successful attempt to draw suburban commuters out of their cars, has convinced transit officials to consistently spend all of their capital expansion resources on hub-and-spoke systems to support jobs that are not there. In the most extreme cases, of which there are far too many, this leads to an exclusively and profoundly hierarchical (one center, everything else edge) hub-and-spoke system of transit, which is antithetical to the original homogenous (no center, no edges) North American streetcar grid. Hub-and-spoke systems, as the name suggests, have a single hub location, always a traditional downtown node, served by a set of "spoke" lines that run out through first-ring former streetcar districts to second- and third-ring suburbs.

Metropolitan regions as diverse as Minneapolis, Houston,

[12]The number of people whose usual place of work was in the city of Vancouver rose by 6 percent between 2001 and 2006 compared to an increase of 9.7 percent in the peripheral municipalities (Statistics Canada, 2006). The fastest-growing peripheral municipalities in terms of jobs were Surrey (+17,300, or 17 percent), Burnaby (+7,000, or 6.5 percent), Langley (+6,400, or 18.5 percent), and Coquitlam (+ 5,800, or 17.2 percent). The business parks in metro Vancouver are often located close to residential areas, services, and transit. Instead of being inherently disconnected from the urban fabric, it is the physical site design and single-use zoning that frustrates connectivity, explodes distances between amenities, and generally makes for an unwalkable, auto-dominated environment (Condon, Belausteguigoitia, Fryer, and Straatsma, 2006).

and Denver have fallen into this hub-and-spoke trap. They have expended billions on new at grade and grade-separated "light" rail systems that only get users to traditional downtowns and cannot conveniently move them in any other direction. Meanwhile, the numerous freeway ring roads in these places operate for the cars much like the streetcar and interurban grids of yore, allowing car owners access in any direction in a way prohibited to rail transit users.

If jobs cannot, or perhaps should not, be confined to single or even multiple high-intensity urban nodes, then a regional transit strategy suited to this circumstance is required. The streetcar and interurban transit strategy that worked in the past, and which spawned the still dominant land use and movement patterns extant in most metro areas, is such a strategy. Transportation and land use choices can still be made that promote complete communities across broad swaths of urban landscape without compelling Herculean daily drives or very long trips on transit. No sustainability strategy can ever work that assumes all people will be crossing entire regions twice a day to do their daily business. Traditional streetcar cities were characterized by high mobility but not unlimited mobility. Statistics still indicate that the average trip in both the United States and Canada on buses and by streetcar is short. This is because buses and streetcars tend to operate well in areas where distances are short and the things needed are close at hand. A trip that is five miles on a streetcar moving fifteen miles per hour takes a lot less time than a twenty-five-mile trip on a heavy commuter rail moving at forty miles per hour.

The common complaint that streetcars and buses cannot move at high speeds through urban streets is thus a red herring. It is not how fast you are going but how far you are trying to go. The streetcar city concept works in metropolitan regions where the average trip distance is a short one. Average vehicle-miles traveled (VMT) per day has been increasing for decades. This trend must be reversed. No sustainable region strategy can ever succeed that presumes an infinite increase in the average daily demand for transportation, no matter what the mode. Accepting that the decades-long increase in average VMT must drop, then the rationale for the streetcar city is ever more compelling. Trips by transit are not free. A passenger-mile on the average diesel bus costs more and produces as much carbon per passenger as a fully loaded Prius. Getting people onto transit will not help defeat global warming unless we can find a way to radically decrease the average daily demand for motorized travel of any kind and the per-mile GHG consequences of each trip. Community districts that are complete and that favor short trips over long ones seem an obvious part of the solution. Inexpensive short-haul zero carbon transit vehicles, such as trolley buses and especially streetcars, are a likely feature of a low-energy, low-travel-demand solution.

Precious few cities seem to "get it" in this respect. Portland, again, is the exception. Portland is the only U.S. city to have made a serious effort to restore its streetcar system. The results could not be more promising. Jobs, housing, and new commercial services are flocking to the line, making the community that much more complete and thus incrementally reducing aggregate per capita trip demand. In Portland, jobs, housing, clubs, and commercial services are coming closer together. A ten-minute ride on the Portland streetcar gets you where you want to go. Its speed between these points is irrelevant.[13]

Other regions should follow Portland's example. Wherever the original streetcar city fabric is still in place, planners should reenforce that structure with transit investments. Citizens and officials in most U.S. and Canadian cities need only search archives for historical maps to discover exactly where these systems existed and how amazingly extensive they were. Transit investment should then shift back to fund modern tram systems using the same alignments of the former streetcars, rather than, or at least in addition to, hugely expensive long-distance, grade-separated systems. A gradual reinvestment in these traditional lines will provide strong stimulus to the kind of urban re-investment in mixed use so dramatically demonstrated in Portland, and will hasten the day when average VMT drops to sustainable levels. It also restores the universally accessible and democratically nonhierarchical regional system that is the defining characteristic of U.S. and Canadian regional cities, a characteristic that we have sadly lost sight of but that it is not too late to recover.

Citizens and officials in newer suburbs should examine the essential street structure of their arterials, almost always a grid with increments of either one half to one mile, a legacy of the Land Ordinance Survey, and should support a transit system

[13]In the United States, it was only after the effort of Congressman Earl Blumenauer, of Portland, and his congressional supporters that federal transit monies could be used to support shorter range, lower speed, and much cheaper streetcar systems. Prior to that, Portland had to pay the entire cost of the first phase of its streetcar system with local funds.

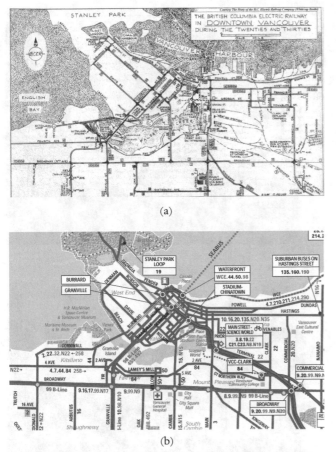

(a)

(b)

Figure 2.16. The map of Vancouver's historic streetcar lines (a) matches up with existing transit routes (b) in Vancouver. (Source: Henry Ewert, *The Story of BC Electric Railway Company* (North Vancouver: Whitecap Books, 1986; Translink 2008)

that best serves local trips along these lines. To do otherwise is to consistently disadvantage their own community interests. This is particularly important if one accepts that "complete communities" should be a feature of any sustainable urban region. Complete communities are communities where one needs to travel far less during the average day than is standard now; they are cities that dramatically reverse our ever increasing demand for transport.

BUSES, STREETCARS, LIGHT RAIL TRANSIT, AND SUBWAYS

When National City Lines disassembled the Los Angeles streetcar systems, they marshaled strong arguments in favor of rubber-tired buses (Bauer, 1939). They argued that initial capital costs for streetcars were much higher and that the cost of operating buses per vehicle-mile was at that time half the cost of operating streetcars. Many of the arguments they used then are still used when streetcar systems are proposed today. Streetcars are inflexible, it is said. They are on rails, so if one gets stuck the whole system gets stuck. Streetcar vehicles cost more than buses. Buses do not need overhead wires to run. Buses do the same job as streetcars but do a lot more too. These arguments are often enough to end the matter. But let's approach the question from a different angle. It is not a question of buses versus streetcars, really. Since most metro areas are now investing in some form of rail transit, it is a question of what kind of rail transit makes the most sense: lightweight streetcar, medium-weight light rail transit (LRT), or heavyweight Skytrain or subway technology.

It is generally agreed that rail systems are a good thing and that they should be a major part of any region's transportation expenditure. But until very recently, rail funding could be used only for traditional hub-and-spoke type transit systems, using grade-separated LRT technology. To call these systems "light" is a misnomer. They are heavy rapid-transit systems that cost many billions to construct. Portland's regional hub-and-spoke commuter system, the MAX (Metropolitan Area Express) line, operates like a large streetcar in the center city, moving at slower speeds on crowded streets.[14] But once out of

[14]Portland's MAX system is one of the most successful light rail systems in North America. According to the American Public Transportation Association's Ridership Report (2007), Portland's MAX system accommodates 104,300 daily trips and is the United States' second most ridden standalone light rail system, behind only San Diego.

the small downtown area, it operates as a grade-separated system with a dedicated right-of-way, widely spaced stations, and travel speeds of up to sixty miles per hour, similar to many other hub-and-spoke commuter rail systems.

Given these speed demands, Portland-style MAX technology costs a lot, about $50 million per two-way mile to build. Fully grade-separated systems, such as the Vancouver Skytrain system, cost four times as much: $200 million or more per two-way mile. In the mid-1990s, Tri-Country Metropolitan Transportation District (TriMet) planned a north–south MAX line to complete the basic hub-and-spoke system. The new line would have run from downtown Portland to serve the north side of the city before connecting across the Columbia River to the city of Vancouver, Washington. Voter approval via a referendum was required to authorize the substantial local cost share. The bond measure was narrowly defeated, constituting a major setback for transit in the region.[15] Officials in Portland were initially inclined to give up, but they didn't. They still needed a system to serve the northwest part of the city so they cast about for more affordable alternatives.

What they found was modern streetcar technology. Europe had never abandoned streetcars, and many companies there still manufacture them. A Czech company, Skoda Transportation, was able to provide the components of a system that could be installed, including rolling stock, for $20 million per two-way mile—only one fifth the cost per mile compared to MAX technology and one tenth the cost of Skytrain. Why so cheap? Car size was the same as Skytrain, so it was not that. The system is cheap because while it can run in dedicated rights-of-way at speeds of fifty miles per hour, it can also very easily run on existing street rights-of-way. It can either share lane space with cars, as it does in Portland, or move faster on dedicated lanes in the center of streets, as it does on the Green Line in Boston. The vehicles are so light that streets and bridges do not need to be rebuilt to support them. On regular streets, all that is needed is a twelve-inch-thick concrete pad within which to set rails. Aside from the pad construction, the street and the businesses that line it are not disrupted.

In Europe, streetcar and tram systems are being expanded much faster than heavier rail systems, gradually replacing buses on heavily used urban arterials.[16] They provide a much

(a)

(b)

Figure 2.17. Photo (a) shows a "light" rail Portland MAX vehicle operating like a streetcar in the foreground with a true light rail streetcar in the background. Photo (b) shows Portland's MAX line outside of the central city, where it travels large distances more typical of a light rail system. (Credit: available under the Creative Commons Attribution 2.5 License)

[15]In 1996, Oregon voters rejected a $375 million transportation package that would have funded the north–south light rail project as well as a nine-mile extension from Vancouver to Hazel Dell, by a vote of 53 percent to 46 percent. Although the measure failed statewide, it was approved by a majority of voters within the TriMet service area (Metro, 2007).

[16]The majority of European cities rebuilt or upgraded their streetcar systems following World War II in response to "lower automobile ownership, a lack of domestic petroleum resources, plentiful electricity and a desire to not allow automobile usage to disturb the traditional economic and social patterns of these centuries-old cities" (Gormick, 2004). A few large cities, including Stockholm, Rotterdam, and Milan, built heavy rail, but most decided to restore or upgrade their streetcar services instead (Black, 1993). In 1975, there were 310 cities in the world with streetcar/

LRT systems in operation, including most West European nations and Japan (Diamant et al., 1976).Great Britain and France were two notable exceptions to this trend in Europe. Very few tram lines survived in these countries after World War II; however, more recently many cities in the United Kingdom and France have been reintroducing streetcars from scratch, after having had no light rail or tramway for more than a generation (Hyden and Pharoah, 2002).

[17]The average cost of new light rail construction in North America is $35 million/mile, excluding Seattle, whose $179 million/mile price tag is well outside of the norm (Light Rail Now, 2002). This calculation includes new streetcar systems, which are significantly less expensive. Portland's modern streetcar line was constructed for $12.4 million/mile (although some sources have it at $16.4 million/mile; Light Rail Now, 2002). The streetcar line in Tampa, Florida, was built for $13.7 million, and the one in Little Rock, Arkansas, was built for $7.1 million/mile (Weyrich and Lind, 2002). The typical price for a modern streetcar vehicle is in the range of $3 to $3.5 million, while a forty-foot transit bus costs between $0.4 and $0.5 million and articulated buses range between $0.6 and $0.9 million. Higher vehicle costs for streetcars can be partly offset by increased efficiency in operating costs. In most cases, the operating cost per boarding rider for light rail and streetcars is significantly lower than for buses, primarily because of their higher capacity per driver. For example, the operating cost per rider trip for buses in St. Louis is $2.49, while for light rail it is only $1.32 (Lyndon, 2007). Streetcars also have a service life of twenty-five years, while that of transit buses is only seventeen years (City of Vancouver, 2006). For detailed notes on the life-cycle costs per passenger-mile quoted in the main text, see Foundation Research Bulletin No. 7: A Cost Comparison of Transportation Modes (Condon and Dow, 2009).

[18]Cervero (2007) cites the streetcar system as a major driving force in the development of the Pearl District in Portland, which now has an average density of 120 units per acre net, the highest in Portland. The streetcar has stimulated housing and transportation in the area as well as an estimated $1.3 billion in investment (Ohland, 2004).

[19]Hovee & Company, LLC, "Portland Streetcar Development Impacts" (2005), in Portland Streetcar Loop Project Environmental Assessment (January 2008).

smoother ride for elderly people than do buses. With an aging demographic in which those over age sixty-five will soon constitute more than 33 percent of the population, a 200 percent increase over today, this is a key factor. Body balance is compromised as one ages. Unsteady rides on rubber-wheeled vehicles and buses that are hard to mount and stand in become increasingly difficult after age fifty-five, and almost impossible past age seventy-five. Low-floor streetcars are mountable at grade and are free of any lateral or orbital rocking motion.

Streetcars are always electric and thus generate no GHG direct emissions, and very low indirect GHG emissions. Finally, and most compellingly, they are cheaper than buses when all costs are considered over the useful life of the system. Over the life-cycle period, tram systems cost $1.23 per passenger-mile compared with $1.62 per passenger-mile for diesel buses.[17] The GHG consequences of this choice are much more dramatic. Diesel buses produce almost 200 grams of CO_2 per passenger-mile, whereas modern trams produce between 0.45 grams and 23.4 grams per passenger-mile (depending on electricity source). More details on these cost and energy relationships follow.

STREETCAR AS AN URBAN INVESTMENT

Most discussions of streetcar focus solely on transit issues, but the implications are much wider. Streetcars stimulate investment and buses don't. This has been powerfully demonstrated in Portland, where the introduction of a modern streetcar line spurred the high-density development that helped the City of Portland recoup construction costs through significantly increased tax revenues.[18] Between 1997 and 2005, the density of development immediately adjacent to the new streetcar line increased dramatically. Within two blocks of the streetcar line, $2.28 billion was invested, representing over 7,200 new residential units and 4.6 million square feet of additional commercial space; even more impressive, new development within only one block of the streetcar line accounted for 55 percent of all new development within the city's core.[19] To put this in perspective, prior to construction of the new streetcar line, land located within one block of the proposed route captured only 19 percent of all development.

Most attribute this impressive increase in investment to the presence of the streetcar line. Developers for the new South Waterfront development at the other end of the downtown from the Pearl District would not proceed before the city guaranteed to extend the streetcar line to the site. These developers, the same ones who had created the highly successful streetcar serving Pearl District, knew from experience how important the streetcar is to success. If the free market tells us anything at all in this case, it is that the economics of the streetcar, when the value of new investment is included, is much more cost effective than an investment in rubber-wheeled diesel buses or heavy transit.

CARS, BUSES, STREETCAR, OR HEAVY RAIL? CASE STUDY OF THE BROADWAY CORRIDOR IN VANCOUVER

Broadway is the dominant east–west corridor in Vancouver, running from its eastern border at Boundary Street to its western border at the campus of the University of British Columbia (UBC). Broadway has always been a good street for transit, even after the streetcars were removed. All of the density and access features described earlier in this chapter are found there. The corridor has a continuous band of commercial spaces for most of its length that are within short walks of residential densities greater than fifteen dwelling units per acre to ensure a steady stream of riders and customers on foot.

Residents who live near Broadway can survive without a car. Many of the residents along the corridor are students at UBC who have always enjoyed a one-seat ride to school on buses with three- to five-minute headways. More than half of all trips on the corridor now are by bus, with over sixty thousand passenger trips per day.[20] Very frequent bus service has reinforced the function of the Broadway corridor even without the streetcar in place. Buses are both local, stopping every second block, and express, stopping every one to two miles. The street has no dedicated bus lanes, although in some portions curb lanes are transit only during peak hours. Walkable districts, sufficient density, three-minute headways, hop-on-hop-off access to commercial services, and five-minute walking distance to destinations at both ends of the trip all contribute synergistically.

---

[20]G. Leicester, *Implementation of Transit Priority on Broadway Corridor*, prepared for GVTA Board of Directors (2006).

The buses on Broadway work very well; if they were never upgraded to streetcars, it would not be end of the world. But the corridor, because of its high ridership, is a candidate for substantial new transit investments. Using a modest amount of proposed funds to restore streetcars to Broadway makes good sense. Streetcars will reduce pollution, better accommodate infirm and elderly passengers, add capacity, provide everyone a more comfortable ride, cost less per passenger-mile over the long run than is being spent now, and attract investment where it is most desired.

WHAT IS THE OPTIMAL TRANSIT SYSTEM?

What evidence exists that streetcars are more cost effective over the long term than either rapid bus transit, which the corridor has, or heavier "rapid" transit, such as the Skytrain, which is being proposed? To get a useful answer to this question, it must be further asked: Cost effective for what? Over what distance? To serve what land uses? The question quickly becomes complicated. It helps to start by asking what the optimal relationship is between land use and transit, and what transit mode would best support this optimum state. Similarly, how do an increasingly uncertain oil supply and rising concern over GHG emissions factor into our long-term transportation planning? Investment decisions made in Vancouver and elsewhere over the next ten years will determine land use and transportation patterns that will last for the next one hundred years. How can we choose the system that helps create the kind of energy, cost, and low-GHG region that the future demands?

A research bulletin completed by the Design Centre for Sustainability at UBC compiled the information needed to begin to answer these questions. The results are organized in the context of three basic sustainability principles: (1) shorter trips are better than longer trips, (2) low carbon is better than high carbon, and (3) choose what is most affordable over the long term.[21]

First, shorter trips. It does us no good to shift car trips to transit if average transit trips become longer and longer over time. Eventually, energy and resource reductions will be eaten up by increased vehicle-miles traveled per person on these new

---

[21]The full bulletin, summarized below, can be downloaded at http://www.sxd.sala.ubc.ca/8_research/sxd_FRB07Transport.pdf.

transit vehicles. If shorter vehicle trips are the long-term goal, what then is the best option to achieve this goal? In traditional streetcar neighborhoods, local buses and streetcars extend the walk trip, allowing frequent on and off stops for trip chaining, and accommodating typically short trips to work or to shop when compared to other modes. Thus, the walk trip is the mainstay mode of movement in streetcar neighborhoods, with the streetcar itself acting as a sort of pedestrian accelerator, extending the reach of the walk trip.[22]

While both buses and streetcars are effective ways to extend the walk trip, streetcars are much more energy efficient than diesel buses and even somewhat better than electric trolley buses.[23] Electrically powered vehicles also give the flexibility to incorporate "green" sources of energy into the mix—electricity from hydro, wind, or solar power that could, in time, completely eliminate carbon emissions from the transit sector. But even streetcars that get their energy from coal-burning power plants generate far less GHG per passenger mile than do diesel buses, as electric vehicles are far more efficient in converting carbon energy into motive force than are internal combustion engines.[24]

The capital costs for transportation modes such as streetcar, LRT, and Skytrain are relatively easy to determine because the large initial investment to build the transportation infrastructure (tracks, platforms, stations, and so forth) is generally tied directly to the project.[25] However, many costs associated with the use of personal automobiles, local bus service, and to a lesser extent bus rapid transit and trolleybuses are more difficult to determine because they operate on existing roadways, the construction and maintenance of which are not included in most cost calculations for these modes. For this reason, external costs that begin to place a value on the land and resources dedicated to automobile infrastructure are necessary to accurately represent the true costs of the system. Estimates for the capital and external costs per passenger-mile for each transportation mode are show in figure 2.20.

The next consideration is ongoing operation and maintenance expense. Figure 2.21 shows these costs, together with the capital and external costs. Energy costs are isolated from the operating expenses and shown separately according to present energy costs for each mode as well as the future increase in energy

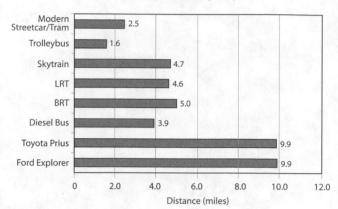

Figure 2.18. Average trip length by transportation mode. Data from APTA, 2009; Buehler et al., 2009; IBI Group, 2003.

[22]This hypothesis is borne out by data that shows that North American districts still served by streetcar or electric trolley buses or both exhibit shorter average trip lengths than other modes (2.5 and 1.6 miles, respectively). On the other hand, the average daily trip length in a personal automobile in the United States is 9.9 miles (15.9 km). Other trip length averages across the United States were found to be 3.9 miles (6.3 km) for local bus, 5.0 miles (8.0 km) for bus rapid transit, and 4.6 miles (7.4 km) for light rail transit (American Public Transportation Association, 2009; Buehler, Pucher, and Kunert, 2009; IBI Group, 2003). These values are represented in figure 2.18.

[23]According to Strickland (2008), internal combustion engines typically convert, at best, one third of their energy into useful work while electric motors generally have energy efficiencies of 80 to 90 percent. In addition, rail vehicles lose less energy to frictional resistance than do rubber-wheeled vehicles, and they are typically capable of much higher passenger capacities.

[24]Although the Design Centre for Sustainability's research bulletin focused primarily on the carbon emissions from the actual movement of vehicles, significant carbon emissions are also associated with vehicle manufacturing and maintenance, infrastructure construction, and fuel production. Recent research by Chester (2008) provides some insight into this question. He found that life-cycle greenhouse gas emissions are 47 to 65 percent larger than for tailpipe emissions from automobiles, 43 percent larger than for buses, and 39 to 150 percent for rail (streetcars, with their minimal construction requirements, would be on the lower end of this range, while Skytrain would be on the higher end) (Chester, 2008).

[25]To make a sound comparison of the long-term aggregate costs per passenger-mile associated with each transportation mode, we incorporated capital costs associated with acquiring the vehicles and constructing the infrastructure necessary to support them. The total cost was then amortized over the expected life of the system, and this annualized cost was divided by the actual annual passenger-miles recorded by various transit authorities for each mode.

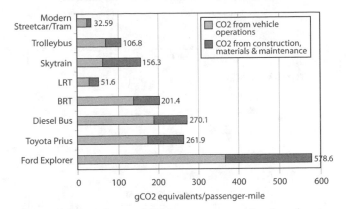

Figure 2.19. Carbon emissions per passenger-mile when electricity source is coal. (Source: Strickland, 2008; U.S. Environmental Protection Agency, 2005; Spadaro, Langlois, and Hamilton, 2000)

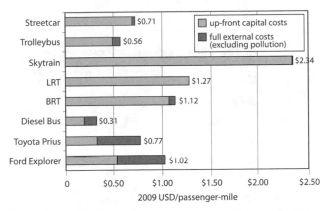

Figure 2.20. Total capital cost per passenger-mile by mode. Capital costs were calculated using construction costs and/or vehicle costs amortized over the expected life of the system. This annualized cost was then divided by the annual passenger-miles reported for each mode. Data from American Automobile Association, 2009; Translink, 2008; TTC, 2007; IBI Group, 2003; National Transit Database, 1998–2007; Portland Bureau of Transportation and Portland Streetcar Inc., 2008; Buchanan, 2008.

---

[26]Litman (2006) found that "cities with large, well-established rail systems have significantly higher per capita transit ridership, lower average per capita vehicle ownership and annual mileage, less traffic congestion, lower traffic death rates, lower consumer expenditures on transportation, and higher transit service cost recovery than otherwise comparable cities with less or no rail transit service." Studies have found that 30 percent of residents moving into Portland's new transit-oriented development own fewer cars than they did at their previous home and that 69 percent use public transit more often than they did in their previous community (Podobnik, 2002; Switzer, 2003).

costs that can be expected as nonrenewable fuels such as oil become more scarce. Using full external costs (excluding the very difficult to assess costs associated with air and water pollution caused by transport), the Toyota Prius scores best per passenger-mile, with a total cost of $1.09, followed by the streetcar at $1.23. Even with negligible energy costs, the Vancouver-area Skytrain system is by far the most expensive, at $2.66 per passenger-mile.

The results shown in figure 2.21 show the cost of moving one person one mile. This kind of calculation tends to favor modes of transportation that typically travel longer distances. But since shorter trips are, in the context of this argument, more sustainable, it is useful to also look at the cost per average trip. Low average trip distance is a marker for a more sustainable district, as it indicates that the relationship between mode and land use has been optimized. Conversely, low costs per mile gain us nothing if the relationship between mode and land use is such that all trips are unnecessarily long.

The cost per average trip for each mode is shown in figure 2.22. In this scenario, the transportation modes encouraging land uses that support shorter trips (trolleybus and streetcar) are significantly more cost effective than modes that facilitate more spread out land use patterns (that is, modes designed for high-speed, long-distance trips).

It is important to note that the benefits of streetcar city development do not come solely from the construction of a streetcar system itself. The streetcar city concept is systemic and necessarily incorporates an integrated conception of community structure and movement demands. When applied to low-density suburban developments absent a comprehensive urban infill strategy, modern streetcars are doomed to low ridership and anemic cost recovery (Gormick, 2004). The streetcar city principle is thus about more than just the vehicle, more than just the track. It is about a balance among density, land use, connectivity, transit vehicles, and the public realm. The streetcar city concept is compatible with single-family homes yet can be served by transit. It ensures that walking will be a part of the everyday experience for most residents and provides mobility for infirm users. It has been shown to induce substantial shifts away from auto use to transit use and can conceivably be introduced into suburban contexts.[26] It has also been shown to dramatically increase investment in a way that neither buses nor expensive subway lines can. It is compatible with the trend toward increasingly dispersed job sites and seems to be the form that best achieves "complete community" goals.

The streetcar city principle, whether manifest with or without steel-wheeled vehicles, is a viable and amply precedented form for what must by 2050 become dramatically more sustainable urban regions. Other sustainable city concepts that presume extremely high density urban areas linked by rapid regional subway systems seem inconceivably at odds with the existing fabric of both prewar and postwar urban landscapes, and beyond our ability to afford. At the other extreme, assuming that some technological fix, such as the hydrogen car, will allow us to continue sprawling our cities into the infinite future seems even more delusional. To heal our sick cities, we must recognize the physical body of the city for what it is and implement a physical therapy calibrated to its specific capacity for a healthier future. The physical body of our regions was, and still is, the streetcar city pattern. The streetcar city principle is intended to provide both simple insight into our condition and a clear set of strategies that have proven themselves for decades.

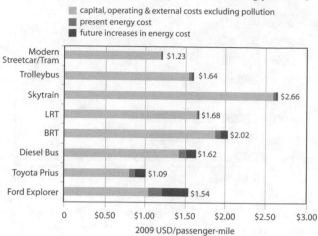

Figure 2.21. Total cost per passenger-mile. The total cost per passenger-mile was calculated by adding the capital, external, operating, and energy costs for each mode.

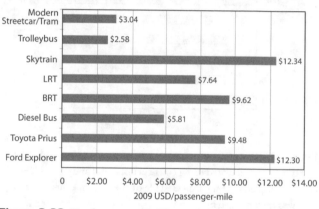

Figure 2.22. Total cost per trip. The total cost per trip was calculated by multiplying the cost per passenger-mile by the average trip length for each mode.

CHAPTER 3

Design an Interconnected Street System

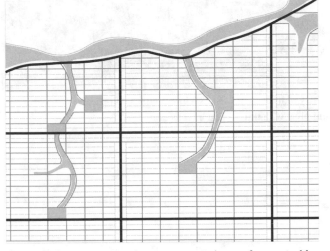

Figure 3.1. Interconnected streets are a vital part of a sustainable community. This diagram shows a rectilinear grid, but many variations are available. Curved, axial, and informal grids are all workable.

Street systems either maximize connectivity or frustrate it. North American neighborhoods built prior to 1950 were rich in connectivity, as evidenced by the relatively high number of street intersections per square mile typically found there.[1] Interconnected street systems provide more than one path to reach surrounding major streets. In most interconnected street networks, two types of streets predominate: narrow residential streets and arterial streets. In this book, for reasons explained in chapter 2, we call these arterial streets in interconnected networks "streetcar" arterials.

On the other end of the spectrum are the post–World War II suburban cul-de-sac systems, where dead end streets predominate and offer only one path from home to surrounding suburban arterials. This cul-de-sac–dominated system can be characterized as dendritic, or "treelike," the opposite of the web of connections found in interconnected systems. Streets in this system all branch out from the main "trunk," which in Canadian and U.S. cities is usually the freeway. Attached to the main trunk of the freeway are the major "branches," which are the feeder suburban arterial streets or minor highways. These large branches then give access to the next category down the tree, the "minor branches," which are the collector streets. Collector streets then connect to the "twigs and branch tips" of the system, the residential streets and dead-end cul-de-sacs.

The major advantages of the interconnected system are that it makes all trips as short as possible, allows pedestrians and bikes to flow through the system without inconvenience, and relieves congestion by providing many alternate routes to the same destination. The major disadvantages of the interconnected street system are that no homes are completely cut off

---

[1]A gridiron street system typically has a greater number of intersections per square unit area than a dendritic street system.

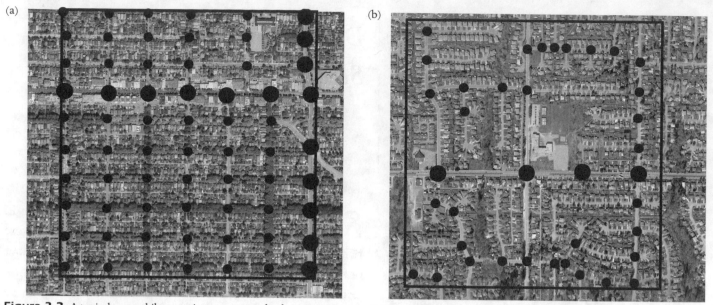

Figure 3.2. A typical square kilometer in a streetcar suburb (a) in Vancouver, British Columbia, with sixty-six intersections compared to a typical square kilometer in an automobile-oriented neighborhood (b) in Surrey, British Columbia, with thirty-eight intersections.

from the irritation of outside traffic and that it uses more linear feet of street per standard-sized lot than does the dendritic system.

The major advantages of the dendritic system are that it shifts trips away from homes lucky enough to be located at the ends of cul-de-sacs, allows cars to flow easily through the system if it has been optimally designed, and requires fewer linear feet of road length per standard-sized lot. The major disadvantages of the dendritic system are that almost all trips are made longer than they would be if the system was interconnected and that it is prone to congestion since it provides no alternative routes away from main intersections.

Despite its disadvantages, the dendritic system has become a ubiquitous feature of urban districts built since 1950.[2] The complex industry that creates new communities is so thoroughly committed to the dendritic street system that alternative thinking is no longer supported. Most municipal and regional transportation planners and engineers speak only in the language of the "street hierarchy," or the hierarchical categorization of streets.

[2]The street hierarchy was first elaborated by Ludwig Hilberseimer in 1927 and has since prevailed as the dominant model for suburban development (Ford, 1999). Between 1930 and 1950, residential street standards became institutionalized by the Federal Housing Administration (Southworth and Ben-Joseph, 1997), and by the late 1950s the "normal" suburban street network was dominated by cul-de-sac streets within vast areas of single-use residential zoning (Ford, 1999).

Figure 3.3. This grade school in Surrey, British Columbia, is located in the middle of a super block, far from the high-traffic arterial highlighted above. The closest bus stop is more than a half-mile walk from the front entrance of the school.

CHALLENGES OF THE DENDRITIC STREET SYSTEM

Jurisdictions typically have a full set of regulations that assume all road systems are dendritic, making it impossible for interconnected streets to be understood. For example, the Salem, Oregon, planning department requires new developments to assign categories from this hierarchy to all streets in a proposed land subdivision before the proposal can be approved.[3] In 2003, the proponents for a sustainable new community at the former Fairview State Training Center in Salem argued that their proposed interconnected street system was essentially without a flow-concentrating hierarchy and, rather, was designed to distribute traffic throughout the network. Unfortunately city planners and engineers did not have the discretion to accept this argument, feeling that their own policies made a categorization unavoidable.

Having failed, the proponents reluctantly identified as the "arterial" the community's proposed "High Street," where shops and community facilities such as libraries and schools were proposed. Unfortunately, this designation triggered a reaction in the school district where one of their policies prohibited elementary schools located across "arterial" streets from the majority of its students. Here, too, the school officials felt that they had no discretion in the matter and could accept only a plan where the school was placed less accessibly on a "quieter" part of the site. They recommended putting the school at the end of a cul-de-sac, with ample space for "mothers to drop off their children in cars every morning." At no point did they take seriously the master plan's imperative that the school should be "centrally located to make walking convenient and to make the school the symbol of the community."[4]

A second example: In 1998, the City of Surrey, British Columbia, partnered with the University of British Columbia's Design Centre for Sustainability to design a new "sustainable community" based on principles similar to the ones in this book. An interconnected modified grid system was designed. All of the charrette participants, including the consulting engineer, understood and supported the logic of the interconnected grid. But when the engineer was required to model the performance of

---

[3] A key objective of the Salem Transportation Plan (City of Salem, 2007, 3-1) is to "develop a comprehensive, hierarchical system of streets and highways that provides for optimal mobility for all travel modes." This is to be achieved through creating a street network made up of peripheral arterial streets linking outlying districts to one another and the central core area; collector streets that connect local traffic to the arterial system; and local streets that provide property access and neighborhood circulation (City of Salem, 2007). This is a community that otherwise encourages sustainability and alternatives to the car. The contradictions between the street regulations and the broader sustainability goals are not recognized in Salem, Oregon, or in most other jurisdictions in the United States and Canada.

[4] Recollection of the author, who participated in these meetings.

the system, she had to artificially assign a hierarchy to the road system or the traffic-flow software simply would not run. Thus, even the modeling software acknowledges only one kind of system—the dendritic system.

These decisions, driven by a deeply flawed street taxonomy and a tendency to narrowly focus on one issue to the exclusion of all the related sustainable community demands, has left us with neighborhood configurations were people are forced to drive more than they should. Studies show that the dendritic configuration forces residents to drive over 40 percent more than residents in older, streetcar city neighborhoods. This results in a 40 percent increase in greenhouse gas (GHG) emissions per car; given that households in these systems are likely to own two or more cars, their GHG contribution per household is easily double that of residents of traditional streetcar districts.

Dendritic Streets: Good for Cars, Bad for People

The basic problem with the dendritic system is that all trips collect at one point, usually at the major intersection of two suburban arterials or at the on ramp to the freeway. With all trips in an area feeding to one point, that intersection will typically receive up to four times more trips than an equivalent intersection in an interconnected system (Allen, 1996). With all of these trips forced through one pinch point, congestion is inevitable. It is only through dramatically widening these intersections that such congestion can be alleviated. Huge expenditures for widening suburban intersections are now routine, with nine or ten thirteen-foot lanes, and right-of-way intersections that are two hundred feet (or more) wide.[5] While many of these intersections admirably handle the turning motions and through trips for sixty thousand or more car trips a day, they are almost impossible to cross on foot, particularly for infirm pedestrians.

One study of pedestrian deaths in the Orlando area identified just such a landscape as a pedestrian death hot spot, the worst in the region.[6] Apparently, many customers were foolhardy enough to try to trek on foot from one popular restaurant to another across the ten-lane arterial street that separated them, and there these pedestrians met their end. It would have been infinitely more intelligent to drive.

[5]Contemporary suburban street patterns are characterized by wide spacings of arterial streets that typically provide six through lanes, right turn lanes, and single or dual left turn lanes (Levinson, 1999). In his report *Traffic Circulation Planning for Communities*, Marks (1974) specifies that arterial streets should be spaced one mile apart; accommodate ten thousand to thirty thousand vehicles per day; feature four to six lanes with a physical median, turn lanes, and signalized pedestrian crossing; and have considerable building setbacks. On-street parking is prohibited, and pedestrian use is meant to be minimal.

[6]In 2001, the fatality rate per 100 million miles traveled for public transit riders was 0.75, for drivers and their passengers it was 1.3, but for walkers it was 20.1 (Ernst, 2004). Using the Pedestrian Danger Index (PDI) to compare metropolitan areas, Ernst and Shoup (2009) found that the most dangerous metropolitan areas in the United States for walking in 2007–2008 were Orlando, Tampa, Miami, Jacksonville, Memphis, Raleigh, Louisville, Houston, Birmingham, and Atlanta. An overwhelming proportion of pedestrian deaths "occurred along roadways that were dangerous by design, streets that were engineered for speeding cars and made little or no provision for people on foot, in wheelchairs or on a bicycle" (Ernst and Shoup, 2009, p. 7). From 1997 to 2006, over 66 percent of pedestrian fatalities occurred on principal and minor arterial roadways (NHTSA, 2008). Miles-Doan and Thompson (1999) state that "the long-range solution to the arterial road safety problem begins with reevaluating the planning practice of designing urban arterials as traffic-moving facilities and nothing else" (p. 217). Typically, pedestrians who want to cross arterial streets need to contend with several lanes of traffic making a variety of movements at street intersections. The City of Orlando Transportation Planning Bureau (2002) found that when these discouraging conditions were minimized by reducing road width, the number of pedestrians crossing the street increased by 56 percent.

Transit systems seldom work well in dendritic systems either, since the passenger drop-off point is still hundreds of yards from their destination, separated from the street by acres of sun-scorched or wind-blown parking lot.

Major streets within interconnected street systems often work quite differently than in suburbs. The interconnected Broadway corridor in Vancouver (discussed in chapter 2) carries sixty thousand vehicle trips a day. Were it redesigned to suburban (dendritic) standards, Broadway would require at least nine wide travel lanes, including three turn lanes at each intersection. It currently operates with only four narrow through lanes, no turning lanes, and two parking lanes. The parking lanes are used for through traffic during rush hours, a double use of a lane that is common in older communities but unheard of in new ones. Left turns are restricted at many intersections to keep traffic moving smoothly. The lanes are a relatively narrow ten feet, with a consequent curb-to-curb crossing distance of sixty feet, less than half the distance of the comparable suburban intersection. Crossing times for pedestrians, even infirm ones, are reasonable over this distance. The remaining space is taken up by fifteen-foot-wide sidewalks serving a continuous line of storefronts. The surrounding grid of streets provides alternative options when this intersection is congested, alternatives that do not exist in the dendritic systems. Drivers frustrated from making lefts always have the option of using the adjacent street grid to position their car on a perpendicular intersection and reach their destination that way.

Big Boxes

Another consequence of dendritic street systems is that they favor big box developments over other, more neighborhood scale developments. When tens of thousands of trips are made through an intersection per day, the major big box chains take an interest. Their store location formulas depend almost entirely on a combination of two factors: (1) the income range of families in the service area as taken from the census data, and (2) the number of trips per day through the intersection adjacent to the site they are considering.[7] The service-area calculation is based on the distance potential customers might be willing to

---

[7]Hahn (2000) looked at two case studies of agglomerated big box retailer developments that were thought to be representative of the industry as a whole and found that in both cases the developer chose a location adjacent to a high-traffic intersection and in an area where the average household income was above the national average.

drive to get to the store (for example, twenty minutes). Obviously, the more the public spends on a smooth-flowing, auto-oriented infrastructure, then the longer the radius line for the service area, the larger the potential customer base, and thus the bigger the store must be.

In this way, we see the connection between ever greater expenditure on suburban road infrastructure and ever larger stores that capitalize on this public expenditure. As more stores locate in busy commercial areas, the gravitational forces these stores exert on the system lead inevitably to congestion, as whatever capacity the system provides is used up by the decisions of big box corporations. Interestingly, Home Depot Corporation has recently changed the way it calculates store locations and size, moving to smaller stores more frequently located in the urban landscape. Why? Because increasing congestion in U.S. and Canadian cities is shrinking the distance consumers can dependably drive in twenty minutes, and as it shrinks the Home Depot "big" box is shrinking as well.

Gated Communities

Whatever one's opinion of gated communities, they are highly compatible with dendritic systems and generally incompatible with interconnected systems. Dendritic systems by their nature require developments to occur in pods, with usually only one access point into surrounding collectors or arterial roads. These arterials are usually unattractive and pedestrian unfriendly ("car sewers," in the words of *Geography of Nowhere* author James Howard Kunstler). The gate serves less to ensure safety than to mark a congenial and attractive inside from the threatening and often very unpleasant exterior of the suburban arterial. Social critics often remark on the insularity and inherent inequity of gated communities but seldom link their emergence with the dendritic street network, which makes them inevitable (Kunstler, 1993, 2005).

On the other hand, interconnected systems leave development increments that are usually too small for gated communities. Even exclusive projects located on typical five-acre urban blocks cannot be truly gated and are therefore less appropriately

Figure 3.4. Atlanta National gated community, Alpharetta, Atlanta, Georgia.

Figure 3.5. Seagate, the oldest gated community in New York, features an interconnected street network and relatively high density.

Figure 3.6. It is easy to see why people living in a cul-de-sac development prefer it to the busy arterial environment created as a result of the dendritic street system.

Figure 3.7. From the air, one can easily see the difference between heavy-traffic arterials and light-traffic cul-de-sacs.

subject to the criticisms leveled at typically much larger gated projects in suburban dendritic street systems.

Cul-de-sacs

It is often said in defense of dendritic systems that people like the enhanced perception of safety from crime and the much reduced traffic flows in front of their houses on cul-de-sacs; these points are then cited as justification for the dendritic system. While the evidence of that appeal is not universal, there is no doubt that many people do prefer the dead-end street for these reasons. It is also understandable that, given the hostile environment that characterizes the arterial and even collector streets in dendritic systems, it is quite rational to want to be as far upstream from these traffic impacts as possible. Unfortunately, it is just not possible to design these urban landscapes such that everyone lives at the end of a cul-de-sac. An achievable number might be in the order of 25 percent of all people living on streets that serve fewer than fifty homes and their twelve trips per family a day by car (for a total of six hundred cars past your window, or one every eighty seconds). As a result, those unfortunates who reside between the cul-de-sacs and busy arterials will have to tolerate many more cars past their homes than would the average resident living within an interconnected street system. Thus, the advantages of the cul-de-sac are paid for at double cost by residents less fortuitously situated.

FOUR TYPES OF INTERCONNECTED STREET SYSTEMS

Given that interconnected street systems are walking and transit friendly, reduce VMT, and are compatible with community-scale "streetcar city" corridors, they are the more sustainable approach. When most people think of interconnected systems, they picture the classic gridiron pattern of perfectly straight streets arranged at ninety-degree angles to one another. Certainly, this is the most common form, but not all interconnected streets systems are grid patterns. In addition to the grid, there are at least three other identifiable and distinct but still interconnected systems: the radial system, the informal web, and the warped grid.

Gridiron Pattern

As the name suggests, the gridiron pattern is the highly uniform grid pattern of straight streets at ninety-degree angles that are usually aligned with the cardinal axes. The pattern is most common in the United States and Canada in cities built between 1840 and 1950. This block pattern is best understood as a finer-grain subdivision of the larger, agricultural forty-acre quarter section. Typically, one forty-acre quarter section would be subdivided into two 640-foot segments in one direction and four 320-foot segments in the other, resulting in eight blocks of five acres each.

This pattern has two principal advantages over all others. It automatically aligns all intersections perfectly at even right angles and can be extended infinitely in all directions as the city grows. It is often criticized as dull but can be extremely dramatic in some circumstances. Manhattan, Vancouver, and San Francisco are three good examples. It is also easy to get oriented in a grid pattern because it provides vistas to distant parts of the city or countryside down the uninterrupted visual corridors of the street.

Radial Pattern

The radial pattern is highly interconnected, but the major streets do not typically align with the cardinal axes. Rather, in this system the major streets typically radiate from significant squares or public monuments. Orientation is not to the north, south, east, or west but to key landmarks in the urban fabric. Blocks are not cut evenly from the fabric of forty-acre quarter sections but are typically close in size to the 320- by 640-foot module of the gridiron. It is undoubtedly a dramatic pattern and can function as well as the gridiron. However, moving traffic and pedestrians through complex intersections where more

Figure 3.8. The traditional urban blocks in Vancouver, BC (top) share the same dimensions as the blocks in Seattle, Washington (bottom).

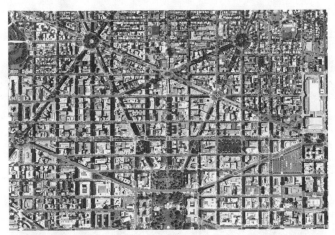

Figure 3.9. A radial street layout in Washington, D.C.

than two main arterials intersect can be difficult. Washington, D.C., is the best North American example of this pattern.

Informal Web Pattern

Boston and Cambridge, Massachusetts, are two characteristic U.S. examples of this pattern. In the absence of the organizing grid of forty-acre squares, earlier U.S. and Canadian cities organized themselves around a web of streets that connected key villages and crossroads. This resulted in a web of major streets that connected these key locations using whatever street angle necessary. The spaces between these major connections were eventually filled in with generally rectilinear blocks, again in the natural increment of between 250 and 350 feet in width and 400 and 700 feet in length. Navigation in such a system is from one city "square" (they are seldom actually square) to another. For example, in Cambridge, Massachusetts, the main streets

Figure 3.10. An informal web street layout in Cambridge, Massachusetts.

connect Kendall Square to Inman Square to Harvard Square to Scolly Square and so forth.

Warped Grid

Grids do not need to be rectilinear and aligned with the cardinal axes to be grids. A grid can be twisted and warped so that the streets curve, usually to match the contours of the landscape. When twisted and warped like this, the blocks will naturally vary somewhat in size. Warped grids create more opportunities for dramatic landscape features than do gridirons. This form is usually associated with the romantic period in American city design, with Frederick Law Olmsted as its most significant proponent. No complete American city is designed this way, unfortunately. However, most cities have at least one district built in this style, usually dating from the period between the 1860s and 1930, when this style was popular. The Chicago suburb of Riverside, Illinois, designed by Frederick Law Olmsted and Calvert Vaux in 1868, is the most famous of these districts.

BLOCK SIZE

The land left inside surrounding streets is called a block. Traditional cities have blocks of about five acres, including street space, and between three and four if one counts only the developable land outside the street "right-of-way" (ROW). Many exceptions exist, of course—notably Manhattan, with its much smaller blocks of less than three acres each, at 200 feet wide by 500 feet long, and Portland, with its extremely small but very walkable blocks of only 200 feet square, or just less than one acre each.

At the other end of the size spectrum is the suburban "super block," a large block with attributes that are harder to describe and understand. Super blocks are always very large, frequently forty acres or more. Super blocks can even be as large as one square mile, the norm in Phoenix and much of Florida. Whether blocks are two hundred feet wide urban scale, or a quarter mile or full mile wide superblock scale, blocks are still defined as the land inside a continuous surrounding road. De-

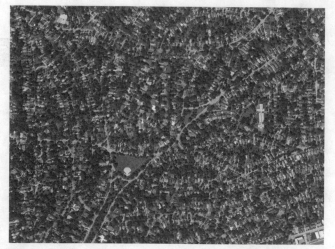

Figure 3.11. A warped grid street layout in Riverside, Illinois.

Figure 3.12. This super block in Pembroke Pines, Florida, is one square mile, with only two entrances from the surrounding streets.

velopable land inside the large super blocks most often requires additional streets to access interior parcels, which results in dead-end interior road networks that could connect across the block but do not. In Phoenix, almost all of the streets on the one-mile grid serve a variety of essentially gated complexes inside the one-mile squares. The result is a city where the through streets on the one-mile grid are all heavily loaded with traffic and generally incompatible with pedestrian-friendly commercial uses. They simply accept too much traffic load from the interiors of the one-mile superblocks they serve.

WHY IS THE INTERCONNECTED SYSTEM BETTER?

Trips on an interconnected street system are more efficient and shorter than those on the artificially lengthy and circuitous dendritic systems. A five-minute walk covers much more ground in interconnected street systems—easily as much as or more than twice as many total acres—making it much easier to provide services or recreational amenities that are accessible without a car. If an intersection in an interconnected system is congested, parallel streets allow for "rat running," obviating the need for expensive intersection widening and associated expensive property takings. While residents do not like rat running, it occurs only during times of peak congestion, can be slowed, and is much less damaging to neighborhood quality and much less expensive than adding lanes to main intersections. Interconnected street systems are also safer for pedestrians. A landmark study by Peter Swift (1998) determined that pedestrian injuries were four times more likely on wide, dendritic suburban streets than on typically narrower, interconnected urban streets (street width issues are discussed below).

Finally, it must be admitted that arterials in interconnected systems must be designed for slower speeds than in dendritic contexts. This is because frequent intersections are an elemental feature of interconnected systems and the streetcar arterials that serve them. This frequency of intersections requires that the streets be designed for lower average speeds and that stops be more frequent. Thus, under ordinary circumstances, a suburban arterial will deliver drivers to their destinations faster than will a more traditional streetcar arterial street. Here suffice it to say that slower average speed in a system that resists congestion and is compatible with urban uses is probably a good thing rather than bad. As mentioned above, the Home Depot Corporation's decision to downsize their stores is instructive. As speeds are slowed in a system, the scale of enterprises shrinks with them. If our objective is to reduce distances between desire points, it would seem that a strategy that allows for smooth flow but not necessarily fast flow has a certain utility value.

The super blocks created by the dendritic system have the advantage of excluding through traffic across the block, provide more options for parcel configurations inside the block, and require less road length to serve parcels than do gridirons. On the other hand, by blocking through movements across the block, they force traffic onto arterials and overload arterial intersections, prevent congestion flows from exercising any optional routes, make pedestrian trips frustratingly indirect, provide bicycles no option but to compete with cars and trucks for road space on the arterials, and degrade the value of parcels fronting arterials for pedestrian-friendly commercial use.

Traditional smaller urban blocks are much more permeable for both car and pedestrian traffic and allow for more frequent "streetcar" arterials (Vancouver, for example, has a streetcar arterial every half mile on average, which means that one is never more than a five-minute walk from a commercial "streetcar street"). The distribution of traffic and the more frequent provision of streetcar arterials within walking distance make this form inherently more compatible with a strategy to promote transit, biking, and walking. For example, bikers who are not enthusiastic about keeping pace with traffic on the arterials can take advantage of the parallel street network for a safer and slower ride without sacrificing directness. Vancouver has a very successful network of designated bike streets that typically run parallel to the streetcar arterials.

PARCEL SIZE

Block size of course determines the range of parcel sizes possible. It is remarkable that in such cities as Seattle or Vancouver every single land use has somehow been fit into parcels that fit

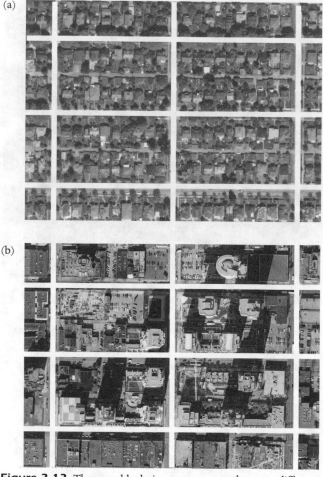

(a)

(b)

Figure 3.13. The same block size can accommodate very different building configurations as shown in these examples from Vancouver, BC.

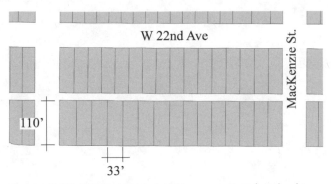

Figure 3.14. This typical block in Vancouver, British Columbia, yields thirty-two lots with the standard size of 33 feet by 110 feet. (Source: VanMap)

inside traditional 660- by 330-foot blocks. Accounting for lanes, this means almost all development parcels in the city are less than two acres in size. Thus, forty-story towers and single-family homes and everything in between have been fit onto the same size block. So while block size will limit the range of parcel sizes and types, it is astonishing to see how many different ways the blocks have been designed and utilized.

Single-family Home Parcels

The most pressing issue in sustainable urban design is probably the single-family home parcel. This parcel type has been the driver for many, if not most, of the symptoms of illness described in chapter 1. Some have argued that the single-family home is anathema to sustainability and should be eliminated entirely. Yet, the desire for single-family homes remains very strong, and it is unlikely that this will shift dramatically in the next few decades, despite ups and downs of the real estate market.

Fortunately, there is a way to configure the single-family parcel that is compatible with sustainable community design: by building on the small lot. Traditional streetcar cities were largely organized around small single-family home lots, in neighborhoods that were pedestrian friendly and where alternatives to the car existed. The secret is the 3,000 to 4,000-square-foot lot. Virtually all lots in Vancouver are 33 feet by 110 feet (making it roughly a 3,600-foot lot). At this size, the lot yield is about thirty-two lots per block. The gross (inclusive of street space) density of the block would thus be about six or seven parcels per acre. Since duplexes and secondary suites are allowed throughout Vancouver, the density—when computed in dwelling units rather than parcels—is typically over ten units per gross acre. Our analysis of two traditional Vancouver blocks that appeared to be all single-family homes actually had a density of over seventeen units per gross acre.[8] The secret was that most of the homes actually had a hidden secondary suite, and some of the homes contained three units.

By using small lots for detached homes, it is easily possible to preserve the single-family home option, and certainly the single-family home "feel" of the street, and still create sustainable communities. Single-family home lots can be as small as

---

[8]This study is available online at http://www.jtc.sala.ubc.ca/projects/ADS/HTML_Files/ChapterTwo/matrix_us_2.htm

2,300 square feet if the footprint of the new home is small and the home is high rather than wide or deep. (This issue is discussed further below under the "different dwelling types on the same street" principle.)

IDEAL BLOCK AND PARCEL SIZE

Various arguments have been forwarded favoring the small "Portland block" (two hundred feet by two hundred feet from street center line to street center line) for its abundance of corner opportunities and its walkability. The longer but equally thin "Manhattan block" has been promoted for similar reasons. However, these two blocks have very shallow parcels, never deeper than eighty feet, tightly constraining the building form options available and making it almost impossible to provide vehicle lanes in the middle of the block for service and secondary access. For this reason, Portland residential neighborhoods are afflicted with driveways that cross sidewalks at every house lot, compromising the safety and comfort of the sidewalk and eliminating at least a third of on-street parking spots. In downtown Portland, lacking lanes, all loading and delivery must compete for space with pedestrians on the sidewalks. The same is true in Manhattan.

Conversely, in Vancouver and Seattle, where blocks are the more common 640- by 320-foot increment, parcels can be over 110 feet deep, even after subtracting 20 feet for the rear lane. These somewhat larger blocks have provided suitable footprints for the proliferation of new condominium high-rise buildings, for which Vancouver is now famous. Ideally, these towers should be between 60 and 80 feet square. Any smaller and they are uneconomic; any larger and they are too fat to get natural light into the core of the building (not to mention ugly). The point tower on the podium base pioneered in Vancouver would not have been possible on a much smaller or much larger block. Indeed, in Portland, where new tower developments are now coming on line, the smaller block is creating a trend toward single building blocks where a whole block is occupied by one podium building of about 200 feet on a side and a usually somewhat fat tower in the middle of the base. While some good results are possible with this form, it tends to predetermine design

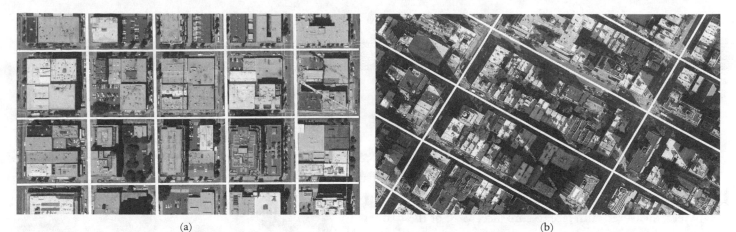

(a)   (b)

Figure 3.15. Portland, Oregon, is known for its 260-foot by 260-foot block size (a), whereas Manhattan blocks (b) are three times as long as blocks in Portland.

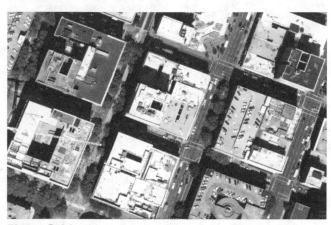

Figure 3.16. The smaller block size in Portland, Oregon, favors single-building blocks.

Figure 3.17. The larger block size in Vancouver, British Columbia, allows for more diverse design solutions.

outcomes more decisively than the larger "Vancouver block" and would in time lead to a city of single buildings surrounded by a square of streets—probably not a good thing.

In residential areas, the larger Vancouver block allows for a rear lane to keep driveways from crossing sidewalks and the front facade, keeping building fronts free of garage doors. Narrow-lot homes have many advantages, but most of them are compromised if half or more of the frontage is given over to wide driveways and garage doors. The phenomenon of the "snout house," a house that is all garage and no facade to the street, is common for this reason in California, where small lots are popular but rear lanes are not.

Finally, the deeper lot allows many creative options for the site, including front-to-back duplexes and "lane houses" (small residential structures where the garage was or is typically located, which as of 2009 are legal in all of Vancouver), or generous rear yard gardens. There is a limit to how deep the lot wants to be, however, and thus how wide the block should be. If blocks were 400 feet wide rather than 320 feet, lots would gain rear yard space but would end up with no additional frontage and, thus, fewer 33-foot-wide parcels per gross acre.

What about block length then? Here there is more flexibility. The breaking of the quarter mile into two even 640-foot increments makes a certain intuitive sense and has proven itself to be walkable, but it is by no means a universal increment. One can reduce the length down to 400 feet without tremendous loss in land use efficiency, or increase it up to 800 feet before the blocks become a very serious barrier to easy pedestrian movement or start to compromise the overall permeability of the system.

ROAD WIDTH

No single feature of sustainable community design is more important than road width. Prior to 1940, most residential streets in the United States and Canada were less than twenty-eight feet, measured curb face to curb face. Most of these streets allowed parking on both sides of the street in seven-foot-wide parking lanes. This left only fourteen feet of travel lane in the middle to handle two-way traffic. The typical car is about six feet wide, so two cars approaching from opposite directions on a street where cars are parked on both sides are going to have to go quite slow to avoid hitting each other. This presumably unsafe condition motivated a change in standards after 1950, when typical curb-to-curb width became thirty-four feet, composed of two ten-foot-wide travel lanes flanked by two seven-foot-wide parking lanes. This width allowed the free flow of two-way traffic without the need to slow down when cars approached from opposite directions. As time passed, many municipalities decided it would be a good idea to widen residential streets even more, allowing additional space for parking and travel ways such that forty-foot-wide suburban residential streets are found in many parts of North America.

A number of unanticipated negative consequences have been associated with this road-widening trend. Most surprising is that streets that were made wider to be safer turned out to be much more dangerous. A study by Peter Swift (1998) found that wide suburban residential streets were associated with four times more pedestrian deaths per unit population than were narrower traditional urban streets. How can this be explained? The answer appears to be induced speed. Pedestrians hit by cars traveling thirty-five miles per hour are ten times more likely to be killed than pedestrians hit by cars traveling twenty-five miles per hour. Wider suburban streets designed to allow free-flowing two-way traffic and generous parking strips signal drivers that it

Figure 3.18. A snout house is characterized by a protruding garage that takes up most of the street frontage, squeezing out front yards and making it hard to find the front door. (Source: Dolores Hayden, *A Field Guide to Sprawl* (New York: Norton, 2004) / photograph by Jim Wark)

Figure 3.19. Curb-to-curb street widths in many neighborhoods across the United States and Canada—such as Nashville (a) and Cleveland (b)—are the same dimensions.

is acceptable to travel at speeds much higher than on narrower traditional streets.

This phenomenon is even more extreme when one considers that the parking strips on most suburban streets are rarely used, since these landscapes also include generous driveway space. Thus, drivers are provided with as much as forty feet of clear width to command when driving. Even when these streets are posted with twenty-mile-per-hour speed limits, as they often are, it takes a tremendous act of will to slow to that apparent crawl when the freeway-scale generosity of the road width invites speeds at least twice that fast.

It took decades for the engineering community to begin to come to grips with this phenomenon and to coin a term— *side friction*—to describe it.[9] Traditional urban streets have high side friction because the travel way is too narrow for passing oncoming cars at speed; combined with the abundance of parked cars on both sides, the trees in the boulevard, and the pedestrians on the sidewalks that one may or may not be able to see behind the cars and trees, all of these things conspire to create an atmosphere of uncertainty and caution in the mind of the driver. Thus, the driver responds by driving slowly, no matter what the posted speed.

Alternatively, wider suburban streets have low side friction. The travel way is generous enough to pass oncoming cars at speed; parked cars are rare, providing an even greater enticement to move quickly; and nothing is hidden from the driver's

[9] The first mention of the term *side friction* seems to be in 1936 in a paper for the Highway Research Board (Barnett, Haile, and Moyer, 1936). Sources in the 1940s and 1950s continued to use it within a highway context (Barnett, 1940; Holmes, 1958); however, understanding how the concept applied to residential streets took far longer.

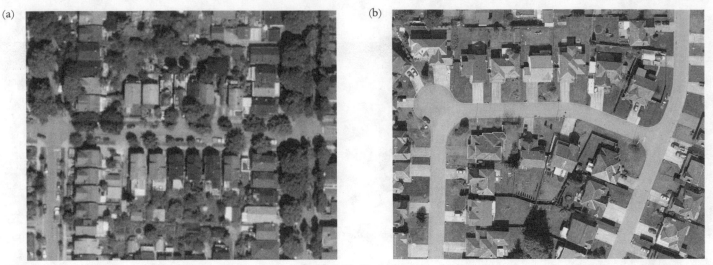

(a) (b)

Figure 3.20. Narrow "queuing" streets (a) create conditions with high side friction compared to the suburban street (b), which has very low side friction.

field of view by trees. All of these things conspire to psychologically license the driver to feel safe at speeds much higher than those posted, resulting in increased pedestrian fatalities.

FIRE ACCESS

Pedestrian and auto safety were not the only motivations for wider streets. Fire access was also a powerful motivation. The average size of fire trucks in the United States and Canada has been steadily increasing. It is common for ladder trucks to require fifteen or even twenty feet of street width to set up stabilizer arms extending from their sides. Concerns about the need to speed to the scene of a fire can lead to demand for thirteen-foot-wide travel lanes in both directions on even short cul-de-sac roads that serve only twenty to thirty homes. A similar concern about cornering at speed can lead to standards for corner curb radii so generous as to seriously lengthen pedestrian crossing distances at intersections and thus compromise pedestrians' safety.

Sadly but predictably, the increased width in these standards has not led to enhanced safety. Peter Swift's study (1998) also found no difference in fire-related fatalities when comparing districts with narrow streets to those with wider ones. More depressing still were the results of a study on fire response times

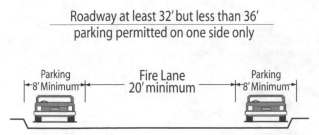

Roadway at least 32' but less than 36'
parking permitted on one side only

Parking
8' Minimum

Fire Lane
20' minimum

Parking
8' Minimum

Figure 3.21. A typical emergency-access standard, with thirty-six-foot (11 m) curb-to-curb width. (Source: Ontario Fire Department, California)

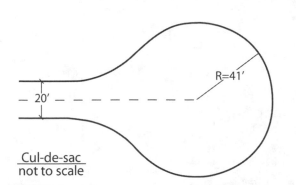

R=41'

20'

Cul-de-sac
not to scale

Figure 3.22. A typical emergency-access standard for cul-de-sacs takes up approximately one sixth of an acre. (Source: San Joaquin County, California)

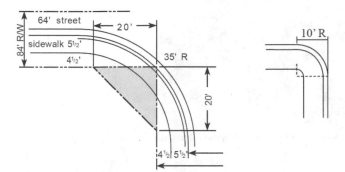

64' street
84' R/W
sidewalk 5½'
4½'

20'

35' R

20'

10' R

4½ | 5½

Figure 3.23. A typical arterial curb radius in a hierarchical street network is thirty-five feet, while a typical neotraditional curb radius is ten feet. (Source: Standard of the Division of Transportation, Salt Lake City Community Development)

[10]Bill Dedman wrote in an article for the *Boston Globe* (January 30, 2005): "Few communities in Massachusetts are adding firehouses to serve new subdivisions resulting in slower response times, which frequently result in deaths. Communities of all income levels are facing these problems."

in the Boston metropolitan area. The study found that response times became dangerously long as one moved away from older streetcar city districts to the suburbs—in exactly those same suburban communities where wider streets were required. It seems that whatever fire-safety benefits were achieved with wider streets were far outweighed by the difficulty of getting quickly and directly to the fire via circuitous dendritic road systems. Given the overall low density of these landscapes, there is not sufficient tax base to build fire stations within a short distance of all homes.[10] In other words, an urban service area for a fire station serving twenty thousand people might be one square mile in a streetcar city area. In suburban areas, the same population might be spread out over twenty times more land, and thus the fire station serving the area would be that much farther away from homes. This, of course, suggests a larger contributing symptom to the disease of our unsustainable metropolitan areas. Fire officials are typically called on to speak only to issues of road width and design. Seldom, if ever, are they asked to speak to the larger issues of density and interconnectivity—issues that seem more significant to their mission when the operation of the entire urban system is examined.

QUEUING STREETS

From this evidence, it seems that the traditional twenty-six- to twenty-eight-foot residential street in an interconnected system is better after all. This kind of street is now called a "queuing" street, a somewhat misleading name that tries to signify that one approaching car will typically pull over (take turns as in a queue) into an empty parking space to allow the other to pass. Coupled with short blocks and frequent stop signs, a queuing street is a more effective traffic-calming strategy than speed bumps. It saves pavement and makes for a much more attractively scaled pedestrian-friendly streetscape. A recommended right-of-way for a sustainable queuing street, capable of handling a large number of car trips but at speeds compatible with pedestrian and bike safety, is as follows: six-foot sidewalk, ten-foot tree boulevard, seven-foot parking lane, fourteen-foot travel way, seven-foot parking lane, ten-foot tree boulevard, six-foot sidewalk. All of this fits within sixty feet, which happens to be the

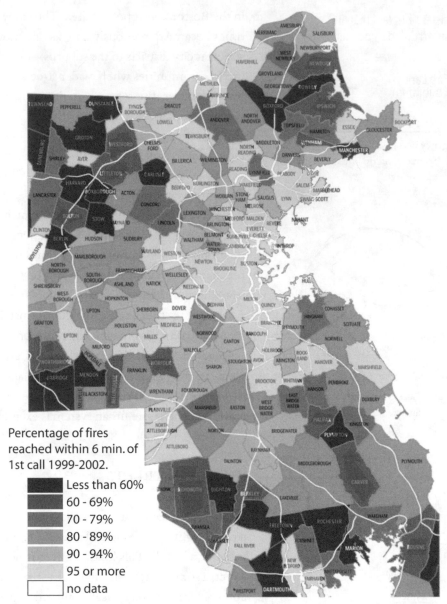

Percentage of fires reached within 6 min. of 1st call 1999-2002.

Less than 60%
60 - 69%
70 - 79%
80 - 89%
90 - 94%
95 or more
no data

Figure 3.24. The emergency response times in the Boston metropolitan area. (Source: *Boston Globe* analysis of National Fire Incident Reporting System data; graphic: GLOBE STAFF/ David Butler, Bill Dedman)

most common right-of-way width found in streetcar city residential districts. Developers will often want to reduce right-of-way widths even more to increase the proportion of lands available for sale in comparison to lands reserved for public right-of-way. Some narrowing can occur in the tree boulevard and sidewalk to get the right-of-way width below sixty feet, but it is not recommended. Wide sidewalks on both sides are crucial for walkable neighborhoods (presuming destinations have been

Figure 3.25. An example of a queuing street with on-street parking and a narrow through lane.

[11] Local levels of government can have a great deal of input when it comes to the adoption and implementation of design standards, but they commonly fail to exercise it. In Oregon, for example, land use laws allow local governments to establish local subdivision standards for street widths that shall "supersede and prevail over any specifications and standards for roads and streets set forth in a uniform fire code adopted by the State Fire Marshall, a municipal fire department or a country firefighting agency" (Neighborhood Streets Project Stakeholders, 2000). Organizations like West Coast Environmental Law advocate and empower local governmental agencies to adapt their standards and guidelines to be more in line with social and environmental perspectives (West Coast Environmental Law, 2002).

preserved and created), while tree boulevards, in addition to being beautiful, provide protection for walking and space for green infrastructure (as described in chapter 7).

THE CORNER

Like all elements of street design, intersection design is far more complex and contentious than one may at first imagine. But, to radically oversimplify, the challenge is to reconcile the issue of moving large vehicles around corners with the need to safely and comfortably get pedestrians across them. The two are in conflict. Fire safety and school bus vehicles, the vehicles that will most often be invoked when setting performance standards for turning motions, have long wheel bases and thus corner more easily when there is a wide radius curve to navigate round. But wide radius curves at corners shave off sidewalks right where pedestrians need them most, where people need to stand and look before crossing. Most jurisdictions apply minimum standards for turning radius based on the needs of fire trucks and school buses rather than on the needs of pedestrians. As with any other standard, turning radius requirements are seldom absolute, even though they are often presented as if they had legal standing. Municipalities are free to set their own standards even if they digress from practices adopted by the majority of other municipalities, *if* they have a reasonable rationale and their decision has been exercised in an atmosphere of due diligence.[11]

One very effective way to satisfy both the fire truck turning demand with the pedestrian safety demand is by using "neck downs," areas at intersections where sidewalks have been extended into the street, usually taking the parking lane space to do so. Since cars are always prohibited from parking near intersections, this space can be given over to sidewalk and boulevard uses. Curbs are extended farther toward the center line of streets, eliminating the parking bays and allowing for twenty-foot curb face to curb face distance used exclusively as a two-way travel lane. Changing to a two-way travel lane from the fourteen-foot queuing street is required to allow space for turning or approaching cars to easily fit next to a car that may be waiting at the stop sign. Thus, the recommended cross section at the neck down would be six-foot sidewalk, fourteen-foot boulevard, twenty-foot travel way, fourteen-foot boulevard, six-foot sidewalk, for a total of sixty feet. The much wider boulevard provides a more generous area to shave back with the radius curve that might be required by fire trucks or school buses. It also pushes the pedestrian safety zone farther out toward the center line of the street and thus shrinks the pedestrian crossing distance.

Streets with neck downs cost more than streets without them, however. The additional cost is for the extra curb (if supplied) and the frequent need to double up on storm drain inlets. If neck downs are absent, proponents of sustainable design should ensure that engineers remember the existence of the parking lane and that measurement of the radius curve is not from the edge of the curb but from the edge of the travel lane. Figure 3.26 provides one common configuration for a residential street with neck downs in place with a radius that has been tested against the longest school bus wheelbase known. Of course, school buses are both a symptom of the problem (no one walks to school) and a geometric demand that makes it worse (everything must be designed to conform to their monstrous proportions). But here, suffice it to say that the school bus issue is just one more example of how intricately nested all of the elements are that conspire to make our new communities unhealthy.

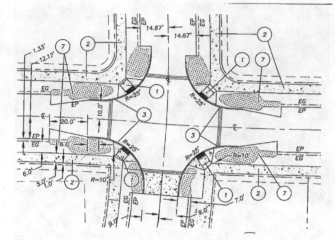

Figure 3.26. Engineering drawing from the Pringle Creek development showing "neck downs." (Credit: WH Pacific Inc.)

LANES AND ALLEYS

Most North American cities built primarily between 1840 and 1950 have blocks equipped with rear lanes (I use the term *lanes* to refer to both rear lanes and what are known as alleys in many jurisdictions). After 1950, when lot frontages increased from thirty-three to fifty feet or more, lanes were generally no longer required. At a width of fifty feet, there was enough space out front to get the car in and still have room for the house facade. After 1950, buyers considered lanes unfashionable, and developers were understandably unwilling to pay money to provide two public access ways—the street and the lane--to every parcel. Some jurisdictions, notably Calgary, continued to require lanes in more modern suburban areas (even when lots were wide and driveways were connected to the streets, not to the lanes) to preserve utility and fire access, but most did not.

Recently, the rationale for lanes has been strengthened. Af-

Figure 3.27. The aerial photograph taken in Surrey, British Columbia, (a) shows shallow lots with large frontages dominated by driveways, while the aerial photograph taken in Kitsilano, British Columbia, (b) shows deep, narrow lots with lane access.

[12]In 1976, the median lot size of new one-family houses sold in the United States was 10,125 square feet. In 2008, it was 8,854 square feet (U.S. Census Bureau, 2009)

[13]For more information on the relative benefits of providing lane access versus driveway access, see the James Taylor Chair in Landscape and Livable Environments, *Technical Bulletin*, No. 7 (January 2001), http://www.jtc.sala.ubc.ca/bulletins/TB_issue_07_Lot_edit.pdf.

ter nearly four decades of steadily increasing lot sizes, starting in the 1980s they began to shrink. For two decades, the average house lot size in typical middle-class subdivisions had been steadily shrinking back toward the original standard 3,600-square-foot lot.[12] As average lot sizes shrink, the rear lane makes sense again. When lots get this small, there are only two choices. They can be configured wide and shallow with frontages over 45 feet but with depths of only 73 feet. This leaves room on the facade for the one- or two-car garage but precious little for the backyard, putting rear windows of houses within 40 feet of each other.[13] The other problem is that driveway curb cuts will occur every 40 feet and be about 20 feet wide, meaning 50 percent of the front yard space and street edge will be consumed by driveway, covering nearly half of the front yard space with impervious surfaces and cutting the number of parking spaces on the street by nearly 50 percent.

The other option is the narrow deep lot with a lane. A 33-foot, 3,600-square-foot lot is 110 feet deep. This lot requires a lane to avoid the "snout house" effect, where streets are all garage doors and no facades. Installing the lane steals 20 feet from the middle of the block, of course, but it eliminates the need for driveways of any kind and therefore does not add to the total amount of pavement required per block. Unfortunately, it adds to the *developer's* costs. Typically, street infrastructure is installed by the "horizontal" developer, who buys the land, subdivides it, and sells off lots to the "vertical" developer, or the house builder. If lanes are installed, they are a cost to the horizontal developer. If there are no lanes, then the cost of the necessary driveways is off-loaded to the vertical developer.

For this and other reasons, it can be very difficult to work through the geometric, cost, and amenity trade-offs associated with lanes. Fear of crime is often cited as a reason to avoid them, even though in the city of Vancouver no correlation has been found between crime rates and the presence or absence of lanes. Municipalities are often averse to lanes for maintenance reasons as well, feeling that it is hard enough to take care of streets without the added responsibility of publicly owned lanes. For this reason, many developers who see the attraction of lanes but have fought a losing battle with municipalities to get them accepted as city land will be offered the option of privatization. A city will often refuse to accept ownership of lanes but may approve them if they remain a private responsibility, to be managed and cared for by a neighborhood association. Neighborhood associations, increasingly common in many states and provinces, have neighborhood-wide taxing authority (in the form of required association fees enforceable via liens on property) and assume the responsibility for maintenance of all common infrastructure. The political trend, particularly strong in the United States, toward citizen-initiated voter initiatives to cut local taxes has forced municipalities to off-load as many formerly city-borne costs as possible. Typically, any digression from standard street designs will trigger an opportunity for municipalities to suggest that developers privatize streets, shifting the cost of perpetual maintenance to the homeowners.

Whether the privatization of urban public realm infrastructure is a good or bad thing lies beyond the scope of this book. The important point here is that any discussion of lanes in municipalities that do not currently allow them is likely to trigger a move to privatize the street system of the proposed development. Citizens and developers should be prepared for this. The tendency of cities to capitalize on any proposal to improve the sustainability of streets as an opportunity to off-load costs constitutes a huge disincentive to more healthy urban infrastructure and is yet another in an all too lengthy list of cultural impediments to healthy change.[14]

GREENHOUSE GAS AND STREET PATTERN

Street pattern has been conclusively tied to increases in GHG production per capita (Burchell et al., 2005; Ewing et al., 2007; Litman, 2001; Mezza and Fodor, 2000). An interconnected street system inherently reduces trip length, as all trips in robustly interconnected street systems are necessarily by the shortest practical route. When combined with a reasonable minimum residential density of ten dwelling units per acre, and a fine-grain distribution of land uses such that commercial areas and frequent transit are within a five-minute walk, per capita GHG production will be reduced by at least 40 percent. Of perhaps greater significance, neighborhoods with interconnected streets and the proper land uses are already walkable. If a gradual shift

[14]The City of Chicago's Green Alley program is a notable exception to governmental resistance to alternative infrastructure. The program began in 2006 as a pilot; as of 2008, more than eighty Green Alleys had been installed with permeable pavement, catch basins, and high albedo, recycled materials.

is to be made away from auto-dominant transportation, these areas are "pedestrian ready."

But in districts with dendritic street patterns (which now cover more than 60 percent of the North American urban landscape) and widely distributed land uses, it seems impossible for a similar shift to occur. Certainly during periods where gas prices rose quickly, such as 2007, we saw immediate reductions in car use in these areas, but not in car dependence. While residents in areas already served by frequent bus service and walkable design shifted significantly away from car use, residents in auto-oriented districts had fewer options. In those districts, reductions were achieved by chaining errands, by carpooling to work, and by forgoing weekend family trips. If fuel prices rise as dramatically as is likely in the next ten years, then residents of suburban districts are in for a very rough ride.

But, fortunately, vast areas of our suburbs are available for retrofitting as complete communities. Most of these lands are located on the many auto-oriented arterials that lace these landscapes. Recent dramatic disruptions in global real estate markets have led to the collapse of many of the financial underpinnings of the suburbs, from the economics of strip commercial developments to the value of McMansions. Certainly, the lowest-hanging fruit in suburban locations is the hundreds of miles of strip commercial arterials, where commercial projects are fast approaching the end of their useful life and commonly lie abandoned. These strategically located parcels, close to transit and potentially walkable, are logical locations for intensive densification. Suburban arterials are usually still arranged as some form of grid, usually rectilinear and at one-half- to one-mile increments.

Whatever new investment occurs in these regions should logically occur on these accessible and geographically well situated arterials, especially given that the demographic forecasts for most metropolitan areas show a huge new demand for housing for older citizens (Berlin, Ramlo, and Baxter, 2006). Infilling presently underutilized arterials for mixed-use transit streets and housing for this burgeoning demographic seems the only possible way to capitalize on our previous investments, meet our housing needs, and retrofit our suburbs for low GHG production. By adding density to these formerly commercial locations, the level of land use activity can as much as double, adding customers for local services, workers for new jobs, and riders for transit.[15] Through this strategy, the land use elements of the streetcar city can be put in place with the expectation of eventual synergy between land uses and transit choices (as described in chapter 2). The market is already confirming the practicality of this trend. The market for "closer in," transit-accessible homes in walkable urban locations as opposed to outer-ring residential zones has been much stronger, in relative terms, during the first decade of the twenty-first century than at any time since the 1940s (Leinberger, 2008; Dunham-Jones and Williamson, 2008).

It's a simple idea: interconnected streets, good; dendritic streets, bad. What gets complicated is unpacking all the unhealthy habits that conspire to block a logical return to interconnected worlds and neighborhood health. The interconnected street system is the very armature of a healthy urban landscape. Preserving interconnectivity in areas where it exists and finding ways to build it into areas where it has been frustrated should always be part of the therapy. In new suburban developments of forty acres or more, interconnectivity should be a first principle, even if this results in a small island of connectivity in a sea of dendritic pod development. Many New Urbanist projects hold firm to this principle even though the value of internal connectivity is limited in such a context, and good for them. But a forty-, sixty-, or even two-hundred-acre area of interconnected street systems will do little to reduce VMT if the surrounding area is still dominated by the dendritic road hierarchy. Once you reach the edge of your walkable world, you are still stuck needing a car. Thus, a willingness of developers to produce walkable neighborhoods is futile unless policy makers responsible for the larger landscape address rules governing the development of the larger transportation pattern and find ways to ensure that the regional street system stays interconnected.

Portland, Oregon, again provides a good example for how to do this. Portland's Metro Planning Council is working hard to impose an interconnectivity standard requiring a through street at least every six hundred feet. The brilliance of this standard is its simplicity. It represents a measured and reasonable requirement from the public sector, ensuring the public good is repre-

[15]Between 2001 and 2056 in the Vancouver region, the average persons per household is expected to drop from 2.6 to 2.3 and the percentage of households with children is expected to drop from 41 percent to 36 percent. Given these trends, and the existing supply of ground-oriented housing, by 2056 ground-oriented single-family units are expected to constitute only 15 percent of the 800,000 new dwelling units needed in the region by 2056 (Design Centre for Sustainability, 2006). Research recently conducted by the Design Centre for Sustainability found that by using mid-rise, mixed-use development along existing corridors and higher density around key nodes, the city of Vancouver could accommodate more than 360,000 new dwelling units on just facing lots lining the hundreds of miles of city streetcar arterials (Condon and Belausteguigoitia, 2006).

sented while not unduly proscribing the actions of the development community. It would lead inevitably to some set of patterns that would emulate the function of the traditional North American 640- by 320-foot block and the streetcar city districts within which such blocks were situated. Finally, it creates a policy framework where individual projects with interconnected internal systems can be integrated into an interconnected whole, allowing new projects to be *extensions* of a predetermined system rather than mere *subdivisions* of discrete parcels of land.[16]

Of all the challenges presented in this book, getting the street system right may be the most daunting. Once a street is in place, it is almost impossible to change. Rome, Italy, is a brilliant example of this, where buildings have been built and then destroyed many times on the same parcel while the streets have stayed the same. Although there is still time to adopt a more reasonable standard for necessary *new* development, existing suburban areas dominated by dendritic street systems will always remain obstacles in the way of cutting car dependence and the GHG that this inevitably generates. Wherever large areas of dendritic streets exist, ways must be found to mitigate their failures, notably by capitalizing on the latent capacity of arterial strip commercial streets. Wherever existing interconnected streets exist, they must be protected and fortified with increased activity. Wherever opportunities for appropriate new greenfield development exist, they must be designed with interconnected streets with an eye toward re-creating the streetcar city form that has served us so well in the past.

---

[16]Prior to World War II, cities commonly predetermined a simple road network geometry that developers were bound to follow. Gridded street systems, classically laid out as numbered streets in one direction and as numbered avenues in the other (as in Manhattan), could be easily completed incrementally by *extension*. As each new development occurred, developers would simply extend whatever street ends were at the edge of their parcel across it, making the same streets ready for attachment when adjacent parcels were later developed. Gradually after World War II, the extension system was replaced by the *subdivision* system, where typically developers were required not to extend a predetermined road system but only to attach their internal road system to an existing arterial. The subdivision system is thus part and parcel with the hierarchical, dendritic road system pattern, and incompatible with an interconnected street system pattern. To effect long-term interconnectivity into our new and retrofitted districts will require a return to something akin to the land extension system employed extensively and ubiquitously throughout the early twentieth century.

CHAPTER **4** Locate Commercial Services, Frequent Transit, and Schools within a Five-minute Walk

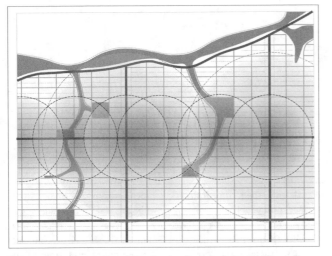

Figure 4.1. Proximity of destinations to where people live is important in creating walkable communities. This diagram shows five- and ten-minute walking distances along a major corridor.

Many believe that electric cars and windmills will solve the climate change crisis, with no need for fundamental change in city form. This belief excludes an acknowledgment of the gargantuan energy and material demands consequent to such an ever more sprawling metropolitan pattern. Professor William Rees of the University of British Columbia, co-inventor of the ecological footprint concept, maintains that we are, as a species, already in "ecological overshoot" mode. Ecological overshoot is the point at which human activities are draining down more resources from the planet than the planet can resupply. In Rees's estimation, we are "draining down" the planet's "capital" now. Even more depressing, he also maintains that if every person on the planet enjoyed the same consumption levels as North Americans, it would take six planets to supply them. And these calculations do not even include the consequences of greenhouse gas (GHG) buildup in the atmosphere, and the extent to which climate change would further drain the planet's "capital" resources and the ecological services that the planet can supply. Accepting these calculations then, a much more radical restructuring is required, as technology and manufacturing cannot save us. In fact, they are what created the problem in the first place.

The conclusion is inescapable. The per capita consumption of materials and energy must be dramatically cut if we are to find a balance with the planet's ability to supply them. Since 80 percent of North Americans now live in cities, it follows that the form and function of the city, along with the resource content of the food and material goods that flow into it for our use, must be substantially changed. Given that transportation is responsible for up to 40 percent of the problem, and that walking is a zero carbon substitute, a careful look at walking seems like a good place to start.

In our current situation, in which the car is always at hand, North Americans will walk only if it is easier than driving. The break point for walking trips seems to be five minutes, which is enough time to walk approximately one quarter mile, or four hundred meters.[1] Most people think that walking five minutes is easier then firing up the car, pulling it out of a parking space, negotiating streets, finding a place to park, and exiting from the auto driver's crouch. Humans are incredibly sensitive to the minor benefits and costs of choosing one mode over the other, no matter how short the trip. Naturally, some people will choose to make longer walks, while others will opt for the car even if the walk is ridiculously short, but the average threshold for walking is five minutes.

But the five-minute walk rule is meaningless if there is no place to walk to. Many new suburban developments are equipped with walking trails, but while these trails may be used every day by people who are in the habit of walking and jogging for exercise, the average person will use them much less regularly if at all. For the average person, the most compelling destination for regular walking is the corner store. If a convenience store is located less than a five-minute walk from home, the average person will walk there many times a week to pick up bread, eggs, milk, newspapers, and many other impulse items. In suburban-sprawl locations, there is a different kind of five-

[1]A pedestrian shed, or pedestrian catchment area, is determined by the distance most people will typically be willing to walk and is generally defined as a five-minute walk to the center of each neighborhood, creating a unit with approximately a quarter-mile radius (Watson, Plattus, and Shibley, 2003). Studies at the Port of New York Authority bus terminal found that a five- to seven-minute walk is typically the maximum amount people will walk, although this varies somewhat depending on the trip purpose, walking environment, and available time (Watson, Plattus, and Shibley, 2003).

Figure 4.2. The corner store (a) is located within a five-minute *walk* of residences in a more densely populated neighborhood. The gas station (b), on the other hand, is located within a five-minute *drive* in a low-density, auto-oriented district. Photos: Kari Dow.

Figure 4.3. The five-minute walking distance from the old street-car line on Fourth Avenue in Vancouver, British Columbia, is highlighted here.

---

[2]According to Metro Vancouver's Livable Region Strategic Plan 2000 report, 22 percent of households in Vancouver do not own a car and only 26 percent have two or more cars, while in Surrey and Delta only 5 percent of households do not have a car and 52 percent have two or more cars. South Surrey/Langley residents took about the same number of trips as residents in Vancouver, but 88 percent were by automobile (Canadian Facts, 2000a) as opposed to 58 percent in Vancouver (Canadian Facts, 2000b). Between 2005 and 2007, 30.1 percent of commuters in the New York metropolitan statistical area (MSA) used public transportation, 6.1 percent walked, 7.5 percent carpooled, and 50.5 percent drove alone (U.S. Census Bureau, 2005–2007). During the same time period, only 3.5 percent of commuters in the Atlanta MSA used public transit, 1.3 percent walked, 10.8 percent carpooled, and 77.9 percent drove alone (U.S. Census Bureau, 2005–2007).

[3]Figure 4.3 shows the historic grid of streetcar arterials in Vancouver distributed in regular intervals. A five-minute walking distance is indicated along Fourth Avenue in Kitsilano. As you can see, the majority of Vancouver is within a five-minute walk of a historic streetcar arterial.

minute rule in play. There you will usually find "gas and go" stores distributed evenly throughout the suburban matrix, but at a five-minute *driving* distance; these stores are usually inaccessible on foot, further exacerbating auto dependence in these landscapes.

If the basic corner store is joined by a video rental, a hair stylist, a tavern, and a café, then it is that much more likely that walking will be a daily part of life for nearby residents. If conditions are perfect, these stores will be joined by coffee shops, hardware stores, used book stores, fruit and vegetable stands, pizza shops, accountants, dentists, and the local grocery store. When most of residents' daily commercial needs can be met within walking distance, not only do they walk more but they use the car significantly less. Residents of Vancouver, for example, where most residents can satisfy their daily commercial needs on nearby streetcar arterials, use their cars over 30 percent less than do residents of South Surrey/Langley, British Columbia, a car-oriented community. Residents of Vancouver also own fewer cars, 1.25 per family compared to1.7 per family in Surrey, British Columbia.[2] Access to commercial services and frequent transit seems to explain these differences, as average family income in the two communities is nearly the same.

Among sustainable community advocates, the five-minute walk rule has become axiomatic. However, it is usually imagined and applied as a walking distance radius or a circle surrounding some fixed commercial point. This is indeed the way it works if there is only a small commercial node with one or two stores, but in Vancouver and other vibrant streetcar cities, commercial activities spread many miles along the streetcar arterial. Where this occurs, the five-minute walk is no longer a circle but, rather, a continuous band that extends a quarter mile perpendicular in both directions to the streetcar arterial. The basic pattern for streetcar cities is a grid of streetcar arterials spaced at half-mile intervals (see chapter 3).[3] This means that everyone will be within a five-minute or quarter-mile walk of some streetcar arterial, and often able to choose between two. These long linear commercial corridors comprise the bulk of public realm spaces in streetcar cities. This linear public realm, so characteristic of most Canadian and U.S. cities, has implications for our understanding of their qualitative aspects—their "sense of place."

SENSE OF PLACE IN CORRIDORS

As touched on in chapter 2, planners and urban theorists have focused on urban *nodes*, even though streetcar city *corridors* are the unique and defining characteristic of the North American city. It seems likely that their training and good intentions have made it difficult to cherish the seemingly undifferentiated linear corridors that are such a humble and ubiquitous datum for our experiences in most U.S. and Canadian cities. It may be that this inattention to the meaning and value of the corridor came from the careful study of older European and East Coast cities, whose web of streets usually focused on key "five-corner" intersections or squares, as in Kevin Lynch's Boston.[4]

What may appear to outsiders to be miles of undifferentiated shops in the commercial corridor of the streetcar city appears quite different to those who use these corridors every day. Local users do not experience every mile of the corridor, but just the transition from their residential block to the more active arterial. Along the way, they might pass the community school, a number of gardens, some townhouses on the block closer to the corridor, and then the streetcar arterial itself. Once at the arterial, they turn either ninety degrees right or ninety degrees left to take advantage of services on the two or three blocks in either direction. Thus, their sense of the place is determined by their walk to the arterial and their eventual familiarity with the blocks immediately in either direction. People who live two or three blocks away in one or the other direction will have a similar and overlapping, but not identical, experience. Some of the shops they use and the people they encounter will be the same, but others will be different.

In this way, corridors are unique and different from urban nodes. They allow for shared and similar experiences, but ones that gradually change depending on where you reside along the corridor. Vibrant streetcar streets are experientially very rich, with buses or streetcars arriving and departing every few minutes, familiar shopkeepers sweeping sidewalks, denizens of ethnic social clubs arguing on sidewalks, school kids walking to the local library branch, and teens showing off. They offer a unique dialectic between the freedom of action allowed by the apparently infinite length of the corridor and the proxemic familiarity that characterizes the best of village environments.

More can and should be said about the undervalued expe-

[4]Kevin Lynch, *The Image of the City* (Cambridge, MA: MIT Press, 1960).

Figure 4.4. Images (a) and (b) show two examples of the experiential diversity along Fourth Avenue, a streetcar arterial, in Vancouver, British Columbia (Photos: Kari Dow)

riential qualities of these overlooked spaces, but for our purposes it is only necessary to add a qualitative argument to the practical, as the streetcar city principle must work in both practical and experiential terms to be of value. This discussion of the experiential value of the corridor is not intended to supplant the articulate explorations of the sense of place attributable to urban *nodes*, just to give *corridors* equal standing. Most of the eloquent arguments of Christian Norberg-Schulz (1980) and Christopher Alexander (1977) can be equally applied to corridors, if one leavens these insights by also appreciating how corridors create both a personal and a communal sense of place. The sense is personal depending on what side street you live on, providing an individualized experience based on your own habitual trips to and from the corridor; and it is communal, providing a shared sense of place for thousands of residents who use some or all of a corridor that is many miles long.

TRANSIT, DENSITY, AND THE FIVE-MINUTE WALK

Transit has a synergistic relationship with pedestrian-dependent commercial services. If the solitary corner store has a bus stop outside, both the store and the transit service are enhanced. The store is enhanced when bus riders pop in to buy a newspaper before jumping on the bus. The transit service is enhanced because riders can now use the trip to the bus to do more than one thing—ride to work and pick up the paper, ride back from work and pick up milk—making the bus that much more attractive. The more commercial functions at the stop the better, as this makes it even more possible to "trip chain," meaning to perform more than one errand on the same trip.

On streetcar arterials, trip chaining is even easier. Riders can hop off the bus or streetcar to stop at the pharmacy, the toy store, the electronics store, or the wine shop, and then hop back on to continue their trip home. In this way, stores located along highly functional streetcar corridors gain customers from both the pedestrians who walk from nearby homes and the transit users passing by on the corridor. Some of these synergies also accrue to developments that are commonly known as transit-oriented developments (TODs), although as pointed out previously, anyone who lives outside a five-minute or at most a ten-minute walk from the center of the TOD will not gain these advantages. Only through chaining TODs in a pattern can these advantages be equally available. The streetcar city corridor is the simplest way to chain TODs in a pattern that is universally accessible.

DESIGNING FOR THE BUS OR STREETCAR

At headways (or frequencies, the length of time between one bus leaving and the next arriving) of seven minutes or less, users no longer need to consult schedules. They know that their wait will be four minutes on average—sometimes less, sometimes more—but never more than seven minutes. These waits are insignificant in the minds of most riders, making it that much more likely they will use transit. For this reason, many transit authorities make achieving seven-minute headways their Holy Grail.

In suburban areas of Vancouver, the transit authority has provided bus service within four hundred meters of almost all homes (thanks to the legacy of the agricultural grid and its quarter-section roads on the half-mile interval), although this is often

Figure 4.5. Lonely bus stop in a car-oriented suburban development.

as the crow flies. But the dendritic street system of "loops and lollipops" inside the half-mile super blocks often forces walks of ten minutes or more. Given the low riderships characteristically generated by these suburban landscapes, regional transit authorities cannot justify buses at seven-minute headways. More typically, they are at thirty-minute intervals and in some cases an hour. In low-density landscapes dominated by the dendritic pattern, destinations usually require one or two transfers, thus taking many times longer than car trips. Furthermore, stops at the most common suburban destinations, such as shopping malls, are notoriously unfriendly for transit customers. With so many disincentives for transit built into the suburban dendritic street system, it is no surprise that transit captures only a few percentage points of all trips in such landscapes. Short of a major and gradual urban retrofit, nothing short of $10-per-gallon gasoline is likely to change this.

With so few customers to serve per square mile in such landscapes, transit officials are hard-pressed to provide frequent transit. At these headways, users must organize their whole day around the schedule of the bus, not just on their departure trip but also on their return. Long headways combined with long multiseat trips and pedestrian-unfriendly destinations make it unlikely that residents with a car will choose transit, and they don't. The large majority of transit users in most suburban areas are the infirm, the young, and those too poor to own a car.[5]

Conversely, in streetcar cities, this kind of entropy toward failure is reversed. Features of the landscape conspire to reinforce pedestrian and transit use, making it more and more likely that residents will choose transit for its convenience and economy, resulting in a more efficient transit system, more revenue for the transit agency, and a compelling justification to reduce headways on the corridor even more. But the key factor in this success is density.

It is now accepted that the higher the density in a service area the more likely it is that residents will use transit. Evidence for this comes from analysis of real places. Almost everyone in high-density Manhattan uses transit; almost no one in low-density, sprawling Phoenix does.[6] A density of ten dwelling units per gross acre, or twenty-five residents per gross acre, is the usual minimum standard for frequent bus service.[7] This guideline is borne out by transit ridership figures from the Vancouver

[5]Income is the primary determinant of auto ownership, which in turn is the main determinant of modal choice. In the United States, transit use drops from 19.1 percent of trips in households with no car to 2.7 percent of trips by households with one car (Pucher and Renne, 2003).

[6]Based on data from the 2000 census, the commuter public transit rate for New York City, for workers over age sixteen was 59.6 percent, while in Phoenix this number was only 3.3 percent (U.S. Census Bureau, 2000b).

[7]Dittmar and Ohland (2003) state that transit agencies in the United States generally use a planning criteria of seven dwelling units per acre to support basic bus service. Densities of thirty dwelling units per gross acre can easily support light and heavy rail transit.

region, where the average density is between ten and fifteen dwelling units per acre. Here, less than 50 percent of all commuters use the single-passenger automobile to get to work. Conversely, in third-ring suburban locations, such as Coquitlam, British Columbia, where gross density is less than five dwelling units per gross acre, and despite the availability of express buses, more than 90 percent of all commuters get to work in the single-passenger automobile.

While density is the most important factor influencing transit use, other more subtle factors also have an influence. An interconnected street network, which helps users get to buses; the even distribution of commercial services along streetcar arterials, which makes trip chaining possible; and lots of jobs located on the corridor all play a crucial role but have proven more difficult for researchers to definitively link to ridership.

If the average density of a very large area—say, greater than ten thousand acres or fifteen square miles—is ten dwelling units per acre or more, and if this area is balanced with one job per household, and if there are convenient transit connections to the larger metropolitan region, and if a full range of commercial services is available in the district, then transit may be able to provide an alternative to the car. That's a lot of ifs. Fortunately, many streetcar city areas already meet these criteria, and many suburban areas, as they mature, are approaching those thresholds as well. Most U.S. and Canadian suburbs start out with average densities of between one and four dwelling units per gross acre. Newer suburban areas in many parts of the nation—Las Vegas for example—are higher, at about six dwelling units per gross acre.[8] Other metropolitan areas are finding ways to add density to previously built low-density areas. Vancouver and Portland, for example, are adding density and jobs to formerly car-dependent areas in numbers that make it possible to provide additional transit service and anticipate viable commercial services within walking distance from most homes, in locations that could not previously support them.[9]

Ten dwelling units per acre is the accepted figure at which buses can be economically supplied at short headways. For streetcars or trams, the accepted figure is closer to twice that.[10] Densities of seventeen to twenty-five dwelling units per gross acre are not uncommon in streetcar cities and not unachievable in new communities. Also, as discussed in chapter 2, there are

[8]In 2000, the density of Las Vegas's suburbs rose to between five and six dwelling units per gross acre (U.S. Census Bureau, 2000a). Today, even higher density communities are being planned and built under new comprehensive community plans (Smith, 2006).

[9]According to Nelson and Lang (2007), up to 35 million of the 40 million new housing units needed to meet the demand of the next 100 million people living in the United States will likely be built for childless occupants. This group is already helping to fuel the resurgence of in-town living, high demand in many transportation-oriented developments, unprecedented demand for central city and close-in suburban infill and redevelopment, and greater stability of housing prices outside of more distant suburbs.

[10]Pushkarev and Zupan (1997) found that seven to fifteen dwelling units per acre can support moderate levels of convenient transit of all type, including streetcar and light rail, which is reasonably sustained at nine to twelve dwelling units per acre.

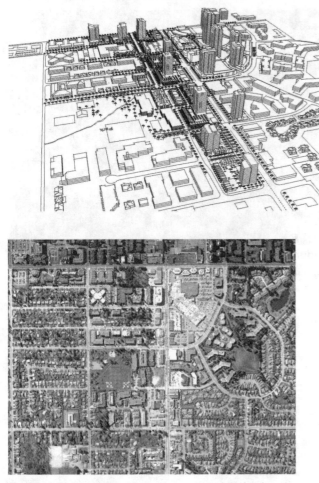

Figure 4.6. Semiahmoo Town Centre, British Columbia, as planned and as it existed in 2009.

many reasons other than ridership for investing in the streetcar, which may make the streetcar an intelligent economic development strategy at average densities between ten and twenty dwelling units per gross acre. Trams or modern streetcars cost less to install and run than buses if you look at the thirty-year amortization costs. And trams, no matter what the power source, produce only a fraction of the GHG per passenger mile that diesel buses do (Condon and Dow, 2009).

The greatest opportunity for making suburbs more sustainable is along strip commercial corridors. While whole-scale alterations of existing single-family fabric are not conceivable in most suburban communities, the gradual intensification of low-density commercial strips is. These vast areas that typically have a residential density of close to zero could easily accept redevelopment where the residential component could be forty dwelling units per gross acre or more. Conversions of this type are already widespread in the Vancouver area and in many communities across the United States.[11] As these developments proliferate along suburban strips, they increasingly exhibit the defining characteristics of streetcar arterials—higher densities within walking distance, continuous commercial, an even distribution of jobs and services along the corridor—and thus provide transit authorities with sufficient justification for reducing headways. Strip commercial zones often occupy between 8 and 15 percent of developed land in the suburbs. Were 10 percent of this land developed at forty dwelling units per gross acre, it could move what might be average gross residential densities from six dwelling units to ten and would likely be more effective at increasing walking and transit use than that figure implies, since all the new residents would be within one or two minutes of commercial services and a bus stop.

THE WALK TO SCHOOL

In many suburban locations, the neighborhood school is indistinguishable from the shopping center; it is a sprawling one-story box set behind a parking lot and a drop-off loop, attached to the arterial via the umbilicus of the cul-de-sac stem. With more and more school kids getting to school by bus, the need to scale schools in relation to the population within a walking

---

[11]In Surrey, BC Bosa Properties is converting a suburban strip mall into a high rise urban village called the Semiahmoo Town Centre. This development features mixed use, pedestrian-friendly streets and high residential densities. An example in the United States is Belmar in Lakewood, Colorado, where a mixed-use renovation and redevelopment of a failed mall site has become one of the most successful grayfield transformations in the nation (Dunham-Jones and Williamson, 2008).

distance circle, formerly assumed to be ten minutes or less, has been eliminated. For decades now, single-minded school parcel size standards, issued by the Council of Educational Facility Planners (CEFPI) in "The Guide for Planning Educational Facilities," have set minimum "recommended" land area requirements for schools—forty acres for a middle school, for example, or sixty acres for a high school. Although the figures are offered as "recommendations," many states and provinces have turned them into requirements. Such minimum school site size standards have made small schools within walking distance impossible to build or preserve, ensuring that virtually all students will need a motorized trip twice a day just to go to school. If these same standards for school sizes had been in use when streetcar cities were laid out, over 25 percent of all development land would be occupied by elementary school grounds, rather than the less than 5 percent they used.

In the streetcar city, a school was provided for each 160-acre half-mile square, with each square surrounded by streetcar arterials. The school was almost always located in the middle of the square, meaning no child was more than a six-minute walk from the school, and very few children had to cross the arterial to get there. With a residential density of at least ten dwelling units per acre (and larger family sizes than now), those 1,600 units usually produced enough kids to fill two classrooms for each grade 1–7. This meant that schools had about four hundred kids in them, a school size now considered "small" but one that the Small Schools Foundation considers ideal.[12] The principal of the Bayview School in Vancouver's Kitsilano district, my son's school, knows the names of all four hundred students, and the kids know the names of almost everyone who goes there too.

When you get much over this four-hundred-student size, however, it becomes more and more difficult to establish a "first name" school community. A school for four hundred students ideally should fit into one four-acre block. This likely means a school that is tall rather than spread out. Traditional schools were three stories served by stairs. This is still an efficient form. Elevators for physically challenged students can be installed at less cost than the building and land costs of sprawling one-story schools. A three-story school for four hundred will have a footprint of under an acre, leaving three acres for recreation, enough for a large playground and a soccer field. Whatever

Figure 4.7. This aerial photo of a new school site built in a sprawling suburb near Boise, Idaho, shows a school site that takes up over forty acres.

[12]See http://www.smallschoolsfoundation.org/.

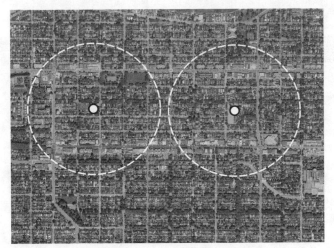

Figure 4.8. This diagram shows an example of smaller school catchment areas in Vancouver, British Columbia. The circles indicate a 2,300-foot (700 m) walking radius. These school sites take up less than three acres each.

parking is necessary should be accommodated on surrounding streets. The full perimeter of the block is usually more than ample for this purpose.

A four-acre site would be a very hard sell with most school districts. The habit of large sites is so strong that it won't be easily overturned. The compromise is the two-block site of eight acres. The negative consequence of a two-block site is that it marginally impedes interconnectivity and, assuming schools stay below the four-hundred-student threshold, removes an additional 2 to 4 percent of land otherwise available for housing or services within the five-minute walk circle, increasing the difficulty of achieving sustainable densities with the detached housing forms so heavily favored in many metropolitan areas.

Fixing this problem usually requires action at the state or provincial level, where funding for school construction and the standards governing construction most often originate. This is the case in Minnesota, where until 2009 CEFPI standards had the force of law, in effect mandating the construction of a few oversized schools far from students and the closing of older neighborhood schools when it came time for major rehabilitation. It took a new law, the Minnesota Education Omnibus Law (HF 2), signed by Governor Tim Pawlenty in June 2009, to fix what should not have even been a problem.[13] The law includes provisions to eliminate minimum acreage requirements for schools and to remove the bias against renovating, rather than rebuilding, old schools. School requirements, such as "recommended minimum" parcel sizes for new and retrofitted schools, are just one strand of the Gordian knot that must be untied before low-carbon communities can be built and rebuilt.

All of our attempts to substantially reduce GHG will fail unless we can make walking and taking transit easier than driving. And this will be possible only if the things we need and want every day are within a five-minute walk. If this five-minute walk brings us to zones where buses and streetcars abound, then it becomes equally convenient to hop on and hop off regularly, until at some point life without a car seems like not such a bad idea. None of this works without a balance among density, street network, frequent bus and streetcar headways, and even sensible locations for schools. Miss one of these components, and you compromise the others. Streetcar city models provide

[13]See http://blog.smartgrowthamerica.org/2009/06/09/.

many lessons for reapplying to other newer contexts, and they impel us to protect these features in landscapes where they are threatened.

Creating new communities and retrofitting old ones for walkability and alternatives to the car will be the challenge of our time. The various monumental pathologies identified in chapter 1 have their source in what seems like a humble decision. Should I drive to get that loaf of bread, or can I walk? That decision amplified and repeated by many millions results in impossibly overloaded freeways and ridiculously expensive and unsustainable patterns of movement. Reconstructing our urban landscapes around the five-minute walk is a key part of restoring their health.

CHAPTER **5** | *Locate Good Jobs Close to Affordable Homes*

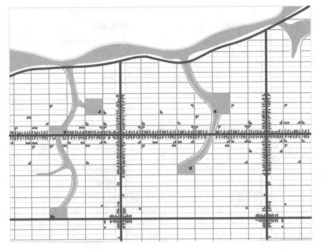

Figure 5.1. This diagram shows the distribution of jobs. The highest concentration of jobs is along the corridor, within easy walking distance of transit.

---

[1]Emissions from industry accounted for about 20 percent of U.S. GHG emissions in 2007. Unlike electricity generation and transportation, emissions from industry have in general declined over the past decade due to structural changes in the U.S. economy (that is, a shift from manufacturing based to service based), fuel switching, and efficiency improvements (U.S. Environmental Protection Agency, 2009a). Globally, primary energy consumption and CO_2 emissions in the industrial sector are projected to continue increasing until 2010, when developed countries will peak and start declining. Emissions from developing countries and economies in transition are forecast to continue their growth after 2010, although at a much slower pace (de la Rue du Can and Price, 2008).

[2]The energy use per square foot for single-family, detached housing dropped from 59,000 btu (British thermal units) in 1980 to 42,000 btu in 2001 and 39,000 btu in 2005 (Energy Information Administration, 2004; U.S. Department of Energy, 2009).

[3]By plotting speed and flow on lane 1 (the fast lane) in one section of I10-W in Los Angeles, Chen and Varaiya (2001) found that by 7:00 a.m. in the peak morning period, speed is a stop-and-go fifteen miles per hour and

Private car use is responsible for an increasing share of total U.S. and Canadian greenhouse gas (GHG) production. Short of an immediate increase in fleet efficiency (not possible) or a dramatic breakthrough in battery technology (not likely), this share is likely to continue its climb for years to come.

On the other hand, the relative contribution of other sectors to GHG production, notably industry, is declining because industry has made major efficiency gains in how it produces and uses energy per unit output.[1] The per square foot use of energy for buildings is also declining, particularly in the residential sector.[2] But these gains are more than offset by the increase in per capita vehicle-miles traveled (VMT) per person per day, a rate of increase that has held amazingly consistent since the 1940s, with tiny interruptions for the oil shock of the 1970s and the spike in gas prices to over $4 per gallon in 2008 (Federal Highway Administration, 2009; Valdez, 2009).

As mentioned in chapter 1, the construction of the interstate highway system, and the girdling of metropolitan regions with one, two, or even three interstate highway ring roads, induced the dramatic rise in average commute distances, making the relationship between home location and job location irrelevant. Any point in the entire region could be accessed from any other point in the region by car if the commuter was willing to drive up to an hour—at least, that is, until the inevitable increase in VMT per capita overwhelmed the capacity of even this bloated system. Los Angeles, appropriately, became the first victim of this phenomenon. Now, speeds on its most congested freeways average only twelve miles per hour during peak hours—ludicrous for a road engineered for eighty miles per hour.[3] Many Los Angeles drivers have taken to the surface arterials for commuting, out of frustration with their long slow drives on clogged freeways. There, they often find that the still robust system of former streetcar arterials delivers them to work in less time, despite numerous traffic lights.

Investment in transit is often posited as the long-term solution to this transportation crisis. Recent changes in U.S. federal transportation funding (the Safe, Accountable, Flexible, Efficient Transportation Equity Act: A Legacy for Users, or SAFETEA LU, signed into effect in 2005) have allowed a proportionately small amount of "gas tax" money to be funneled to transit if states so desire, funds that were originally allocated exclusively to road construction.[4] Metropolitan regions as unlikely as Dallas, Texas, have devoted a portion of their transportation funds to new light rail systems as a result. But virtually all of these expensive transit systems share a characteristic. They are hub-and-spoke systems that are designed to get people from the edge of the region to the center——in forty minutes or less. This pattern is based on a false assumption: that people live at the edge of the region and commute to the center for work. As discussed in chapter 2, this assumption may have been true between 1960 and 1985 in many U.S. and Canadian metropolitan areas, but is no longer the case.[5]

As a consequence of the overbuilding of freeways, the authority of older regional centers has been undercut. While jobs may continue to grow in center cities, their capture rate as a percentage of all new jobs in the region continues to decline. Most new jobs are located far from metropolitan centers, typically clustered around freeway ring road intersections. While commuter rail lines may be reasonably close to many residential origins, they are usually very far from most new job sites, rendering them ineffective at drawing commuters from their cars. Between 1990 and 2000, transit's work trip market share dropped 23 percent in Dallas. This decline continued until recently when ridership on DART's (Dallas Area Rapid Transit's) network of buses and trains began to increase. Between December 2007 and December 2008, ridership on buses increased by 3.4 percent while ridership on DART rail increased by 8 percent (Public Purpose, 2002; Dallas Area Rapid Transit, 2009).

Newer cities, such as Phoenix and the vast conurbations of Florida, are structured in a way that makes them extremely hard to retrofit for transit. Regional transit authorities try hard to provide service to these auto-dominated landscapes for poor

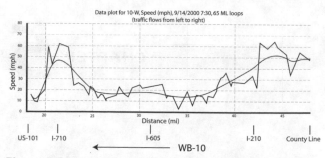

Figure 5.2. Speed is plotted along Interstate 10-W in Los Angeles during the morning peak period. The average speed on this freeway designed for eighty miles per hour is less than thirty miles per hour—and even less than twenty miles per hour for much of its length. These speeds are no higher than what surface arterials allow. It is clear that congestion is significantly reducing the efficiency of the freeway system.

flow has decreased from a maximum of 2,100 vehicles per hour (vph) to 1,300 vph. Figure 5.2 shows similar results for this length of freeway at 7:30 a.m., where nearly half of the total distance is traveled at speeds less than twenty miles per hour (Choe, 2001). Even outside of peak hours, all-day average traffic speed estimates for freeway travel in Los Angeles is the worst in the country, at 34.6 miles per hour (Texas Transportation Institute, 2009). In 2007, congestion caused average annual delays of seventy hours per traveler in Los Angeles (Texas Transportation Institute, 2009).

[4] The SAFETEA-LU bill is set to expire in fall 2009. A draft of the House Surface Transportation Authorization Act 2009, which will replace it, was released on June 22, 2009.

[5] In the Greater Vancouver Regional District, the share of all office jobs located in the region's "regional town centres" declined from 12 percent to 10 percent between 1990 and 2000 while suburban business parks' share grew from 21 percent to 30 percent. The Metropolitan core's (downtown Vancouver and the Broadway corridor) share of office jobs declined from 68 percent to 60 percent over the same period (Royal LePage Advisors, 2001). In 2006, 22 percent of all employment in the Vancouver metro area was located in the Vancouver metro core, 40 percent in all urban centers, 22 percent in frequent transit development corridors, and 38 percent in other areas (Metro Vancouver, 2009). Canadian metropolitan areas (CMAs) continue to have a strong concentration of jobs in the downtown core; however, the relative economic importance of the inner core declined in most CMAs (Heisz and Larochell-Cote, 2005). From 1996 to 2001, areas located within 3.1 miles (5 km) of the city center decreased their shares of employment, and the average distance from a job's location to the city center rose in nearly all CMAs (Heisz and Larochell-Cote, 2005). Between 2001 and 2006, job growth in American suburbs grew six times faster than it did in urban cores (Kotkin, 2008).

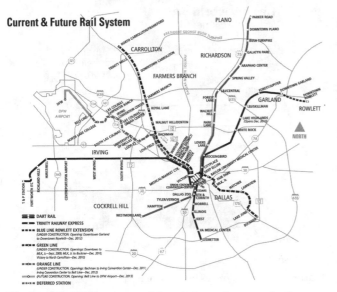

Current & Future Rail System

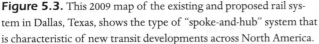

Figure 5.3. This 2009 map of the existing and proposed rail system in Dallas, Texas, shows the type of "spoke-and-hub" system that is characteristic of new transit developments across North America.

Figure 5.4. This aerial photograph shows suburban business parks clustered around a freeway intersection in Dallas, Texas.

and infirm residents by providing on-demand community shuttles to and from stores—but at enormous cost per ride. The cost of providing transit in our increasingly autocentric metro areas has led auto enthusiasts from Demographia, the Reason Foundation, and the Cato Institute to suggest that it would be cheaper to simply buy a car for every person in the United States who is dependent on the bus (meaning mostly the poor) (Public Purpose, 2000). The sad truth is that, given the impossibility of providing efficient transit in most new areas, they may have a point.

THE HISTORIC RELATIONSHIP BETWEEN WORK AND HOME

Even if a zero-GHG electric auto that could travel long distances were widely available, the resources required to continue to build more than 60 million personal autos a year[6]—autos that last less than ten years on average[7]—would drain the planet, not to mention the cost and consequences of adding at least another 25 percent per capita of electric power to fuel such an electric fleet. And, when a full assessment of the GHG consequences of not just the automobile use but its manufacture; the concrete used for its roadways; and the mining, processing, and distribution of

[6]Data from the International Organization of Motor Vehicle Manufacturers indicate that in 2008, over 70 million automobiles were manufactured around the globe (International Organization of Motor Vehicle Manufacturers, 2008). Projects released by the International Monetary Fund in 2008 indicate that the global car fleet is expected to drastically increase as China and India and other developing countries reach the earnings threshold at which car ownership takes off (*The Economist*, 2008).

[7]The median age for passenger cars was a record high at 9.2 years in 2006 (R. L. Polk & Co., 2007).

materials and petroleum is included, the true GHG costs are significantly higher than direct tailpipe emissions.[8]

There was a time in the United States and Canada when jobs and homes were much closer together. With transportation distances constrained by walking distances and, later, by the reach of the streetcar, there was no alternative. Early North American jobs and housing patterns were not unlike those of Venice, Italy, where each neighborhood was dominated by a trade or a "guild" of craftsmen who lived and worked sometimes within the same building but always within a two-minute walk distance. Later in England, during the height of the Industrial Revolution, complete industrial communities were planned and built—notably Port Sunlight near Liverpool, the city organized around Lever Corporation's giant factory.

This same intimate relationship between living and working was imported to industrial North America, most famously in Lowell, Massachusetts, an industrial city on the Merrimack River. Lowell was built all at one time to include industrial, commercial, civic, religious, and residential spaces.

Lowell and other planned North American industrial communities have been extensively studied, but there are other, less formally planned industrial communities that had the same characteristics. Brockton, Massachusetts, the author's hometown, is one of many eastern U.S. examples, where commercial, residential, and industrial spaces organically organized themselves within easy walking and streetcar distance. In Brockton, literally hundreds of workshops and factories profited by providing various parts of the chain of materials and machinery necessary to make shoes. These shops ranged from small tool-and-die machine shops with just a few workers to medium-sized tanneries to large shoe last manufacturers to massive shoe factories employing thousands. Within the city, there existed an entire capitalist ecology, with shops and factories competing with one another to supply the larger manufacturers, while the larger manufacturers competed on the continental scale via a new coast-to-coast rail network.

This intimate industrial and community ecology was broken with the end of World War II and the subsequent construction of the interstate highway system. The economic logic of industrial ecologies such as those found in Brockton was undercut, first by the accessibility to the bigger factories of previously remote suppliers, suddenly brought closer by trucks moving

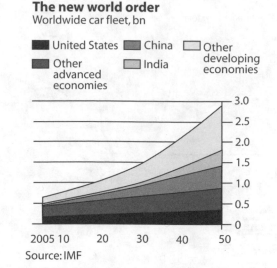

The new world order
Worldwide car fleet, bn

Figure 5.5. World trends in car ownership.

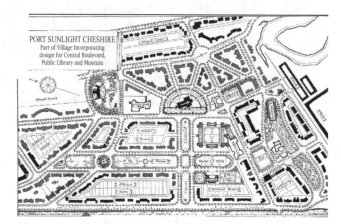

Figure 5.6. Port Sunlight, a village in Cheshire, England, was built in 1889 by soap manufacturer William Hesketh Lever for workers in his factory. Reacting against the squalid slums that had developed as a result of the industrial revolution, Lever wanted to provide a healthy living and working environment for his workers. (Source: Thomas Mawson, *Civic Art* (1911) 283)

[8]In 2006, direct fossil fuel combustion in the transportation sector accounted for 26.3 percent of the total GHG emissions in the United States (U.S. Environmental Protection Agency (EPA), 2008). However, total life-cycle emissions for the transportation sector are estimated to be 27 to 37 percent higher than direct fuel combustion emissions (EPA, 2003). A report by Hydro-Quebec found that direct tailpipe emissions from fuel combustion accounted for 31 percent of Canada's GHG emissions in 2005 (Gagnon, 2006). When production, air-conditioning, vehicle maintenance, and infrastructure consequences were added to this figure, the cumulative percent of total GHG emissions in Canada attributable to the transportation sector rose to an astonishing *52 percent* (Gagnon, 2006).

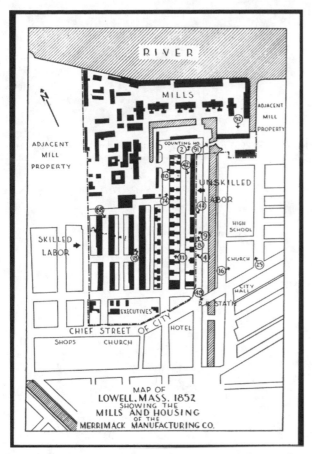

Figure 5.7. Map of Lowell, Massachusetts, in 1852 showing the mills and housing of the Merrimack Manufacturing Company.

rapidly across the continental landscape. It was undercut even further by the national, and then international, trend toward an industrial economy no longer tethered to adjacency efficiencies, which ultimately bankrupted even the largest domestic apparel manufacturers in the rest of the United States and Canada. Now in Brockton, as in other such cities, virtually none of the industry that built this once thriving city still operates (Brockton's last shoe company closed in 2009).

The destruction of place-based industrial ecologies brought one more drastic consequence. Much has been made of the arrangement of the modern metropolis in conformance with the "drive till you qualify" phenomenon (see chapter 1). But a second aspect of the same phenomenon is what might be called the "drive to bed" phenomenon, where poor families move to wherever they can afford shelter, no matter where they work. They too might be spending hours driving to work on congested freeways, cursing the congestion and competing for lane space with the middle class and the rich. The difference is they are probably in older, less dependable (and, for them, less affordable) cars. In Massachusetts, this phenomenon is particularly dramatic. Poor families are disproportionately located in the formerly thriving industrial cities like Brockton, where the

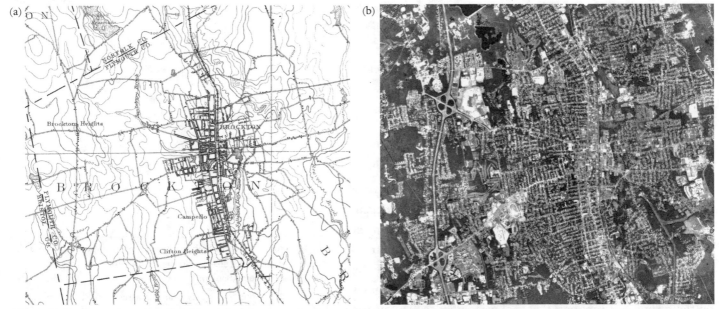

Figure 5.8. Map (a) shows Brockton, Massachusetts, as it was in 1894. Industry, housing, and services were all located in close proximity. Map (b) is an aerial shot of Brockton today. Freeways and sprawling development have led to inefficient relationships between land use and transportation.

jobs are gone but the housing remains. They choose to live there not because it is close to work but because it is what they can afford. Job-intensive sites close to freeway interchanges are far from Brockton and inaccessible by transit, forcing large car-related expenditures for these workers.

These financially stressed families are, in Massachusetts and elsewhere, most likely to have been caught in the trap of subprime mortgages. Foreclosure rates in Brockton are up to five times higher than in its surrounding communities. Brockton now has the single highest foreclosure rate in the state by far.[9]

Massachusetts has tried, with much success, to correct this jobs/housing imbalance through a law passed almost forty years ago: Chapter 40B, the Comprehensive Permit Law.[10] Under this law, developers have the right to overrule local zoning rules with the assistance of state courts if it can be shown that a community has less than 10 percent "affordable" workforce housing and that its zoning is exclusionary. For example, Chapter 40B has helped Lincoln, Massachusetts, to meet its 10 percent affordable housing target. But there is still a long way to go before this housing is located in complete and walkable districts. Most of the new 40B projects are built near the borders of the municipality or close to freeway interchanges (or both), making residents in these 40B projects as or more car dependent than any other suburban dwellers. Wealthy communities still stridently oppose 40B projects, objecting to what they see as an abrogation of the deeply embedded Massachusetts principle of "home rule." Often, they succeed. At this rate, it would be centuries before the suburbs of Massachusetts cease to be segregated by income and class, but 40B provides some hope.

SOLUTIONS

Clearly, any sustained attempt to create more sustainable economies, enhance our security through cutting our dependence on foreign oil, and cut our GHG production by 80 percent by 2050 must tackle the jobs/housing challenge. We find ourselves in an alarmingly vulnerable position. We have made the tremendous mistake of restructuring our metropolitan regions on the wrong assumptions: that fuel was unlimited and its use

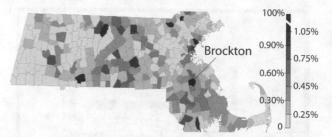

Figure 5.9. 2007 foreclosures. (Source: Federal Reserve Bank of Boston)

[9]In 2007, Brockton had the highest rates of foreclosure of any city or town in Massachusetts, with 365 foreclosures and a foreclosure rate of 1.64 percent (Federal Reserve Bank of Boston, 2008).

[10]For details on the regional planning law, see http://www.mass.gov/legis/laws/mgl/gl-40b-toc.htm.

was without environmental consequence, and that we could always build enough roads to eliminate congestion. Neither is true. The treasure of our progeny is currently being wasted to prop up this gluttonous and inequitable urban landscape, and a devastated planet will be the legacy. A suite of clear and powerful policy tools equal to the gravity of the problem is needed—tools that operate at all levels of government. To fix the problem would require sustained application of such tools for decades. The solutions suggested below would be part of such a suite.

State and Provincial Legal Frameworks

The Massachusetts 40B law, while limited in its scope and thus its impact, provides an indication of future policy tools that might help solve this problem. A more aggressive application of this law or a strengthened version of a similar law, passed in every state and province within North America, would be a start. This law and others like it (Oregon's "Land Use Law" Senate Bill 100, passed about the same time as Massachusetts Chapter 40B, is another example) have survived constitutional challenge after constitutional challenge. Communities and landowners do *not* have the right to segregate their communities by class and income, any more than they have the right to segregate their communities by race.

National, State, and Provincial Infrastructure Investments

The political ground under this issue is shifting. Notable changes have already occurred with the 2008 U.S. presidential election. Barack Obama, the United States' first "urban president" (meaning he mostly grew up in, worked in, and still lives in a major city, Chicago) since Teddy Roosevelt, has pledged to meet the linked security, energy, economic, and environmental goals in the context of redirecting the national infrastructure funds away from new highways and toward infrastructure maintenance and green energy.

Even conservative New York Times columnist and pundit David Brooks, for decades an enthusiast for the suburbs and author on the topic (Brooks, 2004), agrees that the model needs to be changed. In December 2008, he identified the problem and then advanced solutions not unlike those presented in this book. He suggested that we needed a new model for the suburbs whereby they would become less car dependent and more complete: "To take advantage of the growing desire for community, the Obama plan would have to do two things. First, it would have to create new transportation patterns. The old metro design was based on a hub-and-spoke system—a series of highways that converged on an urban core. But in an age of multiple downtown nodes and complicated travel routes, it's better to have a complex web of roads and rail systems." (Brooks, 2008).

In the U.S. government, a fundamental change in thinking is taking hold. The Obama administration's Livable Communities Partnership will, for the first time in U.S. history, align the actions of the U.S. Environmental Protection Agency, the U.S. Department of Housing and Urban Development , and the U.S. Department of Transportation. At long last, they will now be required to coordinate their activities, looking for synergy among their policies—policies that will enhance land use equity and efficiency, meet environmental goals, and advance the most efficient and low GHG transportation solutions.

A transformational change along the lines now being discussed in Washington will not be easy, but the reconstruction of our metropolitan regions has happened once before and it can happen again. The construction of the interstate and provincial freeways in the United States and Canada led to an urban landscape that was utterly transformed. The cost of that effort in the United States alone has been estimated in the range of $600 billion (in current dollars). A similarly dramatic investment, targeted to a different kind of infrastructure, would likely produce similarly dramatic results.

METROPOLITAN AND COMMUNITY SCALE

While it is hard to imagine the reconstruction of our metropolitan landscapes for job equity without the aforementioned policy and financial supports, *with* them anything can happen. Responsibility and power would then fall to the citizens and officials of regions to effectuate these changes over the course of the next five decades. Planning officials, developers, citizens, and elected officials become increasingly important at this scale of enterprise. What would be the rules to guide such a regional and municipal planning effort? Proposed below are some well-precedented rules for new job site development.

Rule 1: Recognize That Most New Jobs Don't Smell Bad

Over the past five decades, U.S. and Canadian heavy manufacturing job growth has slowed to a crawl, with the auto industry only the latest casualty. One might argue that such a trend is unsustainable, requiring as it does the outsourcing of the manufacture of almost all of our material goods to foreign lands. Whatever the long-term trend, it is certain that this trend will likely continue for a number of decades, the same decades within which the retrofit of metropolitan areas must be set in motion. In the 1990s, the Portland region saw manufacturing jobs rise by just 14 percent while nonmanufacturing jobs rose by almost 40 percent. The future looks even bleaker for manufacturing jobs. Between 1990 and 2010, Portland area manufacturing jobs are expected to drop 6.3 percent while nonmanufacturing jobs are expected to increase by 54.6 percent (Yee, 2009). All of these nonmanufacturing job types can be fit into a community without threat of excessive noise, smoke, or pollution. This is a critical point because, throughout the United States and Canada, zoning codes have been based on the premise that the majority of "industrial" zoned job sites should be segregated from other zones, confined to isolated areas usually close to freeways but to nothing else. This zoning habit has not caught up with the changing nature of jobs. Smelly, dangerous, noisy, and industrial-scale jobs, the ones that really require industrial zones, are increasingly rare. Most of the new jobs are clean, quiet, safe, and can easily fit on the second and higher floors of buildings close to streetcar city arterials.

The plan for the Damascus area near Portland, Oregon, demonstrates this principle. This plan was produced at a collaborative, multistakeholder charrette, held to explore how it might be possible to add one hundred thousand people to an eighteen-thousand-acre urban area expansion and at the same time protect the site's ecology, provide alternatives to the car, and create job opportunities close to homes. This 2002 initiative took place in a region where a robust suite of policy tools provided a sophisticated planning context. Not the least of these policy tools was Portland Metro planning district's well-known Portland 2040 Plan, a plan that for the first time identified the regional potential for jobs in both corridors and multi-use nodes. In conformance with these general guidelines, the resulting Damascus Area Design Workshop plan found jobs space for one hundred thousand new jobs, enough for every worker in the district and more—the excess intended for residents in adjoining parts of Clackamas County. The Design Workshop instructions assumed that 15 percent of all new jobs for the district would be in manufacturing. Those jobs were allocated to more isolated sites. But the other 85 percent of all jobs were service, light assembly, financial, education, health care, commercial, government, and other job types that do not need to be isolated. In fact, they should be as deeply embedded into the hearts of mixed-use communities as possible to ensure synergies with housing and transit. The Damascus plan illustrates how these eighty-five thousand jobs were accommodated along the streetcar arterials and adjacent urban blocks of the plan.

The pattern of jobs/housing integration demonstrated in the Damascus plan is not new; prior to 1950, it was the rule rather than the exception. At that time, most jobs—even many types of manufacturing—were knit into the fabric of the city. Absent a gradual return to this historic pattern, it is difficult to imagine a region where access to jobs without a car is even possible. But with such integration, we may have a chance.

Rule 2: Discourage Job-site Space Pigs

After 1950, as jobs moved out of urban blocks and away from streetcar arterials to isolated sites, the density of jobs per acre on those sites also declined. Multistory manufacture, warehouse, and distribution facilities went out of style in auto-oriented sprawl. One-story buildings for all uses became the rule. Since everyone now had to drive to work, overly large parking lots consumed a large percentage of job sites. Required landscape buffers, a well-intentioned attempt to beautify new job-site areas, had the unintended consequence of making the jobs-to-acres ratio even lower. For these and other reasons, the density of jobs per acre was reduced by over 80 percent in just a few decades.[11]

[11]Gordon et al. (2005) found that while some workplace types (such as financial districts and traditional central business districts) had very high job density (ranging from 35 to 436 jobs per acre), the vast majority of California's major metropolitan areas were characterized by job densities lower than 7 jobs per acre. These included less centralized business and office centers, often located in the suburbs (7 jobs per acre); educational and civic centers (approximately 5 jobs per acre); industrial jobs (less than 5 jobs per acre); retail, entertainment, and food workplaces (1.7 to 3 jobs per acre); and exurban workplaces (1 job per acre). The average across workplace types was only 5 jobs per acre. Scott (2001) compared U.S. cities with European and Asian cities. He found that U.S. cities average 2.8 jobs per acre, European cities average 12.6 jobs per acre, and Asian cities average 28.7 jobs per acre.

Figure 5.10. Many of the manufacturing jobs in Portland, Oregon, historically were integrated into the fabric of the city. Here, east of the Willamette River, industry was situated next to the river and the city built up around it.

In the Damascus study, an average job density of fifteen to twenty jobs per acre was eventually set. This was considered an aggressive target, as it is about twice as high as many conventional job-site planners assume and higher than the ambitious goals set by the 2040 Plan.[12] This number, while representing progress in increasing job density on sites, is still influenced by sprawl land use assumptions. This becomes absurdly obvious when you consider that general industrial and "tech flex" jobs require only five hundred square feet of interior space per job on average.[13] If such a building covered 100 percent of its site, even at one story it would provide eight hundred jobs per acre! A more suitable jobs density appropriate to the GHG crisis we find ourselves in would be that of the more recent City of North Vancouver carbon neutral plan that calls for job densities of over fifty jobs per acre.[14]

Rule 3: Link Jobs to Streetcar Arterials

New job sites rarely link to transit. In rare cases, transit comes out to meet the more mature "edge city"[15] jobs centers, as in current proposals to tie Tyson's Corner, Virginia, into Washington's rapid transit system, known as Metro. But providing this

[12]See page 14 of the Damascus Community Design Workshop Design Package (2002), http://www.jtc.sala.ubc.ca/Damascus/Design%20Package_finalMay16_02.pdf.

[13]Damascus Community Design Workshop Design Package (2002), p. 14.

[14]These jobs are to be accommodated along major corridors (at sixty-five jobs per acre), in major employment nodes (at seventy-seven jobs per acre), and within the residential fabric (at twenty to thirty-two jobs per acre).

[15]The term *edge city* was coined by Joel Garreau, *Edge City: Life on the New Frontier* (New York: Doubleday, 1991).

kind of retrofit after the fact can only partially succeed, and it comes at a monumental cost per worker served. In certain cases, enlightened corporations, with the assistance of local authorities, have successfully linked mixed-use job sites to regional transit systems, as in the case of the Atlantic Station in Atlanta.[16] These laudable efforts are the harbingers of a new opportunity, but one that must be systematized. A regional system of street-car arterials close to all districts, where the 85 percent of jobs that are nonpolluting could be located advantageously, is the next step. Existing and new state and provincial policy can and must mandate that municipalities zone mixed-use job sites near streetcar city–type transit corridors, within an interconnected street network, rather than at freeway interchanges.

If an interconnected street system and the streetcar city pattern discussed in chapter 2 have been hopelessly compromised, then jobs must at the very least be accessible by bus. Unfortunately, the configuration of most new job sites makes them extremely difficult to serve by bus or any other kind of public transit. They are not on the way to anything else, and their circuitous interior road configurations doom bus drivers to long, winding trips to serve only a small handful of riders. Even in the otherwise vanguard Portland metro area, the political attraction of such job sites has rendered any other consideration moot (as shown in figure 5.12, at the junction of Sunset Highway and Northwest Cornelius Pass Road, to the west of Portland).

A much more sustainable alternative configuration is shown in figure 5.13, drawn from the Damascus Community Design workshop project.[17] This configuration allows for a jobs node, but one that is knit into the block and street pattern of the surrounding community with job-intensive blocks attached to, or one block away from, a major transit corridor. When compared to conventional office park configurations, this plan provide easy access to transit lines, which serve both these job sites and other land uses along the line.

Figure 5.11. Tyson's Corner, Virginia, is an example of a suburban job center situated at the intersection of two freeways and generally accessible only by car.

Rule 4: Understand That Jobs Fit into Blocks— Really They Do!

Some say that modern job sites cannot fit into traditional block and street patterns. This is simply not true. Assuming a more or

[16]Atlantic Station residents have an average daily VMT that is 59 percent lower than that of the typical Atlanta resident, and employees of Atlantic Station have a daily VMT that is 36 percent lower than that of the average employee in the Atlanta region (Winkelman, Bishins, and Kooshian, 2009).

[17]Available online at http://www.jte.sala.ubc.ca/Damasus/Index.htm

Figure 5.12. Sunset Business Park near Portland, Oregon, is an example of an isolated employment center with circuitous interior road configurations.

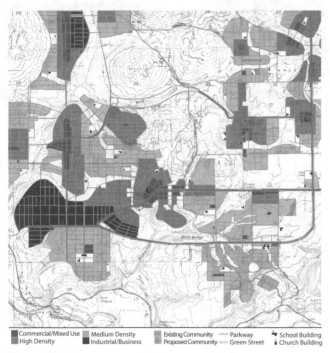

| ■ Commercial/Mixed Use | ■ Medium Density | ■ Existing Community | — Parkway | ♣ School Building |
| ■ High Density | ■ Industrial/Business | — Proposed Community | — Green Street | ♦ Church Building |

Figure 5.13. Damascus site plan.

less standard North American block size of 320 by 640 feet, it can be shown that most jobs-intensive buildings, even the types now used in office parks, will easily fit into the four acres provided. The occasional larger building can fit within two blocks combined to create a 640- by 640-foot ten-acre block. Finally, should a community find itself with the happy circumstance of needing to accommodate a building or buildings that demand an even larger site, blocks up to 640 by 1,280 feet can be provided for a site of twenty acres without dramatically overloading the streets in surrounding blocks.

Rule 5: Accept That No Home Run Is Coming

Here we have what is often the most difficult barrier to sensible integration of jobs within communities. It is the habit, common in many communities, of hoping for the "jobs home run." Communities will commonly protect very large sites, through zoning for industrial use and placing minimum lot size restrictions on parcels so designated, in hopes of landing the massive Intel plant or the like. This happens often enough to whet the appetites of municipal and regional officials (in a way not unfamiliar to habitual purchasers of lottery tickets). Thus, they stridently resist plans for interconnected street networks and traditional urban-scale blocks. Meanwhile, over 95 percent of job sites consume far smaller sites, sites that can easily fit into five, ten, or twenty acres.

Rule 6. Understand That Commercial Strips Are Your Friend

Finally, the reality is that in most first- and second-ring suburban communities, the land is used up. Where are the communities to find the acres required for even high-job-density facilities? Brownfield sites are an option, but they are seldom found in suburban areas and at most cover less than 1 percent of all urban lands. But there is one type of land that is much more common and is ripe for redevelopment in many forms, including job-intensive uses. Low-density strip commercial areas, a legacy of the 1950s, 1960s, and 1970s, are only marginally viable in present market circumstances. These strips are either former streetcar or interurban corridors in degraded form, or the product of freeway-induced devolvement on formerly rural roads. Such sites consume 10 percent or more of the land in first- and second-ring suburbs, land that is ripe for redevelopment and usually has an advantageous location within the region. They are also almost always located on transit corridors, no matter how weak the current ridership, and are typically very suitable locations within which to reestablish the streetcar city form discussed in chapter 2.

Of all the relationships that force our current overuse of energy, and our consequent enormous per capita production of GHG, the chaotic and tortured relationship between jobs and housing, and the impossibility of reasonably connecting them, is the worst. It is, of course, unlikely that the historical pattern where all workers lived close to their jobs will be restored. But it is also true that no real progress in living more sustainably will be made unless we begin to reverse a trend that allows fewer than 5 percent of all workers in the United States and Canada to conveniently access their jobs via transit; no amount of transit investment can solve the problem if the metropolitan matrix cannot be adapted for more equitable distribution of jobs and housing. No amount of goodwill can get workers on transit if the backbone of the region's transportation infrastructure remains the freeway and the single-purpose and often exclusionary landscapes that are the inevitable spawn of such a system. No amount of goodwill or heroic efforts at the local level will succeed without a policy context that enhances integration rather than thwarts it. Finally, none of these proposed rules can hope to succeed unless federal, state, and provincial monies are redirected toward a fundamental greening of the machinery of the metropolitan region—its transit and transportation infrastructure.

Fortunately, simple and constitutional means exist that are equal to the challenge. Regional planning laws to induce housing and jobs equity are no dream; they exist. Oregon's land use law, after thirty years of struggle, threat, and progress, has produced America's best current example of a coordinated jobs, housing, and transportation strategy. Largely because of this law, the Portland region is the only North American region that is on track to meeting its own Kyoto-related GHG reduction tar-

Figure 5.14. This commercial strip in Tulsa, Oklahoma, is located on what was once a pedestrian-friendly commercial corridor. Small-scale, street-fronting buildings are replaced by oversized big box stores fronted with expansive parking lots.

gets (Condon, 2008). Expecting a sea change in the criteria for allocating federal infrastructure dollars is no longer naive; such a change is already under way. In the Canadian context, the Vancouver area's Livable Region Strategic Plan, for all of its struggles and flaws, has produced a region where well over half of all new housing is in higher-density form in areas that are transit friendly.

With these policy and financial structures more broadly in place—not just in Vancouver, not just in Oregon, but in every state and province—local planners, developers, and designers would have the support necessary to cure the disease. It won't happen in ten years; it won't even happen in twenty. Changes to cities take much longer than that. But in fifty years? Yes. It has been done before; it can be done again. Policy tools exist that, if strengthened, could produce equitable and low-GHG communities, communities that provide jobs and housing in equal balance, provide reasonable alternatives to the car for getting to work, and that integrate jobs seamlessly into the network of complete communities. The six rules listed above for achieving this end, or other ones grounded in the same principles, provide a logical and practical way to heal our regions of a sickness. It is a sickness that drains our people of their money and energy while enforcing an economic segregation that violates our democratic principles.

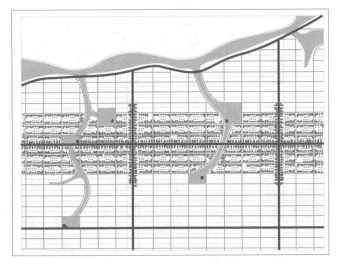

Figure 6.1. This diagram shows the housing diversity along a major corridor in a streetcar city.

CHAPTER **6** | *Provide a Diversity of Housing Types*

Where we live is the other side of the jobs/housing relationship discussed in chapter 5. In this chapter, we look more carefully at how the types of houses we live in and their arrangement on the parcel, on the block, and in the district influence the sustainability of the region and the per capita production of greenhouse gas (GHG) in particular.

In both the United States and Canada, buildings generate a larger share of GHG consequences than any other sector—larger than the transportation sector, larger than the industrial sector.[1] However, the relative contribution of buildings to the total regional GHG produced varies from one part of North America to another. This is due to a few basic factors: (1) the more or less stringent building energy-performance standards in force, (2) the source of energy used for building heating and cooling, and (3) the severity of the climate. In states and provinces where the climate is quite extreme and coal is used to produce electrical energy, and where the fuel for nonelectric

---

[1]Between 1990 and 2005, residential, commercial, and institutional buildings in Canada accounted for 41 percent of all GHG emissions while transportation accounted for 33 percent and industry accounted for 18 percent (Office of Energy Efficiency, 2005; Environment Canada, 2008; Canadian Home Builders' Association, 2008). According to Mazria (2007), building-sector emissions account for 48 percent of total GHG emissions in the United States. This includes the annual energy required to operate residential, commercial, and industrial buildings along with the embodied energy of industry-produced building materials, such as carpet, tile, glass, and concrete. In 2006, CO_2 emissions from residential buildings alone accounted for 20 percent of total U.S. emissions (U.S. Department of Energy, 2009).

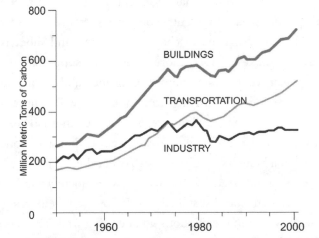

Figure 6.2. United States carbon dioxide emissions by sector, 1950–2000.

furnaces is typically oil, GHG production per square foot of built space will be relatively high. In the United States, the state of Ohio fits that bill. Oil-fired heaters and coal-fired electrical generation provide the bulk of the energy used by buildings there.

In milder climates, where electrical energy comes from hydroelectric, or nuclear power, and where heating is either from electricity or from natural gas, GHG production per square foot of built space will be much lower. The Canadian West and the U.S. Pacific Northwest fit that bill. Due to the ready availability of hydroelectric power and natural gas, the GHG production per square foot of built space is relatively low. Thus, in Seattle, Portland, and Vancouver, transportation accounts for a higher percentage of total metro area GHG than do buildings.[2]

These basic energy differences will influence how various regions approach the GHG reduction challenge. For some, buildings might take priority; for others, it might be transportation. In either case, the arrangement of buildings on the land, and how one moves from one to the other, will be the crucial starting point for analysis.

Residential land uses typically consume between 70 and 85 percent of all developed North American metropolitan lands. How these lands are utilized and configured is likely the most crucial physical factor for determining the social, economic, and social sustainability of the region. Current policies have worked at cross purposes with basic social, economic, and ecological sustainability goals.

The homogeneity of our residential landscapes—in many cases, fostering a residential monoculture that covers whole municipalities—has undercut ecological sustainability in two ways. First, as discussed in chapter 5, zoning and subdivision regulations make it much more difficult to supply affordable housing near work sites. Second, zoning and subdivision regulations ensure that GHG impacts from buildings will be unreasonably high (by favoring building types that are inherently expensive to heat and cool),[3] and in arrangements that gain none of the potential benefits of adjacency to other dwelling units.

Zoning has been used, consciously or unconsciously, as a tool to undercut social sustainability. It does so by enforcing social inequity. Zoning regulations do one thing well. They ensure that large districts are covered by residential lots of one size and

[2]Building-sector GHG emissions in Oregon and Washington State are relatively low compared to Atlantic Canada and the U.S. Upper Midwest because much of their energy generation comes from hydro, nuclear, or biomass facilities rather than from coal-burning power plants (Kerstetter, 1999; Sadler, 2007). Lower emissions in the building sector raise the relative importance of transportation emissions in these regions. In Oregon, 34 percent of the state's GHG emissions are attributable to the transportation sector, while in the Upper Midwest (Iowa, Minnesota, North Dakota, South Dakota, and Wisconsin) transportation accounts for only 28 percent (U.S. Environmental Protection Agency, 2000; PCO2R Partnership, 2006). In Nova Scotia, where a dependence on coal and oil for electricity generation is a significant factor behind the relatively high emissions, electricity generation accounts for 42 percent of all GHG emissions while transportation accounts for only 26 percent (Nova Scotia Department of Energy, 2007).

[3]According to data provided by BC Hydro, electrically heated, single-family detached homes use approximately 21,000 kWh/unit/year, more than twice that of housing units located in low rise multifamily structures. (Marbek Resource Consultants, 2007).

that these lots allow only one tenure type. Neighborhoods regulated this way are inherently exclusionary and thus defy the most elemental definition of a sustainable society. Proscriptive zoning policies lead naturally to neighborhoods occupied by a very narrow demographic band, a narrow range of ages, a narrow range of incomes, and a narrow range of family types.

Such monocultural neighborhoods also undercut economic sustainability; they are difficult, if not impossible, to adapt to changing future circumstances. Most metropolitan areas have dedicated the lion's share of their lands to a housing demographic that is rapidly disappearing: two-parent families with more than two children. Three- and four-bedroom houses, now increasingly occupied by one or two individuals—often aging empty nesters with more than one empty bedroom—dominate many first- and second-ring suburbs.[4] Meanwhile, young singles and couples are likely in search of adequate and affordable places to live in what might be a highly competitive housing market, while all those bedrooms sit empty.[5] Our regulations ensure this imbalance and, because zoning is so difficult to change once set in place, make it almost impossible to fix.

Given that current policies are counterproductive, it may be reasonable to start over with an opposite set of policies. Where previously we insisted on uniform parcel sizes, perhaps we should insist on a diversity of parcel sizes that would lead inevitably to a diversity of housing types. Where previously we insisted on one tenure type covering vast areas, perhaps we should insist on multiple tenure types on every block. Where once we insisted that commercial and residential uses be separated, perhaps we should bar single-use subdivisions. Where once we banned rental units from the neighborhood, perhaps we should find policy tools that could ensure their presence. The strategies listed below for building and arranging sustainable housing provide a starting point for citizens and officials to assemble such a suite of policy tools.

THE INFLUENCE OF BUILDING TYPE ON GHG PRODUCTION

For the purposes of this chapter, at the risk of oversimplifying, there are three basic types of residential structures: residential

[4]See Andrew Ramlo's *British Columbia's Empty Bedrooms* (Vancouver: Urban Futures Institute, 1999) for more information about this phenomenon in British Columbia.

[5]In 1900, nearly half of the U.S. population lived in households of six or more people (Hobbs and Stoops, 2002). By 2007, the average household size had fallen to 2.6 people, and more than 27 percent of households had only one person living in them (U.S. Census Bureau, 2007). Due in part to the trend toward smaller household size, the number of housing units has increased at a far faster rate than population growth. Between 1978 and 2007, the number of housing units increased by over 50 percent while population increased by 30 percent. Surprisingly, as household size has been decreasing, the size of homes has been increasing. According to census figures, the average size of a new home increased by 162 percent from 1970 to 2005 (Lopez, 2007). This trend has only very recently begun to correct itself. In 2007, 15.5 percent of residential architects surveyed in the United States reported that home sizes were decreasing; in 2008, this number had more than doubled to 33.5 percent (Baker, 2008).

towers of between ten and thirty stories, mid-rise structures of between four and nine stories, and ground-oriented detached structures, mostly single-family homes, of three or fewer stories. Each has its own inherent energy performance characteristics and resultant GHG production profile. While it is possible to reduce GHG production by over 70 percent in any type of structure (through special glazing, more insulation, heat pumps, and so forth), for some building types it is more difficult and therefore more expensive than for others. For example, residential towers, through their design, expose themselves to more heat losses and gains from climatic factors than do other building types. Vancouver has pioneered the modern North American version of the residential tower, the "point tower," called this because it is very thin, usually with fewer than eight thousand square feet and as few as four units per floor. The gross density for this type building is generally more than one hundred dwelling units per acre. Between 1990 and 2000, the residential population of the Vancouver downtown peninsula doubled, surging from forty thousand to eighty thousand in just ten years. Virtually all of these new residents were accommodated in point towers. Inspired by Vancouver, other cities, including Toronto, Calgary, San Francisco, Portland, and Seattle, are moving in this direction.

Towers are more exposed to the unwanted heat loads and drains caused by wind and sun than are lower buildings.[6] Wind speeds, even in low-wind areas like Seattle and Vancouver, increase with height. Loss of building heat to wind increases parabolically as wind speeds increase linearly.

The radiant heat provided by the sun is also a problem. Solar heat gain on tower walls during summer can be immense, especially on the east and west walls (which are exposed to the sun for many hours in early morning and late afternoon). No buildings or trees can shade towers, so there is no shield against the sun. Modern towers usually have glass skins because of buyer preference and ease of construction. Glass sheathing is usually partially reflective as a way to mitigate the heat gain inside the shell, but heat still penetrates.[7] Even in perpetually cool climates like Seattle and Vancouver, towers require air-conditioning. B.C. Hydro statistics indicate that, on average, towers consume 50 percent more energy per habitable square foot of floor space than do mid-rise structures, even though energy codes have been tightened for this building type.[8]

[6]*Conduction* is the transfer of heat directly in and through a material. Conduction heat loss or gain results from the transfer of heat directly through the materials of the building envelope. If the outside temperature is greater than the inside temperature, heat is gained from outside the building. *Convection* is the transfer of heat from particle to particle through the movement of fluids such as air or water. This is the process through which hot air rises and cool air sinks. *Radiation*, in contrast, is energy transmitted directly through space and does not require matter in transmission, although it does require a line of sight connection between the objects. All objects radiate energy or heat, which heats all cooler objects around them. Solar radiation passes through space to heat (and light) objects that it strikes.

[7]The G solar factor is the fraction of incident solar energy that is transmitted to the interior of the buildings. Single clear glass has a G solar factor of 89 percent. Clear double-glazed units have a G solar factor of 75 percent; highly insulated triple-glazed units, 35%; and solar control double-glazed units with "soft coating," 31 percent (representing the upper performance range) (Dama, 2005). Generally, gains in G solar factors reduce solar gains but also reduce the visual transmittance or availability of daylight. Evaluating the energy performance of glazing depends on finding a balance between keeping solar energy out (low G solar factors) and letting solar light in (high visual transmittance) (Allesandro, 2005).

[8]In the Vancouver region, high-rise, electrically heated apartment buildings consume 9,363 kWh/unit/yr—almost 40 percent more than low-rise, electrically heated apartment units, which consume only 6,823 kWh/yr (Marbek Resource Consultants, 2007). In non–electrically heated buildings, this discrepancy is even larger, with high-rise units using 56 percent more energy than units in low-rise buildings (Marbek Resource Consultants, 2007). It is important to note that a building's energy efficiency is a result not only of the height of the building. Other factors, including building materials, unit size, and the number and size of windows (the outside of many towers is almost entirely glass), also play a large role in the overall energy efficiency of the structure.

Figure 6.3. The large, single-family detached home (a) is inefficient due to the extremely large surface area per unit while the tower (b) suffers from heat loss and gain from the poor performance of glass as an insulator. The medium-density town houses (c) exhibit the best energy efficiency.

[9] According to the National Association of Home Builders (2007), in the 1950s the average size of a new U.S. single-family house was 983 square feet. By 2005, this number had risen to 2,424 square feet, representing an increase of 148 percent. In many parts of the country, this trend was even more extreme. For example, the standard house built in Austin, Texas, in the late 1940s was about 1,200 square feet. By 2006, the average house size had increased by well over three times this number, to 4,000 square feet (Robinson, 2006).

[10] Post-1976 single-family homes heated with electricity consume three times more energy, at 20,466 kWh/yr, than do low-rise apartment units, at 6,823 kWh/yr (Marbek Resource Consultants, 2007).

At the other end of the density spectrum is the detached, single-family house on its own lot. The density range for this type of structure is very wide but generally cannot be higher than eight dwelling units per gross acre (absent duplexes or secondary suites), and is more typically between one and four dwelling units per gross acre.

In the fifty years since the death of the streetcar, the interior area of the average U.S. single-family homes has doubled.[9] This ballooning of the structure—at the same time that average family size has plunged—has overwhelmed the efficiency gains for this house type. Thus, occupants of this type of house have steadily increased their per capita GHG production consequent to their home size.

This is not the only aspect of the single-family home GHG production problem, however. People could go back to their average pre-1940s per capita square foot interior space and still produce more than their fair share of GHG. Why is this? Single-family homes have the same physical handicaps as towers; they are just smaller. From an energy perspective, a single-family home is the least efficient way to house a family. It has more exterior skin exposed to the elements per family than any other type. Even duplex structures have at least one shared wall, a wall that is consequently not subject to convection losses or radiant heat gains. Townhouses have at least two shared walls. Apartments have at least four shared walls and as many as five. Thus, the intrinsic exposure of apartments to the elements can be up to 80 percent lower than that of a single-family home.[10]

At the middle of the density spectrum lies the most GHG-efficient housing type: low-rise, medium- to high-density structures. This type generally inhabits the density range between twenty and sixty-five dwelling units per acre (parking requirements have a large influence on density for this type). It is efficient because it has the most number of shared walls possible, can be shaded by trees and other buildings from both sun and wind, and requires less elaborate and less expensive to run elevators and heating and cooling systems than do point towers.

In the Vancouver region, homes at densities of over twenty-five units per net acre make up more than half of all new homes built. Seattle and Portland are following similar trends, albeit not so dramatically. The reasons are numerous, but demographic shifts are a major driver. In metro Vancouver, the percentage of families with children is shrinking in proportion to other age and family type cohorts. These other, fast-growing cohorts, notably those over age fifty and younger singles or couples without children, tend to favor higher density options close to urban services over single-family homes on their own lots.[11]

It is fortunate that the Vancouver market is no longer averse to this housing and density type since it is inherently more GHG efficient than the single-family home. But, unfortunately, the arrangement and configuration of these new buildings often defy simple, time-tested rules for good urban districts. Typically, these buildings are arranged around parking lots, preventing them from shading one another, and in arrangements that thwart walking and biking. Configurations like this ensure the same auto dependency experienced by those who live at the end of suburban cul-de-sacs.

The GHG performance of medium-density residential buildings can be enhanced if the buildings are located within an efficient block and street pattern. Tight urban blocks that are not dominated by parking areas reduce convection losses and heat gains, as buildings protect one another from wind and sun. Boulevard trees on streets have always functioned to shade structures, particularly against the low morning and afternoon summer sun. Trees provide this protection more elegantly and cheaply than elaborate wall details and "green gizmos" ever can.[12] This is partly because trees absorb rather than reflect heat energy, using sun energy for the production of sugars and leaving the air that surrounds the tree five to eight degrees cooler

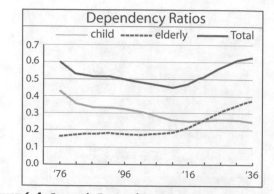

Figure 6.4. Quarterly Regional Statistics, Interim Report, Fourth Quarter 2008: Greater Vancouver Regional District, Ministry of Labour and Citizens' Services. (Source: BC Stats, 2008) **[AU: please provide full source info in references for BC Stats, 2008.—sh]**

[11]According to projections from the Greater Vancouver Regional District (GVRD, 2002), the number of people living in the GVRD who are over age sixty-five will increase by 265 percent between 2001 and 2056. This is in contrast to an increase of between only 44 and 55 percent for all age classes below age twenty. This will create a "top-heavy" demographics distribution in which more than 22 percent of the population is over age sixty-five and less than 5 percent falls within each of the 0–4, 5–9, 10–14, and 15–19 age classes (GVRD, 2002). As shown in figure 6.4, this increase in the absolute number and relative proportion of elderly people in the population will lead to a sharp increase in the dependency ratio for this region.

[12]The term *green gizmo* refers to high-tech solutions for building energy use, such as automatic window-shading machinery. Very often, green gizmo solutions are applied before simpler and more effective strategies—such as block configuration, building type, and street trees—are considered.

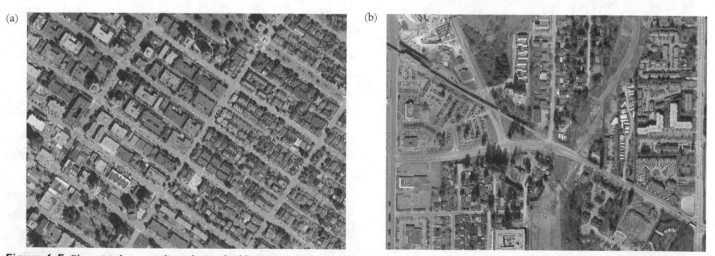

Figure 6.5. Photo (a) shows medium-density building types in a compact, mixed-use, gridiron street network in the city of North Vancouver that supports walkable communities. Photo (b) shows the same building types in a car-oriented suburb in Surrey, British Columbia.

than ambient air.[13] Street trees in healthy situation attain forty-foot heights within twenty years in most North American areas (generally, and understandably, the warmer the temperature and the more the available moisture, the faster trees will grow). If these site planning and urban design strategies are employed, it is likely that the energy savings will be over 30 percent, or even 50 percent, without any changes to the building skin or heating- and cooling systems.

THE SUSTAINABLE SINGLE-FAMILY HOME

Even though mid-rise structures may be inherently more GHG efficient than single-family residential structures, this does not alter the fact that most houses are now single-family homes and that this type still dominates in most metropolitan areas.

Purchasers of new and used single-family homes enjoy the separation afforded by owning all four walls and the exterior spaces that separate one building from the next, and they believe deeply that single-family homes hold their value better than other types.[14] Whatever the case, single-family homes can be designed and arranged in a way that is more socially, economically, and ecologically sustainable than is now typical.

The typical suburban subdivision yields about four dwelling units per acre, even on lots so small that they provide very little space for backyards.[15] We have somehow created a system for producing detached single-family homes that gives us none of the benefits of low density (large yards, green spaces) and none of the benefits of streetcar city density (walkability, stores, transit). Detached houses in most U.S. and Canadian streetcar suburbs retain the advantages of the single-family home without losing the ten dwelling units per acre minimum density necessary for sustainable, walkable, transit-friendly, and low-carbon neighborhoods. Most streetcar suburbs are inherently low carbon due to block size and density (for the reasons discussed in chapter 4).[16]

Perhaps even more important, streetcar city single-family homes often illustrate that the advantages of single-family living can be shared equally by apartment livers and duplex owners. Architectural solutions abound that allow for multifamily housing on one parcel in structures that retain the single family

[13]The energy savings provided by trees has been referenced in a number of studies. McPherson et al. (2005) found that street trees in Minneapolis produced annual savings of $6.8 million in energy costs and provided a service worth $9.1 million in stormwater treatment. These same trees were also responsible for a $7.1 million increase in property values city-wide (McIntyre, 2008). In 2006, McPherson et al. concluded that the 6 million trees in the southwestern United States stored approximately 304,000 tons of atmospheric carbon dioxide, 12,000 tons of ozone, and 9,000 tons of particulate matter (McIntyre, 2008).

[14]This convention has been called into question with the recent foreclosure crisis. Market value data obtained from Zillow.com shows the staggering drop in property values brought about by the recent U.S. mortgage meltdown and indicates that second- and third-ring suburbs are often those hardest hit by the market crash. Home values in Culver City (a first-ring suburb of Los Angeles) peaked in 2006 at approximately $730,000 before falling to $600,000 in 2009, constituting a 17.8 percent decrease in value. The relative decline in property values was far more extreme in Rancho Cucamonga (a third-ring suburb of Los Angeles), where home values fell from $502,000 in 2006 to $324,000 in 2009, constituting a drop of 35.5 percent. This trend could also be seen in the Boston area, where property values in Cambridge (a first-ring city/suburb) fell 5.6 percent between 2006 and 2009 while property values in Stoughton (a third-ring suburb of Boston) fell 13.8 percent. In his article "The Next Slum?" (Leinberger, 2008), Christopher Leinberger explores the steep decline of suburban developments in the United States in contrast to the evident revival of urban living. Per square foot, urban residential neighborhood space goes for 40 percent to 200 percent more than does traditional suburban space in areas as diverse as New York City; Portland, Oregon; Seattle, Washington; and Washington, D.C.

[15]For more information on conventional suburban development specs, see the Alternative Development Standards Project Web site: http://www.jtc.sala.ubc.ca/projects/ADS/HTML_Files/ChapterTwo/figure7_us.html.

[16]The traditional neighborhood pattern (figure 6.6a) has a density of approximately ten to fifteen dwelling units per acre (Condon and Teed, 1998). Given 2.5 people per dwelling unit, this development pattern accommodates 9,500 to 14,250 people within a service circle that fits 380 acres within a five-minute walk. In contrast, the status quo neighborhood pattern (Figure 6.6b), with four dwelling units per acre, accommodates less than 4,000 people within a five-minute service circle (Condon and Teed, 1998). This means that any services placed within the lower density neighborhood have a much smaller population to support their business.

"feel." Various styles of duplex and even triplex living are suitable for these small and deep lots. Lane houses are the most obvious way to add an additional unit, but forming one building with two entrances in a way that respects the desires of owners and the language of the street is another way. In both of these cases, the green space on the parcel in the front yards and backyards can be divided such that each family has a private garden for planting or playing.

BUILD AND ADAPT NEIGHBORHOODS FOR ALL AGES AND INCOMES

In U.S. and Canadian cities, zoning has been used as a tool of separation rather than integration. From the social perspective, zoning by density categories is especially heinous, as this separates families by income and thus by class. Census data confirms an almost one-to-one relationship between a zoning designation for a particular district and a narrow band of incomes exhibited by the families living therein. Discriminatory impulses play themselves out in the process of determining new zoning status for adjacent areas, with many homeowners extremely reluctant to see a designation applied nearby that would allow families of lesser means to purchase a home.

Prior to the 1940s, districts typically had more than one house and tenure type and sometimes a wild profusion of variety. Maple Avenue in Cambridge, Massachusetts, exhibits a level of income, tenure, and house type variety that was banished from virtually all neighborhoods built after World War II (see figure 6.7). On Maple Avenue, you can still find a one-, two-, or three-bedroom apartment. You can also find a sixteen-room house on four floors. The income demographic on the street is tremendously wide and provides residents of all ages and incomes a place to live, residents who can fill the jobs in the district and age in one place should they wish. But the success of Maple Avenue must not be oversimplified. It is not only that the street contains a variety of tenure types; it is also that the buildings make, for all their differences, a unified but diverse visual ensemble. Porches and protruding eaves abound, horizontal clapboards predominate, floor heights are common from one lot to the next, and each house takes pains to acknowledge the

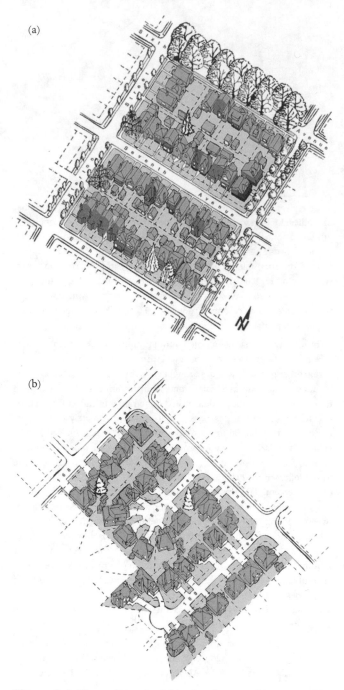

(a)

(b)

Figure 6.6. The traditional neighborhood pattern (a) accommodates ten to fifteen dwelling units per acre, while the status quo neighborhood pattern (b) accommodates only four dwelling units per acre.

Figure 6.7. Maple Avenue in Cambridge, Massachusetts. Here, a large, 3-story single-family home sits next to 2.5-story duplex. In the distance is a large brick structure containing three dwelling units. (Credit: Alanna Mallon)

Figure 6.8. These medium-density (25+ du per acre) residential town houses, designed by Ramsay Worden Architects, are visually integrated with nearby homes and offer a higher density typology without drastically changing the character of the neighborhood. Many of the units remain ground oriented, and the large number of entrances and overlooking windows enliven the street environment. (Source: Ramsey Worden Architects).

---

[17] Inclusionary zoning refers to zoning practices requiring that a given share of new construction be affordable to people with low to moderate incomes. Montgomery County, Maryland, is often considered a pioneer in establishing inclusionary zoning policy. Montgomery County's Moderately Priced Dwelling Unit program requires that developers sell or rent between 12.5 and 15 percent of the total units in every new subdivision or high-rise building of fifty or more units at specified affordable prices. In return, developers are generally granted density bonuses of up to 22 percent (Southern Nevada Regional Planning Coalition, 2005).

importance of the street architecturally. Successful places must be successful in both the quantitative realm (tenure types, numbers, rents, sizes) and the qualitative (architectural details, massing, materials, sensitivity to historical context).

Policy changes whereby all newly developed or renewed and retrofitted areas would be required to include a wide variety of house types are needed. These policies must go beyond Massachusetts' Chapter 40B law, which requires affordable housing somewhere in town but does not govern where, to urban design policies that are applied at the much finger grain scale of the neighborhood.[17]

Vancouver provides a good model for adding housing diversity to existing residential districts, and in two different ways: (1) through building new higher density, low-rise buildings that are compatible with lower density neighbors, and (2) by learning how to convert existing single-family homes into multiple dwelling structures. In the ten years between 1990 and 2000, forty thousand new residents found homes in the city's older single-family and low-rise residential neighborhoods, a number equal to the number accommodated in downtown point towers. During this period, Vancouver architects and city planners learned that residents do not object to added density so much as they do to the *feel* and *appearance* of density. Not wanting to engender unnecessary resistance, architects learned how to design buildings that looked and felt like the low-density buildings next door. Large facades were broken into pieces scaled to the roof, dormer, window, and facade forms of nearby residences. Roof pitches of new buildings were steeply sloped and highly articulated to mitigate four-story heights. Building fronts were provided with as many individual entrances as possible for the same reason. The example proves that NIMBY responses are not knee-jerk reactions to density per se, but understandable reactions to disrupting the unified and comforting qualities of many fine single-family home areas.

The second effective strategy for gradually adding density to existing single-family home areas has been through converting single-family homes to structures with multiple dwelling units. As mentioned earlier in this chapter, because of the way North American cities grew, and given the influence of the baby boom demographic in particular, most U.S. and Canadian metropolitan areas are oversupplied with single-family homes built for large families but now occupied by only one or two people. Vancouver is no exception but has found a way to occupy those empty bedrooms.

Since the 1970s, housing in Vancouver has become increasingly expensive. With rents rising, some homeowners decided to convert part of their homes for rental to capitalize on this demand. Typically, these "illegal suites," as they are known, were located in the basements of Vancouver's most common house type, the bungalow. The bungalows of Vancouver have a peculiar characteristic. Because of unusually wet soil conditions, the slab elevation of the home is very shallow, leaving the basement floor only two to three feet below grade. Thus, tens of thousands of basements in Vancouver have full-size windows and a basement floor that can be reached from the outside at grade or with just a few steps down. These rental units were built without the benefit of code inspection, so they varied wildly in their execution.

Area residents, and thus their elected officials and code enforcement officers, knew of this trend. But rather than closing down these units, as might be expected in U.S. cities, the City of Vancouver adopted a characteristically Canadian response to this emerging trend. The issue of illegal suites came up for debate in council on many occasions, but for every homeowner who complained, there was a renter or a rental-housing advocate who argued that these units were necessary to avert a housing crisis. Thus, no action was taken, but the conversation was prolonged, seemingly indefinitely.

The supply of these units gradually grew until there were tens of thousands. During this same period, the cost of single-family homes more than tripled in real terms. This influenced the behavior of individuals and families seeking not a place to rent but a place to buy. Since average family income had more or less stagnated during these decades, single-family homes, once affordable to the middle class, were now out of reach—unless an income stream were available to help support the mortgage costs. This income stream was the illegal secondary suite. Fully one third of the monthly cost of the mortgage could be met by the rent from the suite, making it at least possible for the schoolteacher, or the merchant, or the bus driver to own a detached home.

Figure 6.9. These Vancouver, British Columbia, homes are typical of homes built in streetcar city districts built prior to World War II all across North America. They originally were home to one large family, but over the years they have been renovated to include at least one additional suite (and sometimes two or three additional suites). (Photo: Kari Dow)

Suddenly, the entire market shifted. Real estate agents would show a home paying specific attention to an existing suite or a space suitable for a suite, providing probable rents, and helping potential buyers calculate what effect this money would have on their monthly payments. In time, reaching well into the 1990s, the vast majority of home buyers were looking for homes where they could also be landlords. During the 1980s and 1990s, proposals to legalize these suites were occasionally floated. Longtime area residents who owned their homes, and who therefore felt none of the financial pressures that weighed on younger home buyers, usually opposed these proposals. Thus, proposals for legalizing secondary suites died during these decades. It was not until the first decade of the new millennium that a citywide blanket allowance for the creation of new secondary suites in single-family homes passed city council. By this time, well over half of single-family homes in the city had already been converted. Thus, voting homeowners were no longer opposed to this new policy, since they already depended on it.

Vancouver has been changed, for the better, by secondary suites. Tens of thousands of affordable new rental units have been created, and a synergy between middle- and upper-middle-class families and lower-middle-class, blue collar, and service sector–employed families has emerged: an economic ecology of the parcel, where neither the landlord nor the tenant could afford to live there without the other.

In time, the creation of suites was legalized, as was the separation of existing single-family homes into two, creating a legal duplex where each side was available for purchase. In some areas, the regulations allow the conversion of single-family bungalow structures into three-unit condominium structures, providing that the original structure is preserved and the architectural quality of additions conforms architecturally to the host structure.

Consequent to Vancouver's slow and organic integration of these new residential units, and the general satisfaction with the results, other B.C. communities have been able to adopt similar polices, with muted political opposition. Now, virtually all of the major municipalities in the metro area, including those profoundly suburban in form, allow for the legal creation of secondary suites.

Housing Type	Interior Space in sq. ft.	Residential Density Units/Acre (gross incl. street ROW	Unit Sale Price	Developed Land Value	Development Cost per Unit	Residual Value per Unit	Mortgage or Rent/month Required to Amortize Cost
Single Family Detatched							
Estate housing	3200	3.5	500,000	100,000	47,000	47,000	$3,200
Medium lot (4,500 sf)	2,150	7.3	280,000	56,000	22,000	22,000	$2,000 – 1,500 with rental suite
Small lot (3,500 sf)	1,700	8.4	220,000	44,000	20,000	20,000	$1,550 – 1,050 with rental suite
Single Family Attached							
Town House	1,100	18.2	150,000	30,000	12,500	17,500	$1,050
Row House	1,300	19.9	180,000	36,000	12,500	23,000	$1,300 – 800 with rental suite :stacked townhouse" form
Duplex	1,750	15.8	170,000	34,000	10,500	23,520	$1,200 – 700 with ground floor suite
Rental Units of Condo Apt.							
1-2 BR Apartments	700	30.3	80,000	16,800	5,800	11,000	$780
2-3 BR Apartment	800	27.6	90,000	18,000	6,500	11,500	$875
Secondary suite in detached residence	600-800	on 25% of all lots					$500

Figure 6.10. The cost to actually live there—a "back of the envelope" monthly rental requirement analysis from the Damascus Area Design Workshop. Calculations courtesy of Rudy Kedlub, Costa Pacific Homes, Oregon.

The same logic applies for new housing developments. Including secondary suites in a new residence can bring the cost of buying a new home, even when land costs are over $400,000 per raw acre, into the affordability range of more than 50 percent of wage earners.[18] The income from rental suites can be affordable and still support mortgage payments, such that all but the lowest 12 percent of families in the Portland region can rent market-rate rental units without the need for subsidies. Those requiring subsidies could, of course, rent there too, providing they have vouchers or cash subsidy, thus fully integrating neighbors to include all income classes.

Although certain cities, such as Vancouver, have managed to attain a relatively high degree of diversity, such conditions often arise more from organic and fortuitous circumstances than from a systematic approach to the issue. When consciously planning for diversity in new communities, a robust methodology is required.

One such technique that can be implemented at the project scale is to directly use the income and family type demographics of a specific area to generate the appropriate palette of building and tenure types for a given neighborhood. The quantitative portion of this undertaking (income and demographics) can be readily attained through census data. Once obtained, this information can be the major driver in selecting the building and tenure types for a particular neighborhood development. In doing so, the project could and would be a physical manifesta-

[18]Including secondary rental suites in new detached and attached homes helps to provide housing for those at the lower end of the income spectrum while also opening up new opportunities for homeownership to moderate-income families. The cost to manufacture secondary suites is up to 30 percent cheaper than apartments built in complexes, and the suites could be profitably rented for as little as $500 per month (in the Portland metro area in 2002 USD). The extra rent generated from these secondary suites allows families who could not otherwise afford to own a home to enter the housing market.

tion of the larger demographic pattern particular to a specific area.

The Pringle Creek Community in Salem, Oregon, serves as a case in point. This project, developed by Sustainable Development Inc., is grounded in a rigorous set of guiding principles that integrate green building, energy efficiency, and environmental responsibility.

One major goal was to make Pringle Creek "look like Salem," meaning to include all of the types of families that are found in that city. Toward this end, the design teams conducted an in-depth analysis of the demographic patterns of the Salem region. This required an understanding of the types of household in the region—single-parent families, extended families, two-children families, and so forth—and their respective average incomes and space needs. Given the direct relationship between spatial requirements and the costs of construction, this information was supplemented by the hard data concerning housing and building. This hard data included the average price of homes throughout Salem and the square foot costs associated with constructing certain building types. This helped the design team understand the economic, social, and construction context within which the project was to be built, methodically bringing together all the elements required to make development decisions in keeping with their housing diversity goal.

With this information in hand, the design team organized the community as a microcosm of the larger Salem context. The number and type of dwellings chosen were directly correlated to the demographic patterns analyzed—each home calibrated in size and costs to the incomes of each type of household to be accommodated. The result is a mosaic of people and places in homes that they can afford and that suit their family needs.

BUILDINGS WITH A FRIENDLY FACE TO THE STREET

The idea of articulating the layers of space between fully private space (the deep interior of the home) and fully public space (the street) was best articulated by Jane Jacobs in her penetrating work *The Death and Life of Great American Cities* (1961). In this work, she stood alone against what were then the dominant urban design canons, those of Le Corbusier manifested in his Radiant City schemes (Le Corbusier, 1964). His vision was of towers and massive apartment lines lifted off the streets on piloti, eliminating any formal connection to the ground and obliterating any clear distinction between buildings and streets, between public spaces and private spaces. Thus, the entire landscape was completely public right up the apartment door, and the only means for controlling that membrane was the peephole device in the door. By the time of Jane Jacobs, a few of the more sensitive observers of the city had become alarmed about the social inadequacies of this form. An increase in lawlessness was observable when neighborhoods were "renewed" to this form, the opposite of the claims made by their enthusiasts.[19]

It was left to Jacobs to explain what had occurred. By removing all of the New York brownstone apartment types that had predominated in much of New York City, renewal officials had erased a subtle but crucial language of behavioral civility—a language that was embedded in these seemingly pedestrian structures. These previous types were built in such a way that the short distance between the sidewalk (fully public) and the front door included three or four distinct layers of space that visitors needed to penetrate before entering. At each of these layers, residents of the buildings had the opportunity to (one might even say they were compelled to) engage unknown visitors with the classic question put in such circumstances, "Can I help you?" Visitors who belonged or were invited were not intimidated, of course, but others were. The key here is that the architecture of the space created zones that residents could easily control. In Radiant City planning, all that had been destroyed. The public spaces below the buildings, far from being available to all residents like the proponents supposed, were impossible to effectively control, and were thus abandoned to various denizens of the night. Crime became rampant, and only the criminals who claimed these abandoned pieces of turf felt comfortable within them.

Forgotten in all this was that the most important part of any building is the part that meets the street: the *face*, or facade.[20] If the streets are indistinct and the buildings are floating in space, you have a problem: no face. Without a face, and the associated layering of the space between the face and the street, you lose control—and thus civility. The primary function of the

Figure 6.11. Pruitt-Igoe was an award-winning modernist housing complex built in 1955 in St. Louis, Missouri. Shortly after its completion, living conditions began to decay, and by 1972 the extreme poverty, crime, and segregation of its inhabitants led the federal government to destroy the first of the complex's thirty-three buildings. When the last residents of the housing project were called on in a meeting to determine the fate of the buildings, the chant started immediately: "Blow it up! Blow it up!"

[19]Newman (1972) states that when yards or landscapes have no association to particular residences, such as those of a high-rise, residents of the building are unlikely to claim ownership over the spaces because they seem to belong to all. Therefore no one, except for the security guards, takes responsibility for their care and surveillance. The best-known example of the breakdown of social systems due to the Le Corbusier style of housing is the Pruitt-Igoe Housing Project in St. Louis, Missouri. The architects tried to eliminate the "wasted space" of public hallways and transitional areas between apartments and the outside public. The result was a lack of semiprivate space that could be claimed by particular apartment dwellers; thus, any public space, such as the stairwells, elevator, and public galleries (on the fourth, seventh, and tenth floors), became a neglected and uncontrolled "no man's land" with frequent occurrences of rape and assault (Yancey, 1971).

[20]Kupfer (1990) theorizes that in the past the front porch dissolved the wall between private place and public space and invited the communal life, which is built on easy and spontaneous social interaction. With the loss of the front porch, and the advent of the new backyard barbecue orientation, we lose the casual sharing of space and with it the cultivation of a sense of community. The house presents on its front a sign of rational order that transcends communal differences. The porch becomes a transitional place where people can negotiate their differences politely (Glassie, 2000). Successful transitions are achieved by regulating devices, such as the arcade, the storefront, the dooryard, and the ensemble of the porch, fence, and front lawn. These transitional devices soften the visual and psychological edges between zones and allow us to move between them with appropriate degrees of ease (Kunstler, 1998). In his book *Bowling Alone*, Robert Putman (2000) shows how Americans are becoming increasingly disconnected from one another and documents the negative impacts this disconnection has on physical and civic health in the United States.

Figure 6.12. This row of "snout houses" presents a particularly illustrative example of the unfriendly facades that garage-dominated houses present to the street.

front of a building is to contribute to the community, while other building "faces" on the street contribute back. Any face presented socially can be either welcoming or off-putting. The best buildings express themselves as welcoming while still suggesting social boundaries. These boundaries are much like human boundaries, where a smile of welcome can quickly disappear if the other person is dense enough to move too close too quickly, invading the personal space in front of us—a space that, while not obvious, we all nevertheless fiercely protect.

Cars backing out of front-yard driveways and crossing sidewalks can easily injure or even kill small children, making it unlikely that parents will allow children to play out front—in the space where they might serendipitously see the kid next door and start to play safely.[21] The presence of garage doors on the street also violates the "friendly face to the street" rule, as the garage door on the facade consumes so much space as to make the part of the facade dedicated to humans an insignificant remnant. With ideal lot sizes of only thirty-three feet wide, a garage door, even for only one car, would occupy more than half of the front facade. Were it a two-car garage, there would be no actual house left. This form of housing, called a "snout house" in many jurisdictions, is the ultimate in unfriendly facades and is incredibly dangerous for pedestrians, particularly small ones. The best solution to this problem is to take car storage off the front of the house and put it to the back, accessible by a lane in the mid-block. With the car removed from the front, the facade can be a human face to the street. With the car removed to the back, the sidewalk can be truly that, a place completely protected from cars.

Housing in North America has reached a crisis point where homogenous communities discriminate against buyers not by race but by income (which in some areas amounts to the same thing). From a social equity perspective, it is not an overstatement to suggest that this apparently intentional breach of the principle of fair play and opportunity is a disgrace of major magnitude and must not stand. As a practical matter, it is equally odious. The radical segregation of our cities and towns by class, often assigning entire towns for exclusive occupation by one income group and another town far distant for everyone of a lower income group, guarantees that our transportation woes will continue indefinitely. Legislation like Massachusetts

---

[21]Researchers from Edinburgh University found that in neighborhoods where high-quality pedestrian-oriented communal spaces were available, 85 percent of children used these communal spaces for play and only 15 percent played on roads or in parking areas. Parents and teachers appreciated the positive advantages of linked open spaces, and the child accident rate was half that of the nearby street-oriented layout of more conventional suburbs (Cooper Marcus and Sarkissian, 1986).

Chapter 40B is a big step in the right direction. Upheld many times in the face of constitutional challenges and political assaults, it clears a path for redress.

But much remains to be done. Chapter 40B, and similar narrowly executed policies, have not yet integrated communities in an organic, holistic way. It helps little in rationalizing our urban landscapes for walking and transit if worker housing continues to be placed in locations that are only serviceable by car. Fortunately, emerging models for suburban and urban retrofit, tools for planning and designing more equitable communities, are emerging.[22] The United States is expected to add 130 million new residents in the next thirty years. Canada is expected to grow at a similar rate. Where and how are these people to be housed? With proper local and regional strategies in place, these new families can be the instrument for a vastly more equitable, efficient, and low-carbon urban landscape. This is enough building mass to create thousands of new walkable centers or to be the vehicle for retrofitting presently car-oriented strip commercial corridors.[23] No new opportunity should be wasted in deploying this growth strategically in an integrated way. There is not a moment to lose.

[22]Zoning and Development By-law No. 3575 in Vancouver, British Columbia, was amended to allow secondary suites in RS, RT, and RM zoning districts (designations that refer to largely single-family-home areas of the city). For details of the bylaw, see http://vancouver.ca/commsvcs/BYLAWS/zoning/zon&dev.htm#sections.

[23]Stapleton, in Denver, Colorado, is an infill development covering 4,700 acres. With a gross density of nine dwelling units per acre, Stapleton will include twelve thousand dwellings, a large commercial area, business parks, schools, a recreation center, and industrial and institutional uses (Girling and Kellett, 2005). In 2008, three thousand of the twelve thousand homes had been built, and between 2007 and 2008 twenty-one thousand trees were planted (Buntin, 2008). A mix of housing types is provided, including single-family detached homes, apartments, townhouses, live-work options, and low-income housing. The development is designed to ensure that the majority of homes and businesses are within a ten-minute walk of one of the four town centers.

Another example is Orenco Station, in Hillsboro, Oregon. Situated on the light rail transit (LRT) line to downtown Portland, Orenco Station will include approximately 1,800 dwellings located within walking distance of the LRT, with a gross density of twelve dwelling units per acre (Mehaffy, 2001). As a third example, the design of East Clayton in Surrey, British Columbia, encourages a compact, walkable community design with a preserved system of natural drainage areas. The community is designed to incorporate a range of housing types and business opportunities and to provide good pedestrian connectivity to transit, services, and green space (James Taylor Chair in Landscape and Liveable Environments, 2003). At build-out, the average density of East Clayton will be ten dwelling units per acre (Canada Mortgage and Housing Corporation, 2001). As of 2009, East Clayton was 60 percent built out.

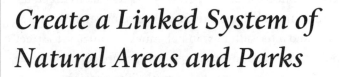

CHAPTER **7** | *Create a Linked System of Natural Areas and Parks*

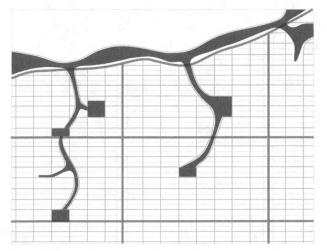

Figure 7.1. A linked system of parks and open space in the urban fabric.

We start by offering this first principle for ecological design: *The site is to the region as the cell is to the body; just as the health of the individual human cell has everything to do with the health of the human body, so too does the ecological function of the individual site have everything to do with the ecological health of the region.* Site-scale elements, when multiplied thousands and even millions of times throughout vast metropolitan regions, do more than *influence* regional environmental systems; they *constitute* regional environmental systems. The most obvious and important regional environmental system is the watershed. Of all the varied influences of the city on environmental function, the influence of urbanization on watershed function is the most profound.

If sites are the *cells* to the *body* of the region, then streams and rivers are the *veins*. If we extend this analogy even further, the rooftops, driveways, lanes, and streets of the urban landscape are the *capillaries* of the system. Capillaries take water to veins through a hierarchy of ever larger channels until this water reaches the sea. These capillaries and veins form a dendritic network common to all urbanized landscapes, whether they be desert or rain forest.

Since the time of the Romans, we have buried this network of rivulets, streams, and rivers under our cities. It is still there; it is just hidden in pipes. This is an expensive, ugly, and damaging strategy. Urban green space is too precious to hide. Absent exposure to green space, children growing up in these districts are experientially impoverished. When all traces of nature have been sterilized from neighborhoods, a vital connection between nature and citizens has been closed. It is far cheaper, far more beautiful, and far more healing to retain this network as is and to incorporate it as infrastructure. It should be revealed and used as a system that works with, not against, nature.

From rooftop to yard to driveway to sidewalk to street, urban elements must behave like forest trees, understory plants, forest soils, and intermittent water channels. From lane to street to schoolyard to park to preserved natural areas, urban areas must emulate natural areas—the swale like the intermittent stream, the park like the wetland, the ball field like the floodplain, and the greenway like the river of the natural order. These elements must be linked together in an ecologically functional chain—a linked system of natural areas and parks.

Linked natural areas and parks reduce greenhouse gas (GHG) emissions. Stream systems, and their necessary forested buffers, can reduce heat island effects in even new neighborhoods by the shade they provide and by the air cooling they produce. Preserved streamway forests also sequester carbon, a significant benefit, even though it takes twenty-five acres of trees, to sequester the average annual amount of carbon produced by one American.[1]

But perhaps of even more importance for our cities, linked parks and natural areas can connect urban districts for human purposes. Stream systems are inevitably dendritic, or "treelike," with branch tips reaching every corner of a watershed. A path system organized around the stream system will thus allow pedestrians and bikes to access every part of the urban district without using streets. Such paths can provide a comfortable, shaded way to travel long distances on foot or on small wheeled vehicles (such as electric scooters), thus offering a logical and organic way to make walking and biking more pleasant and convenient than driving.

These insights are not new. We have a long tradition of designing cities around a linked system of parks and natural areas.

FREDRICK LAW OLMSTED AND LINKED NATURAL AREAS AND PARKS

The movement to design cities around a linked system of natural areas and parks begins with Fredrick Law Olmsted (1822–1902). Olmsted is best remembered as the designer of Central and Prospect parks in New York, and of the Emerald Necklace in Boston.

[1] In a forest ecosystem, carbon sequestration occurs in the soil, trees, forest floor, and understory vegetation. The total amount sequestered in each part varies greatly depending on the region and the type, age, and quality of the forest. Generally, the soil holds roughly 60 percent, the aboveground parts of the trees hold an additional 30 percent, and the rest is mostly in the forest litter (9 percent) and understory vegetation (1 percent) (Haile et al., 2008). Carbon sequestration rates vary by tree species, soil type, climate and management practices; but some forest types have been shown to accumulate roughly one metric ton of carbon per acre per year (U.S. Environmental Protection Agency, 2006). To put this in perspective, the total U.S. GHG equivalent emissions in 2007 were 7,179.7 million metric tons, or approximately 23.8 metric tons per person per year (U.S. Environmental Protection Agency, 2008).

Olmsted was a product of the North American Transcendental Movement, a movement spawned by Ralph Waldo Emerson and Henry David Thoreau. Transcendentalism was itself a part of the broader and more global Romantic Movement. Transcendentalism had a profound influence on the arts of the time. Not surprisingly, its influence on landscape architecture was especially strong. The profession of landscape architecture, started by Olmsted himself, may not have been born without the push that Transcendentalism provided.

Inspired by the cannons of Transcendentalist thought, Olmsted designed and built parks with one purpose: to feed the spirit of their users. It is often wrongly assumed that Olmsted set out to copy nature; he had a much more ambitious agenda. His intention was to create environments that provided a spiritual uplift, an epiphany, in the soul of the user.[2] He used the materials of nature, not to replicate nature, but as media to create powerful works of art.

But Olmsted also integrated other, more practical objectives with the spiritual. He brought unprecedented sophistication in transportation planning, ecological systems restoration, real estate development, and recreational design into his work. The most brilliant example of this genius is the Emerald Necklace in Boston.

The Emerald Necklace is North America's first linked network of natural areas and parks. Extending well over six miles, it is effective in so many ways: it accommodated many different ways of moving, from carriage way to wooded path; it provided a public realm armature for real estate development, ensuring that the newly developing areas on both sides of the system would be much more valuable; it invented an urban design strategy that put nature at the center of civic life, instead of public buildings or traditional urban squares; and it solved a host of ecological problems through radically reengineering the entire landscape for enhanced ecological function.

This last point is worth emphasizing. Users invariably assume that the streams and ponds of the Emerald Necklace were always there. The construction photos of the period tell a very different story, however. Olmsted radically reshaped the landscape and in so doing did more than restore its ecological function, but he reimagined it. Because of Olmsted's aggressive

<hr>

[2]According to Fisher (1986), the organic principle for Olmsted led to a philosophy of art tied to purpose, beauty reflecting utility, and form organized by function. Olmstead believed that organic unity was achieved in its highest form through the creative action of the artist, whose unconscious processes of work simulate the work of God. The result is art. That art is perceived by the observer, whose own unconscious transforms its beauty into spiritual freedom. Fisher argues that Olmsted viewed planning as both a rational and an unconscious process that could be used to offset the deleterious side effects of urbanism and industrial progress and ultimately provide an avenue for spiritual transcendence (Fisher, 1986, 58–59).

Figure 7.2. Photo (a) was taken during construction of Olmsted's Emerald Necklace (circa 1850–1895) around Boston and shows the degree of human intervention involved in the construction of what appears afterward (b) to be a very naturalistic landscape.

reshaping of nature, Robert Smithson, the earth artist who produced the Spiral Jetty in Utah, called Olmsted the "world's first earth artist" (Smithson, 1979).

Olmsted's influence did not die with him. His son, his stepson, and Charles Eliot would carry it forward with plans produced at the landscape architecture firm Olmsted, Olmsted, and Eliot. The most impressive and extensive of these plans was Charles Eliot's 1893 plan for Boston's Metropolitan Park Commission. For the first time in North America, a group of independent municipalities collaborated in creating a linked system of natural areas and parks, a system that linked more than twenty cities and towns and was intelligently organized around the armature of the region's system of rivers, streams, wetlands, and estuaries. The plan, now executed, did more than protect natural function and provide a growing city with recreation; it is, in large part, what makes the Boston region what it is. The sense of place that distinguishes Boston from other East Coast metropolitan regions of similar size is a result of the landscape strategy of linked natural areas and parks.

IAN MCHARG AND THE GREENWAY REVIVAL

Yet, by the beginning of the twentieth century, things had very much changed. The United States was emerging as a world

Figure 7.3. Charles Eliot's plan for Boston's system of linked natural areas and parks. Much of the plan was built and continues to provide recreational and ecological services. This system is crucial to the sense of place of the city and region. Light gray areas indicated proposed additions to the system; dark gray areas show existing parks. Heavy lines indicate proposed parkway systems, many of which were eventually completed.

power, and Transcendentalism had been replaced by American Pragmatism. In the second and third decade of the twentieth century, the arts finally "broke free" of Romantic-era canons to explore more modernist avenues of expression. Nature, previously the motivating concern for all arts, was replaced by more abstract notions of perception and experience.

It remained to the counterculture of the 1960s to revive the concept of a healing nature, again promoting it as an antidote to the spiritual poverty of the city.[3] Into this cultural revival swept University of Pennsylvania landscape architecture

[3]Charles A Reich wrote *The Greening of America* (New York: Random House) in 1970, a canonic piece in its time.

professor Ian McHarg (1920–2001), who was arguably the first twentieth-century figure to restore the authority of nature as an urban and regional design informant. McHarg was without doubt the twentieth century's most popular urban and regional designer, filling stadiums for his lectures and selling more than a quarter million copies of his seminal 1969 book, *Design with Nature*.

Design with Nature was released just before the first Earth Day, in 1970. It provided timely solutions to what was widely recognized as a looming environmental crisis. McHarg introduced a way to heal the land, using a scientific—or what certainly seemed scientific—methodology. He invented ways to map the individual attributes of large landscapes, with each attribute mapped separately, and then to layer these semitransparent maps one over the other. Through examining the transparent maps, one could determine areas of the landscape that were most sensitive, and thus exempt from urbanization, and others where urbanization might occur with minimal damage.

This kind of mapping, called *sieve mapping* (for the way it acts like a series of screens that limit uses from falling through where restrictions are greatest), is now in widespread use. McHarg's system communicated rationally what Olmsted had advanced poetically: that the most crucial elements of the landscape are its streams, river corridors, lakes, and wetlands. Thus, on the resultant composite maps, the architecture of a regional-scale greenway system inevitably emerges, purely as a consequence of the rational assessment of the landscape's material and ecological capacities.

A few caveats are in order. What is lacking in McHarg's methodology is a recognition that river systems, to remain healthy, must function naturally throughout the watershed, not just in stream zones. Seen in this light, the whole watershed is precious, not just the main stream and river arteries. Also lost in this process (although not lost on McHarg himself, as his writings make clear) was a way to credit the spiritual value of nature, a value that was central to Olmsted's earlier conception.

It was at the Woodlands project, north of Houston, Texas, that McHarg first put his methodology into practice. It is a brilliant example of working with, and not against, natural systems. A high water table and a table-flat landscape made the site particularly sensitive to disruption—and almost impossible to

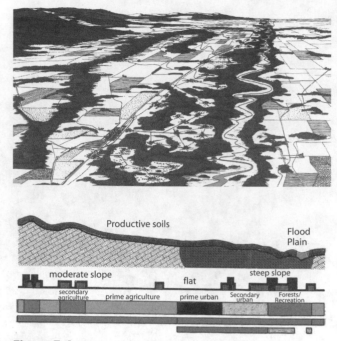

Figure 7.4. McHarg's overlay method produced a composite map that made it possible to identify alternative project locations that would give rise to the fewest environmental impacts.

Figure 7.5. This aerial photo of The Woodlands shows how the natural constraints, primarily waterways, determined the form of the community.

develop using conventional means. The solution was to leave the natural systems armature in place and to find ways to insert roads and houses with minimal disruption to that system. Thus, the natural systems armature serves both as infrastructure, removing storm flows, and as amenity, providing The Woodlands with a unique sense of place.

The Woodlands, while hugely significant for its achievement, also illustrates the dangers inherent to using only natural function and sensitivity to guide design. The deference to the wetland system leads naturally to a dendritic road system that functions for traffic no better than the worst sprawl subdivision (Girling and Kellet, 2005).

MORE RECENT PROGRESS

When the limits of McHarg's process became more apparent, Professor John Lyle (1934–1998) published *Design for Human Ecosystems* (1985). In the book, Lyle argued that the city is an ecosystem and that humans are part of that system. Lyle called for a more nuanced appraisal than what sieve maps could produce. Like Olmsted, Elliot, and McHarg before him, Lyle was reflective of his times. The 1980s were a time when scientific certainty was under assault from many fronts. Building architects, influenced by poststructuralist ideas then current, moved away from modernist self-assured purity to more disrupted and incomplete forms. For Lyle, this meant that humans and nature were no longer distinct categories and that creativity and rationality were no longer opposed.

Even more recent is the work of Professor Julius Fabos. Fabos began his interesting public career by publishing *Frederick Law Olmsted, Sr.: Founder of Landscape Architecture in America* (1968). Incredible as it may seem today, by 1960 Olmsted had been largely forgotten. Fabos, a young man at the time, acted on the insight that Olmsted's legacy, and the profession he created, could be revived by creating a mythology around Olmsted's life and works, a mythology that is accepted as fact today. During the mature phase of his career, Fabos has emphasized the concept that humans can create an intelligent relationship with regional natural systems, and that the core of that strategy is a regionwide system of linked parks and natural areas. He has advanced this argument through his work on implementing greenway policies at scales as large as the New England states, captured in *Greenways: The Beginning of an International Movement* (1995).

But a complete picture of how urban functions can be completely integrated with natural functions has only recently emerged. The first published work to make this connection explicit is *Skinny Streets and Green Neighborhoods* (2005), by University of British Columbia professors Cynthia Girling and Ronald Kellet. In this book, Girling and Kellet document green community case studies, including the Stapleton project in Denver, Coffee Creek in Indiana, and Villebois in Oregon. Each is characterized by a green infrastructure concept that both influences the form of the community and functions all the way to the parcel.

Increasingly, these sustainability strategies are making their way from isolated demonstration projects into broadly applied policy. Particularly noteworthy is the spread of what are called low-impact development standards into city ordinances and bylaws—notably in Olympia, Washington.[4] Low-impact development regulations have two main thrusts: (1) to insist that stream corridors be protected by very significant buffers (often greater than two hundred feet), and (2) to ensure that storm drain systems for streets and parcels emulate natural processes in their performance. These bylaws can, in time, retrofit existing communities around an integrated and healthy green infrastructure system, making that system increasingly valuable for recreation and, as was learned in Boston with Olmsted's Green Necklace, a way to enhance property values in adjacent neighborhoods.

PROGRESS ON THE GROUND

There are no recent North American examples of a regionwide system of linked parks and natural areas to compare to what Olmsted and Elliot accomplished in Boston, but plans are being adopted that could, in time, produce even more powerful results. Portland, Oregon, provides one example. In 1973, the Oregon legislature passed Senate Bill 100, which became known as the "land use law."[5] Oregon was the first, and until very recently

[4]Ordinance #6140 was adopted July 12, 1994. More information can be found on the City of Olympia's Web site, http://www.olympiawa.gov/citygovernment/codes/omc/.

[5]Senate Bill 100, adopted in 1973, established the Land Conservation and Development Commission (LCDC) to establish new statewide goals and guidelines. In 1974, the LCDC adopted nineteen goals (listed in the following note) that had been developed through extensive public review. Goal 5 addresses the protection of resources, including riparian corridors, wetlands, wildlife habitat, federal wild and scenic rivers, state scenic waterways, groundwater resources, approved Oregon recreation trails, natural areas, wilderness areas, mineral and aggregate resources, energy sources, and cultural areas. Oregon's Statewide Planning Goals and Guidelines are available at http://www.oregon.gov/LCD/goals.shtml#Statewide_Planning_Goals.

the only, U.S. state to pass a law giving the state authority over local land use decisions. The law is most famous for its inclusion of the "urban growth boundary" (UGB) tool, and indeed this element has been the subject of much conflict within the state, and of much publicity beyond. Much less well known are the specific goals included in the bill, goals that govern the actions of the state as well as of regional and local planning authorities. There are nineteen goals in all, ranging from process goals such as "Goal 1, Citizen Involvement" to functional goals such as "Goal 12, Transportation." Goals 5, 6, and 7 address water systems but in a disintegrated way, separating them into habitat (goal 5), water quality (goal 6), and natural hazards (including floodplains, goal 7).[6]

In early decades, these goals were narrowly regulated, with no recognition that the region needed to understand streams and natural areas as a system rather than as a set of unconnected attributes. What was previously seen as a mere regulatory problem became a problem of city form and integrated function. Mike Houck, currently the director of the Urban Greenspaces Institute in Portland, was the first to advocate for an integrated planning approach to what he called Portland's "greenfrastructure."[7] What is now known as Title 13 Fish and Wildlife Habitat Plan (regulatory parks) and "Connecting Green" (nonregulatory parks, trails, and natural areas master plan) manifest this integration. Both are official documents of the Portland Metro Council regional government and were produced during a period when Houck and his colleagues worked with and advised the Portland Metro Council. The overall vision, when accomplished, will create a bi-state interconnected system of natural areas, trails, open spaces, and neighborhood, community, and regional parks knitting together the entire urban region.

CASE STUDY AT THE REGIONAL SCALE: THE DAMASCUS DESIGN WORKSHOP

A Portland-area plan that may, in time, realize the full potential of a linked system of parks and natural areas is the Damascus Area Design Workshop plan. For this project, the organizers

---

[6]Oregon's Statewide Planning Goals: Goal 1: Citizen Involvement; Goal 2: Land Use Planning; Goal 3: Agricultural Lands; Goal 4: Forest Lands; Goal 5: Natural Resources, Scenic and Historic Areas, and Open Spaces; Goal 6: Air, Water and Land Resources Quality; Goal 7: Areas Subject to Natural Hazards; Goal 8: Recreational Needs; Goal 9: Economic Development; Goal 10: Housing; Goal 11: Public Facilities and Services; Goal 12: Transportation; Goal 13: Energy Conservation; Goal 14: Urbanization; Goal 15: Willamette River Greenway; Goal 16: Estuarine Resources; Goal 17: Coastal Shorelands; Goal 18: Beaches and Dunes; Goal 19: Ocean Resources.

[7]See the Urban Greenspaces Institute Web site at http://www.urban greenspaces.org/index.htm.

worked to reveal what a community would look like were it to be designed in complete conformance with the goals of Senate Bill 100, and especially its ecological goals.

Senate Bill 100 makes comprehensive landscape-scale planning possible in a way that is not possible elsewhere. Portland Metro Council is now managing the Portland area's largest ever UGB expansion: a twenty-thousand-acre area in the southwest quadrant of the metropolitan region. Unique to U.S. metropolitan areas, the elected Portland area regional government, Portland Metro Council, must approve community development and servicing plans before affected municipalities can approve projects.

When this twenty-thousand-acre UGB expansion was first proposed, it raised many questions for regional officials and interested citizen groups. The most fundamental of these questions was the following: can such a large region be developed sustainably? To provide a partial answer to this question, two nonprofit public interest groups—1,000 Friends of Oregon and Coalition for a Livable Future—collaborated on a regionwide charrette.

This charrette had a simple goal: to see what a community would look like if it lived up to the nineteen goals of Oregon's landmark Senate Bill 100.[8] Could they really do it all? Or would some of the goals be unachievable on the ground? Would the environmental protection goal be compromised by the transportation goal? Or by the affordability goal? Only through an on-the-ground exercise where apparently competing goals were applied in design could they tell.

Finding a design that would protect natural areas while still being practical to build was the most difficult and most important challenge for the charrette team. Could it be done? The answer was yes, if they returned to many of the strategies that make Olmsted's Emerald Necklace scheme so successful. There, Olmsted proved that nature, real estate value, and transportation need not compete. Correctly handled, they can integrate synergistically. Several fundamental lessons could be learned from the Emerald Necklace project: (1) use nature out front, not out back; (2) use the seam between nature and the city for transportation of all kinds; (3) integrate natural systems into the fabric of more formal recreation areas and civic spaces; (4) expand the system indefinitely; and (5) provide an alternative

---

[8]The charrette report is available online at http://www.jtc.sala.ubc.ca/Damascus/Final%20Report.htm.

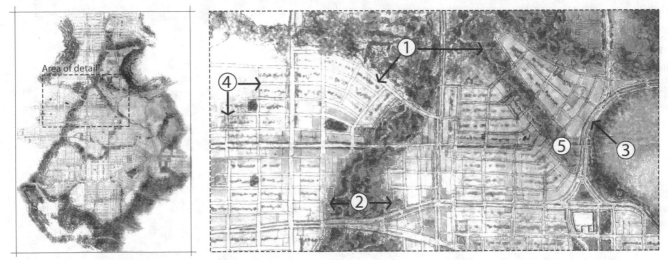

Damascus Master Plan   Area of Detail

Figure 7.6. The Damascus Area Master Plan demonstrates at the district scale the five principles of a linked system of natural areas and parks: 1) Nature Out Front, 2) natural areas to bind and protect, 3) ecological parkways, 4) expand indefinitely, and 5) an alternate movement system.

movement system. These lessons, which can be generally applied, are explained below.

Linked Parks Strategy 1: Plan for Nature out Front, Not out Back

Current regulations now typically require developers to preserve stream channels. But these channels are usually located not at the edges of public ways but along rear property lines. This is a waste of a valuable amenity. Such streams become the destination for stray shopping carts and a convenient dumping area for construction waste. Research has shown that protected and preserved nature contributes to increased average property values many blocks away, but only if it is designed as a visible and accessible public amenity.[9] The only way to truly make natural systems into a visible public amenity is to locate them on the "front door" of the community, not out the back—that is, abutting public rights-of-way or parks rather than rear parcel lines.

In practice, this means using roads to put nature on one side of the street and to put front doors of buildings on the other. Many developers who develop parcels next to protected stream corridors are loath to accept this principle. For them, roads with nature on one side and houses on the other are a waste of money because such streets are "single loaded" and

[9]Bolitzer and Netusil (2000) conducted a study on the influence that open spaces, such as public parks, natural areas, and golf courses, have on the sale price of homes in close proximity to them. They found that proximity to open space and the type of open space can have a positive, statistically significant effect on a home's sale price. Homes that were within one half block of any type of open space were estimated, on average, to experience the largest positive effect on their sale price.

yield only half as many serviced lots to sell per unit length as do "double-loaded" streets. But with that approach, the lesson of Olmsted goes unlearned, the amenity ignored, the development diminished, and nature hidden. Municipal district plans are seldom, if ever, specific enough to show and later require roads fronting nature. Absent such requirements, it is a rare developer who will provide it proactively.

The revived "nature out front" rule is evident in the completed Damascus proposal. In no case in this plan is nature hidden in back at the rear edge of parcels. In all cases, nature is edged with a two-lane parkway road and associated bike paths and footpaths. Beyond that begins the protected riparian corridor. In certain key areas, civic and formal recreation spaces and neighborhood schools are embedded in the natural fabric of the greenway. It is particularly important that natural areas not be designed as prisons for nature, as protected areas where even pathways are forbidden. Environmental managers are justifiably reticent to allow any sort of recreational use in protected areas, given how few are protected and how fragile are these areas. But in a design as rich with protected areas as in this example, this logic does not pertain. For too long, environmental regulators have taken a myopic view of their charge. Absent a direct connection to nature, neighborhood residents, a natural constituency for natural area protection, lose any vested interest in their preservation. In addition, the damage wrought on stream systems by recreational users is often exaggerated, especially compared to the damage done by humans to "hidden" urban streams, typically full of illegally dumped construction debris and shopping carts.

Developable areas of twenty thousand acres close to a major city are extremely rare. Even more rare are sites this size owned by one entity. When large developable areas are under multiple ownerships, it then becomes the responsibility of the municipal and regional planning powers to insist that this "nature out front" rule be enforced. If a planning power did nothing more than require protected natural areas "on the front door and not the back," along with a requirement for a through road at increments no greater than six hundred feet, most of the benefits described in this section would eventually accrue. As the years pass, a continuous fabric of public parkways would emerge, as was the case in Minneapolis, where W. H. S Cleve-

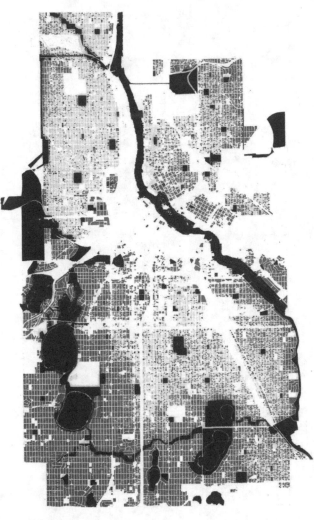

City of Minneapolis
Residential Market Value in Dollars
(land and building)

■ Parks and Open Space
■ Greater than $60,000
□ $0 - $60,000

Figure 7.7. This tax value map clearly shows the positive benefit of being close to the H. W. S. Cleveland "Chain of Lakes" system. (Source: City of Minneapolis and Professor William Marsh, Parsons School of Design).

land's Ring of Lakes took many decades to complete. Such a system would add greatly to the attachment felt by area residents to their neighborhood, as tax value maps from Minneapolis clearly indicate. Property values for similar houses on similar lots are highest right at the parkway edge but also maintain a distinctly higher value for a number of blocks farther into the neighborhood. This emphasis on property value does not indicate that available natural systems have only a pecuniary value; rather, it suggests a quality-of-life value that is naturally reflected in the desirability of the area and thus naturally evident in a financial premium for houses in the district when compared to other districts not so richly endowed.

Linked Parks Strategy 2: Use Natural Systems to Bound and Protect Neighborhoods

Accessible natural areas and park systems can certainly be the center of community life, but they just as often serve as a containing edge. Linked park and natural areas automatically provide firm boundaries to neighborhoods, protecting and defining them. In streetcar city districts, natural areas that bound and protect neighborhoods can provide a real value. They interrupt what might otherwise be an unrelenting grid, and they distinguish one part of the metropolitan fabric from another. Olmsted understood this concept, and his urban forms respond to the surrounding grid of the streetcar city in a way that gives additional power to both, providing both a place to recreate and a vivid, obvious boundary for neighborhoods astride it.

The Damascus plan shows the application of this principle at the very large urban scale. Even a glance at the plan proves that even though the interconnected street strategy is applied universally, each district is placed in a distinct relationship with the natural system that bounds and protects it. It is the dialogue between the interconnected web of streets and the dendritic branches of the linked system on natural areas that produces "place." Any concern that interconnected urban street networks are placeless should be allayed. This point of conjunction between the street system and the greenway system can express a neighborhood edge, or a neighborhood center, or even both: a natural center, a civic edge.

Many contemporary urban designers miss this opportunity for place making. By creating radial street systems to create points of emphasis, they frustrate the easy flow of traffic. Civic buildings are most often proposed for these crucial central points, in order to create sense of place with an obvious civic center for the district. While this strategy is not antithetical to what is suggested here, for these designers the power of greenway systems to create distinct places on a vast scale is easily overlooked. The Damascus project provides ample evidence of this potential, while Olmsted's Emerald Necklace suggests what this might be like in built form.

Linked Parks Strategy 3: Design the Ecological Parkway

An important feature of Olmsted's greenway is the boulevard. In his hands, these wide boulevards were beautifully engineered and heavily planted with large trees, trees that are only now reaching their full majesty. But however green were his boulevards, they performed no ecological services. They were conventionally drained, like the damaging storm drain systems discussed in chapter 8. With a more current understanding of watershed function, urban boulevards can provide an expanded role and their generous green spaces can perform a myriad of ecological services. Medians can be designed to infiltrate water (as shown in chapter 8) while also providing an ephemeral expression of nature's recent gifts in the form of temporary reflecting pools that serve to retain and infiltrate stormwater. A completely pipe-free city, with no buried storm water pipes, is easy to build but requires a few new ways of thinking.

Linked Parks Strategy 4: Expand the System Indefinitely

Another worthy characteristic of the interconnected street and natural greenways system is that it is infinitely expandable. Streetcar cities conformed to simple rules. In the early part of the twentieth century, the only planning done was street planning. City engineers knew that Seventh Avenue would go west until it ran out of land, as would Fifty-first Street heading south. Every four long blocks, the right-of-way was thirty feet wider for the eventual arterial, and that was it. Zoning maps did not exist and were not needed. Commercial uses filled the streetcar arterials, and that was that.

This fundamental planning power—the power to predetermine street networks—has been relinquished in the past fifty years of almost universal "pod"-style development and should be reclaimed. A two-part strategy—where natural systems are protected and formed into linked natural areas and parks, which are then to be layered together with rational interconnected streets—is certainly as simple. But the contingencies of place, an automatic outcome of a revealed natural system, provide the potential for great beauty over the full extent of metropolitan-scale urban landscapes. In short, it almost designs itself.

Linked Parks Strategy 5: Provide an Alternative Movement System

Linked parks and natural areas, by their nature, should connect all parts of a district. In the Damascus plan, the continuous network of parks and natural areas includes avenues for various modes of travel, from bike paths to footpaths to "pleasure vehicles only" parkways to rough walking trails that bring users closest to untrammeled nature. This continuous system provides the potential for users to reach all parts of the district without using conventional streets at all. Such a secondary system can considerably reduce auto dependence and provide a resilient connective tissue capable of accommodating movement in future decades regardless of skyrocketing fuel costs or future limits on car use.

CASE STUDY AT THE NEIGHBORHOOD SCALE: SUSTAINABLE FAIRVIEW AND THE PRINGLE CREEK COMMUNITY, SALEM, OREGON

Modern built landscape–scale examples of this strategy do not yet exist. But certain places already under development give a sense of what such a region might feel like, notably the Pringle Creek Community project in Salem, Oregon.[10]

---

[10]Pringle Creek Community is a project of Sustainable Development Incorporated of Salem, Oregon. For more information, see http://www .pringlecreek.com/. Sustainable Fairview is a project of Sustainable Fairview Associates. For more information, see http://sustainablefairview salem.com/.

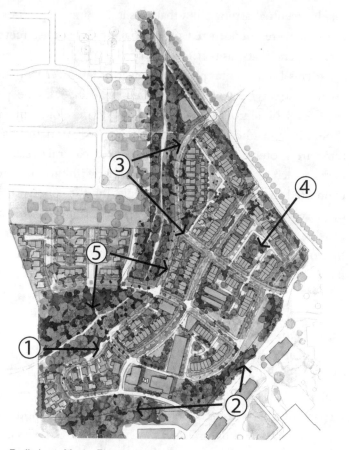

Preliminary Master Plan
Pringle Creek Community - Salem, Oregon

Figure 7.8. The Pringle Creek Community Master Plan responds to the five principles of a linked system of natural areas and parks.

The Pringle Creek Community occupies a thirty-acre portion of the much larger two-hundred-plus-acre plan for the Sustainable Fairview community. This master planned community, approved by the City of Salem, will incorporate the features discussed above: an interconnected street system and an extended green infrastructure system that, in this case, reaches at least one end of nearly every block. Natural water function was a key determinant of urban form, in concert with the other six rules discussed in this book. The plan allows all water to flow through the site naturally, without any buried pipes for stormwater.

The Fairview site is shaped like a large upturned hand with the spaces between the "fingers" being dramatic declivities where water naturally flows. In the palm of the hand is the center of the community, where roads lead naturally to this central wa-

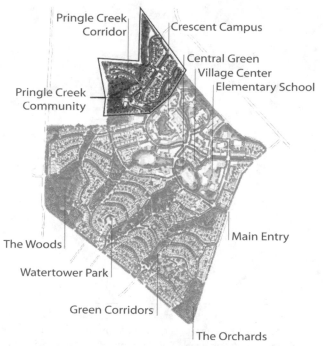

Figure 7.9. The Pringle Creek Community, shown in dark, is part of the larger Sustainable Fairview community, shown in light.

tershed point. The central green functions in the same way as the park spaces in Scottsdale, Arizona, with green space doubling as water storage and infiltration on days of large storms. All other water is absorbed on parcels or in the street cross section.

The Pringle Creek Community is now North America's largest residential area application of pervious streets. There are no pipes at all in the plan. Water is carried naturally from the center line of the site, which is only slightly higher than the two edges. Most water is absorbed by the streets, but on the very rare days when the capacity of the streets is overwhelmed, or in very unusual circumstances when the water table rises within inches of the surface, a series of roadside swales begin to perform, conveying water to Pringle Creek via a system of naturalized artificial streams and wetlands circling the site. These wetlands and streams operate ephemerally only after large rains, animating the site in response to climatic phenomena. Even on this small site, the principle of "front door to nature" is adhered to, with a large percentage of street length "single loaded" as a result. Thus all natural areas are clearly within the public realm. While the streets are pleasant enough to walk on, with sidewalks on both sides of all streets, the site also includes a system of pathways convenient for a more shaded and convenient walk to the center. The commercial center is within an easy five-minute walk of all homes, although it will likely not be self-sustaining until the other two thousand homes are built in the larger Fairview site to the south.

At the center of the community is a more formal square. This square performs a water holding function as well, holding three inches of water across the surface after large storms and turning the whole plaza into an ephemeral reflecting pool for a day or two before infiltrating into the ground. Bringing this ephemeral reflecting pool to the heart of the Pringle Creek Community is, of course, intentional and motivated by reasons that go beyond simple flow control. Water is at the heart of this sustainable community plan, and it would be wrong to physically exile it from its very center.

At the heart of a healthy urban region is water—water that moves through the veins and arteries of the urban watershed. While the fight to reduce our GHG footprint is now at the height of urgency, reducing our water footprint remains crucial as well. Just as the atmosphere, the air itself, may not support human life as we know it unless we acknowledge our role in its destruction, so too are we as a species on the point of irreversibly corrupting the other life support system of the planet: its water. A system of linked natural areas and parks is easily the most cost efficient and effective means of reversing the corruption to natural systems caused by cities.

Using a natural areas and parks strategy to manage the environmental consequences of city building has a corollary with the creation of neighborhood quality, its sense of place. Neighborhoods bounded and protected by nature provide children with ready access to natural areas and to an explanation for how their world works. This is beyond price. Not only does a linked system of natural areas and parks put nature at our doorstep, but it also provides verdant avenues for moving through the landscape—a way of traveling that is both safe and delightful.

The benefits of a system of linked natural areas and parks are thus manifold. But, like all sustainability issues, it is a fatal mistake to focus on just one element of the puzzle at the expense of all others. The secret lies in designing for all of the sustainability issues at the same time. A societal paradigm shift is required, one where it becomes commonplace to work collaboratively and holistically, rather than boxing ourselves into narrow technical, environmental, or economic silos. When this happens, when a community is designed in an integrated way, water will inevitably be at its heart. And when that collaboration occurs, it will be expressed in physical form in a linked system of parks and natural areas. This North American planning tradition, too long moribund, can and should be revived. It is now foolish to ignore the myriad of benefits—social, economic, and ecological—that accrue.

CHAPTER **8** | *Invest in Lighter,*
Greener, Cheaper,
Smarter Infrastructure

In chapter 7, we looked at the main arteries of the watershed and how they can become the main armature for urban design. Here, we look at the most tertiary branch tips in the urban watershed, the streets and the parcels they serve. Road and stormwater infrastructure often destroys the ecological function of the land that supports it and burdens home buyers and taxpayers through its cost to install, maintain, and replace. Since the end of World War II, the per dwelling unit costs for providing, maintaining, and replacing infrastructure (defined here as the physical means for moving people, goods, energy, and liquids through the city) has increased by nearly 400 percent according to some estimates.[1]

Most of this per capita increase has been the consequence of ever more demanding engineering standards for residential

---

[1]A number of studies have shown that alternative development practices can provide significant savings on the cost of installing, maintaining, and repairing infrastructure systems (Guillette, 2008; U.S. Environmental Protection Agency, 2007). For example, in 2004 the National Oceanic and Atmospheric Administration (NOAA) conducted a comparative analysis of three hypothetical development scenarios for a prime coastal residential site. Factoring in the cost to clear land and develop roads, sewers, water lines, trails, and sidewalks, this study found that the New Urbanist (or Neo-traditional) scenario offered potential net revenues 18.5 percent higher than the conventional development scenario (NOAA, 2004). By compiling the various costs associated with infrastructure construction, operation, and maintenance, Condon and Teed (1998) estimated that by reducing road width, allowing gravel lanes with utility poles, and implementing efficiencies in placement and use of utility hookups, the total infrastructure costs per dwelling unit could be reduced to one fifth the cost of a conventional development.

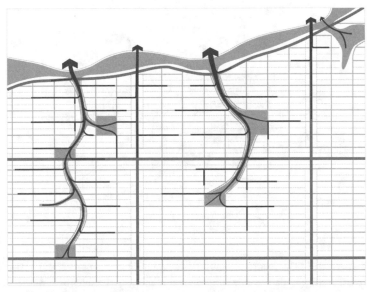

Figure 8.1. This diagram shows road and utility infrastructure working with natural systems to maintain healthy ecosystem function.

roads, coupled with the gradual increase in per capita land demand over the decades (or at least until the year 2000), a consequence of universally applied sprawl patterns throughout the United States and Canada. The first costs of these ever more odious engineering standards and ever more exclusive zoning regulations were often invisible to the taxpayer, buried as they were within the costs of the original home purchase. These costs become more obvious to the taxpayer after two generations, when the costs associated with the necessary replacement of infrastructure fall not on the home purchaser but on all property tax payers.[2] First-ring suburbs built during the 1950s and 1960s now face major costs for overhauling an overextended system of roads and pipes; because of low-density development, these suburbs do not have enough taxpayers to cover those costs.[3] Faced with rising property taxes and falling level of services, residents of first- and second-ring suburbs simply opt out, leaving behind those communities for the greener fields of the third- and fourth-ring suburbs or even exurbia. Decaying oversized infrastructure in need of replacement provides strong financial incentives for residents to move farther away from the geographic core of the region and farther away from jobs and services.[4]

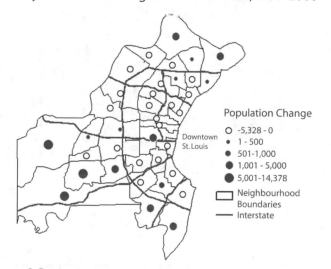

Change in Total Population by Census Tract Neighbourhood Areas, 1990–2000

Figure 8.2. This diagram shows the doughnut-hole effect in St. Louis, Missouri, as the population moved from the center city to the suburbs. (Source: USDC Bureau of the Census, Census of Population and Housing [1990 STF3, 2000 SF3]; prepared by Office of Social and Economic Data Analysis)

[2]Sprawling development increases the cost of building and maintaining roads, sewers, schools, and other public facilities for a number of reasons: (1) because of the initial capital costs of new infrastructure in greenfield developments, (2) because the increased distance between developments increases the length of roads, water pipes, and sewer lines, and (3) because facilities must be more dispersed in the landscape without being able to take advantage of efficiencies from economies of scale (Meredith, 2003). In a 2007 report, the Federation of Canadian Municipalities found that close to 80 percent of Canada's infrastructure is past its service life and the price of eliminating the municipal infrastructure deficit is $123 billion (Globe and Mail, 2007). In 2009, the American Society of Civil Engineers (ASCE) estimated that $2.2 trillion needs to be invested over the next five years to bring the condition of America's public infrastructure—water, sewer, and transportation systems—up to a good condition (ASCE, 2009). As urban centers are left with aging and deteriorating infrastructure, properties are abandoned and property values and tax revenues go down, depriving the municipality of the money needed to maintain, repair, or replace existing infrastructure (Hirschhorn, 2001).

[3]Although the total infrastructure costs for the entire site were greater, the per dwelling unit costs in the sustainable alternative ($4,408) were significantly lower than the per unit infrastructure costs in the status quo development ($23,520) (Condon and Teed, 1998). These cost savings are attributable to a more compact urban form and higher residential density (sustainable alternative development, 17.7 dwelling units per acre; status quo development, 3.9 dwelling units per acre).

[4]Hirschhorn's Traditional Circular Model of Sprawl (2001) describes the mechanisms behind the deterioration of many urban centers during the second half of the twentieth century. It shows how higher taxes and decaying infrastructure did as much to push the nonpoor out of urban centers as the cheap outlying land, new infrastructure, low property taxes, and attractive open space acted to drawn them to the suburbs. Urban centers are left with aging and deteriorating properties, facilities, and infrastructure as property values and tax revenues decline (Hirschhorn, 2001).

An alternative to this gray, expensive, and heavy infrastructure—and a topic of this chapter—is "green infrastructure" for roads and drainage. Green infrastructure is defined herein as roads and drainage systems that work with, and not against, natural systems. It manifests itself in a set of engineering and constructions standards that make road and drainage infrastructure lighter, greener, cheaper, and smarter.

Every dollar's worth of pavement produces a measurable increase in environmental impact. Pavement fundamentally alters where water goes when it rains. Water that should go into the ground goes into a pipe instead, utterly transforming watershed performance. The cure for the sickness inflicted on watersheds consequent to urban development is to spend *less* on infrastructure, not more—less pavement, fewer pipes, fewer inlets, fewer gutters. Infrastructure exists that costs less than what we are currently requiring and that works with nature's systems rather than against them. This is infrastructure that capitalizes on nature's services while minimizing the weight, extent, and cost of the "hardscape"—the streets, walks, lanes, and drainage ways of the site. Green infrastructure can significantly reduce cost while dramatically shrinking environmental impacts.

WATERSHED FUNCTION

We start by repeating in a slightly altered form the first principle for ecological design introduced in chapter 7: *The site is to the region as the cell is to the body. And as the cells in the body are comprised mostly of water, so too is water any site's most important ecological element.*

In most North American natural landscapes, the vast majority of rainwater that falls on the ground is infiltrated by the soil or absorbed into plants. Plant roots draw rainwater from shallow soils and then send it back up into the sky through the leaves (a process called transpiration). The water that the plants do not need or cannot absorb flows through the soil to be stored in the water table or drained from the soil via a nearby stream. The relative ratio of water transpired versus water absorbed varies from place to place and from season to season. For example, during the dry season in certain prairie landscapes, plants can commonly transpire more water than they receive. Thus, the plants draw not only from the supply of new rain but also from moisture stored in soil over the winter and early spring.

Conversely, in coastal Pacific Northwest temperate rainforests, the average percentage of rainwater that is returned to the atmosphere as evaporation and transpiration throughout the year is about 45 percent, while infiltration accounts for the rest. However, during the winter, when it rains the most, it is too cold for much photosynthesis and thus transpiration to occur. Consequently, during winter nearly 100 percent of the winter rain that falls on the forest floor is absorbed by the tree detritus and the soils below. As more water falls, soaking the soils, some of the excess seeps into deep water aquifers, where it might be stored for an indefinite, or almost infinite, amount of time; however, most of the excess seeps a few inches or a few feet below the surface until blocked by a harder soil, called glacial hardpan, the legacy of the most recent period of glaciations that covered all of Canada and much of the United States in a blanket of ice miles thick. Once impeded by this layer, it flows horizontally, emerging eventually at a nearby stream bank, in a process called interflow.

Soils in the parts of the continent south of the farthest extent of the glacier have a more complex and older genesis, some the result of wild volcanic events so far in the distant past that the glaciations occurred only yesterday in comparison. However, infiltration in these soils is quite often similarly impeded, producing similar watershed performance characteristics.[5]

Because of the highly erratic actions of the glacier during its various stages of melt and advance, one acre of land can be the locus of a deep lens of sand left by a particular kind of outwash off the surface of a melting ice sheet, while on the acre immediately next door the soils can be almost completely impervious—a concretized mass of very heavy clayey soils.

As touched on in chapter 7, streamside vegetation plays an important role in preserving fish habitat. Streamside vegetation holds soils in place, retains nutrients in the channel, prevents water from the overheating caused by direct exposure to sunlight, and ensures a steady food supply of insects and forest detritus for fish. Many, if not most, new development sites of more than sixty or so acres will contain riparian areas with this kind of habitat value, areas deserving of protection. Most studies indicate that at least one hundred feet (thirty meters) of streamside vegetation on both sides of any given watercourse is

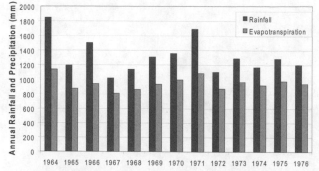

Figure 8.3. The total annual precipitation and evapotranspiration of mostly forested watershed in the Pacific Northwest. Here, precipitation exceeds evapotranspiration; however, most of the water that falls on the forest in this case does not leave the site as stream flow but reenters the atmosphere as water vapor. (Source: Amatya and Tretin, 2007)

Figure 8.4. Ten thousand years ago, glaciers covered all of Canada and many parts of the United States. The thick sheet of ice mixed and compressed soils to form an unstratified, concretized layer of rock called the hardpan. Recently glaciated landscapes are characterized by a dense and fine-grained lacework of streams; the aquatic creatures that inhabit them have acclimated themselves to this hydrological framework.

[5]During and after a rain event on glaciated soils, precipitation infiltrates the soil, percolating downward until it reaches a layer of less permeable soil material that restricts the downward flow, causing the water to move laterally along this layer, eventually discharging into a surface water body. This lateral movement, called interflow, maintains the stream's baseflow during the sometimes lengthy period between storms (Ward, Trimble, and Wolman, 2004). In the glaciated midwestern United States, most present-day groundwater flow is restricted to shallow aquifers that help to maintain this baseflow (Person et al. 2007).

Figure 8.5. The Cuyahoga River in Cleveland, Ohio, has caught fire several times—in 1936, in 1952 (shown here), and in 1969. (Credit: United Press International)

required to maintain a healthy riparian corridor. Some call for as much as three hundred feet (nearly one hundred meters).[6]

Such a canopy cover of riparian vegetation shades streams and helps to maintain cold water in streams. Insects that reside in this vegetation also provide a constant source of food for fish. Fallen trees and branches provide cool resting places for fish as well as protection from predators. Roots and fallen trees reduce the energy of flowing water, which in turn helps to secure streamflow and to stabilize stream banks. Riparian plants bind soils in place and trap moving sediment, replenishing soil and reducing erosion. During times of rising floodwater, vegetation filters surface runoff and slows overland flow. Slow-moving water then has more time to soak into the soil. In healthy, well-managed watersheds, stored groundwater is released back into the stream during periods of dry weather to help maintain a minimum base flow.

Water Quality and Water Quantity

Throughout North America, the conversation about watershed health has been inordinately focused on water quality—the degree to which water discharged into receiving waters carries pollutants—as opposed to water quantity—the degree to which urbanization alters the rate and amount of water discharged into receiving waters. This is a legacy of the first North American environmental movement, when concerns about polluted water (sparked by many notable events, including the Cuyahoga River fire) led the United States to pass the Clean Water Act of 1972.[7]

Today, the Clean Water Act is still the only regulation governing U.S. water quality, and all fifty states have, to a greater or lesser extent, aligned their policies with it.[8] The original act clearly obligates states and lower levels of government to protect America's waterways, with a goal of keeping all U.S. waters "swimmable and fishable," if not drinkable. But the act was mute about the damage wrought on American waterways by alterations in the *quantity* of water that moves through its thousands of streams. At the time the act was passed, very little was known about how devastating changes to streamflow can be. In the decades since originally passed, the act has been updated by adding the "TMDL rule" (for "total maximum daily load" of

---

[6]Erman, Newbold, and Roby, 1977; Steinblums, 1977; Rudolph and Dickson, 1990; Chen, 1991; Spackman and Hughes, 1994; and Ledwith 1996 found that a minimum buffer of 100 feet (30 meters) is necessary to avoid significantly affecting riparian environments. To maintain processes such as sediment flow and contribution of large woody debris, this one-hundred-foot buffer may be increased to the maximum height of a native riparian forest tree. In coastal rainforest zones this can be up to 260 feet (80 m), the approximate height of a mature Douglas-fir (Broderson, 1973; Beschta et al., 1993; Thomas et al., 1993).

[7]Federally, the Canadian Environmental Protection Act, administered by Environment Canada, establishes a regime for identifying, assessing, and controlling toxic substances. Environment Canada also administers the Canada Water Act, enacted in 1970, which provides the framework for joint federal-provincial management of Canada's water resources. For the most part, waters that lie solely within a province's boundaries fall within the authority of that province. Their legislative powers cover flow regulation, authorization of water use development, water supply, pollution control, and energy development. The BC Liberal's new Riparian Areas Regulation (RAR) significantly weakens the Streamside Protection Regulation (SPR) enacted under the New Democratic Party's time in power in British Columbia. For example, the SPR set minimum standards for building setbacks on fish-bearing streams, while the RAR allows the developer to hire a professional to determine the setback while giving local governments more flexibility in choosing whether or not to implement protective measures for Streamside Protection and Enhancement Areas.

[8]For more information on water legislation in the United States, visit http://www.epa.gov/water/laws.html.

suspended solids), which can address stream degradation by regulating siltation. But the act's essential focus on "water quality" has never changed, making it an unwieldy instrument for regulating water quantity.

In the Pacific Northwest of the United States and in Pacific Canada, the water *quantity* changes brought about by urbanization have produced a crisis.[9] By 1999, the U.S. Fish and Wildlife Service, acting in conformance with the mandates of the Endangered Species Act of 1973, listed five species of Pacific salmon as "endangered."[10] This triggered a requirement for other jurisdictions in the states of California, Idaho, Oregon, and Washington to respond in a way that ensured no further harm to these species. Unfortunately, on the list of harmful activities that affected fish, urbanization was second only to forestry.

How is it that a land use that covers less than 10 percent of these states could be so damaging? One reason is that when people build cities they tend to choose the same places where salmon spawn and rear. Spawning and rearing occur on stream runs that are between 1 percent and 5 percent gradient. These gradually sloping but not entirely flat streams occur in gradually sloping but not entirely flat landscapes—exactly the landscapes that are appropriate for building cities. The second reason is how profoundly urbanization, even at suburban densities, alters watershed performance. When an area urbanizes, conventional stormwater practices require the installation of a stormwater infrastructure over potentially vast percentages of salmon habitat. This stormwater infrastructure functions in a way that is 180 degrees contrary to how natural landscapes perform. Rather than holding water in the soil, where it can be cleaned and delivered to streams over weeks or even months via interflow, a network of pipes is installed to ensure that the same amount of water is delivered to the stream within a few hours, or even a few minutes, of a rain event. Thus, water that had previously been slowly metered out by the soil—clean and at the temperature required for fish health—is flushed immediately in amounts that can be tens, or even hundreds, of times more gallons per minute then predevelopment rates.

This rapid flushing of urbanized landscape produces many serious consequences. The destruction of stream banks is the most damaging of the consequences precipitated by these sud-

[9]Modifications of the land surface, specifically the elimination of vegetation and the proliferation of impervious surfaces, results in the loss of water storage in the soil column and drastically alters flow patterns so that the largest flood peaks double or more and frequent storm discharges can increase by as much as tenfold (Booth, 2000; Williamson, Bartholow, and Stalnaker, 1993). Increases in flow volume and peak flow rates erode stream channels and increase the risk of flooding (Ministry of Water, Land and Air Protection (MWLAP), 2002). Eroded material creates turbidity and subsequent sedimentation in low-lying areas, which degrades aquatic ecosystems and is harmful for fish health and reproduction (MWLAP, 2002; Booth, 1991; Vronskii and Leman, 1991; Havis et al., 1993). Water quality is affected when stormwater containing hydrocarbons, heavy metals, nutrients, pesticides, and bacteria is delivered directly to the stream via pipes instead of being cleaned by infiltration and delivered to the stream via interflow through the soil column. Stormwater flowing over large paved surfaces on a warm day raises the temperature of the water to levels that can be harmful for cold-water fish, such as salmon and trout.

[10]Between November 1991 and October 1999, twenty distinct population segments of five salmonid species were listed as endangered under the Endangered Species Act (Buck and Dandelski, 1999).

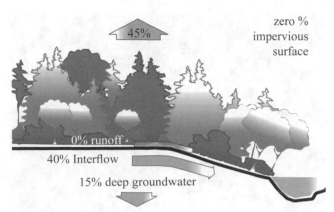

Figure 8.6. Predevelopment hydrology. In a naturally functioning watershed in the Pacific Northwest, 45 percent of rainfall is lost to evapotranspiration, and 55 percent infiltrates the soil, feeding streams through subsurface interflow and replenishing the deeper groundwater aquifer. There is essentially no runoff.

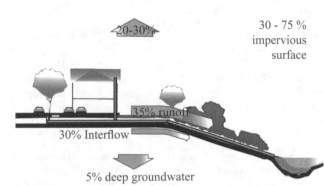

Figure 8.7. Postdevelopment (conventional). Here, runoff increases dramatically from close to 0 percent to 35 percent while evapotranspiration drops from 45 percent to between 20 and 30 percent. Only 35 percent of rainfall infiltrates the soil to replenish streams and deeper groundwater.

den, unaccustomed deluges. Stream banks that have taken ten thousand years since the recession of the glacier to stabilize are suddenly asked to accept ten, twenty, or even a hundred times more water per minute than they can accommodate. The result, unsurprisingly, is erosion of the stream channel, and the delivery of those silts to lower parts of the watershed. Unfortunately, these silts are typically delivered to the very places that the salmon favor for spawning and rearing—gravel beds in stream locations with gradients between 1 percent and 5 percent.

As a consequence of the disruption to urbanized watersheds, the fish-bearing capability of virtually all of our urbanized stream systems has been destroyed. In the city of Vancouver alone, only two of the original sixty salmon-bearing streams still provide habitat.[11] The loss of these systems not only threatens the extinction of an icon of Northwest life, the wild salmon, but also experientially impoverishes city residents, especially children. What was once a profound and peaceful environment teeming with life and palpably expressive of the rhythms of nature has been erased.

Impervious Surfaces and Pipes

Even in low-density developments of four dwelling units per acre, over 50 percent of all surfaces can be impervious. Rooftops, driveways, patios, sidewalks and, most importantly,

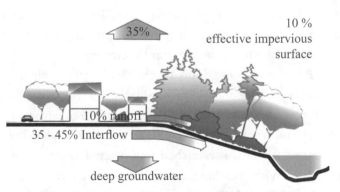

Figure 8.8. Postdevelopment (alternative). Development that limits impervious surface area achieves a much higher rate of infiltration than does conventional development. Narrower streets, smaller building footprints, and riparian vegetation with continuous tree cover work together to mimic the natural hydrology of the site. Runoff is limited to 10 percent of the total rainfall. (Source: Condon et al., 2003)

---

[11]In Vancouver, there were once over fifty salmon- and trout-bearing streams (Kirkby, 1997), but in 2009 that number had dwindled to only two: the Musqueam Creek and its tributary Cutthroat Creek, both of which run through a relatively large regional park. Recently, efforts have been made to restore salmon habitat to waterways such as Spanish Banks Creek, where coho and chum salmon fry have been released in an attempt to develop a viable population of returning fish (Urbanstreams.org, 2006).

Figure 8.9. A typical stormwater outfall seen here at a time of low flow. During high precipitation events, the force of the water is enough to move boulders. (Source: Township of Abington, Pennsylvania)

Figure 8.10. This photo shows the consequence of urbanization on stream banks. Larger volumes of water delivered to streams in the hours immediately after the storms can devastate stream banks and effectively sterilize stream ecology. An example of this type of degradation can be seen here in Little Shakes Creek in Jefferson County, Maryland. (Source: Maryland Department of Natural Resources)

streets cover a surprising percentage of these presumably leafy neighborhoods.[12] Typically, at least 35 percent of all water that falls on such a low-density site is channeled as "runoff" directly and quickly to streams via hard-pipe connections to storm drain systems. Runoff is a category of drainage that does not even exist in natural forested landscapes.[13] As areas urbanize, runoff suddenly emerges as the dominant way that water leaves the site. Evapotranspiration rates, while still significant, fall to between 20 and 30 percent, from over 45 percent in predevelopment landscapes, while interflow and deep infiltration drops to 30 percent from over 50 percent in the forest. This change may not seem extreme until you consider that all of the 35 percent of total rainfall that is drained as runoff is directed to the stream in the hour or two immediately after the storm.

Because of these dramatic changes, it takes only a small amount of pavement in the watershed to kill fish. In the Pacific Northwest, an analysis of a multitude of urban streams revealed that fish counts in urban streams began to fall off when only 10 percent of the urban watershed was covered in pavement and rooftops.[14] When reaching impervious surface levels of 30 percent and above—the minimum coverage conceivable for even low-density suburban development—the news is even worse. At this level, in most cases fish populations have collapsed and salmon runs have been extinguished. At streetcar city densities of ten to twenty dwelling units per acre gross density, up to

[12]To see the breakdown of impervious surfaces for low-density residential developments, visit http://www.jtc.sala.ubc.ca/projects/ADS/HTML_Files/ChapterTwo/matrix_us_2.htm. Status quo development with a density of 4.4 dwelling units per acre was found to have 54 percent total impervious area (TIA), while traditional development with a density of 13.4 dwelling units per acre had 51 percent TIA (Condon, Teed, and Muir, 1998).

[13]Horton overland flow (HOF), commonly known as runoff, occurs when precipitation falls on soil faster than the soil can absorb it. It is most common in regions with periodic, intense rainfall, limited vegetation, and thin soils. Where rainfall intensities are generally lower than the rate at which soil can absorb it, all of the precipitation is infiltrated where it first lands, resulting in surface runoff rates of essentially 0 percent. The coastal regions of the Pacific Northwest, with their gentle rainfall and lush vegetation, provide an excellent example of these conditions. In these regions, rainfall is infiltrated into the soil and moves downslope below the ground surface at much slower rates than HOF (summarized from Booth, 2000).

[14]As a watershed nears or exceeds 10 percent impervious cover, stream health, as measured by the benthic index of biological integrity, deteriorates rapidly (Booth et al., 2004). Urbanized watersheds typically give rise to streams that suffer from what is commonly referred to as the urban stream syndrome (Walsh et al., 2005). Streams suffering from urban stream syndrome are generally characterized by flashier hydrographs, elevated concentrations of nutrients and contaminants, altered channel morphology and stability, and reduced biotic richness, with increased dominance of tolerant species (Paul and Meyer, 2001, Meyer, Paul, and Taulbee, 2005). To protect sensitive stream ecosystems such as those supporting fish populations: cluster development to protect natural vegetative cover, minimize watershed imperviousness (either through minimal development or through the widespread re-infiltration of stormwater), protect riparian buffers and wetland zones, begin landowner stewardship programs and minimize utility crossings (Booth et al., 2004).

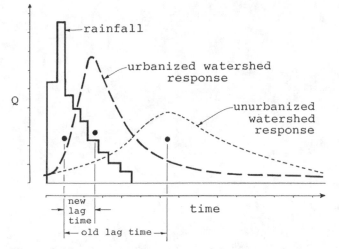

Figure 8.11. Schematic representation of changes in peak stream flow due to urbanization. The lag time between rainfall and peak flow can be significantly reduced as the watershed runoff characteristics are changes by urbanization. (Source: J. David Rogers, 1997)

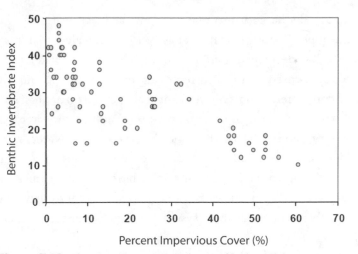

Figure 8.13. This chart shows a compilation of biological data on Puget Lowland watersheds. The pattern of progressive decline with increasing imperviousness is evident on the upper bound of the data; but significant degradation can occur at any level of human disturbance (as measured by impervious cover). (Booth, 2000)

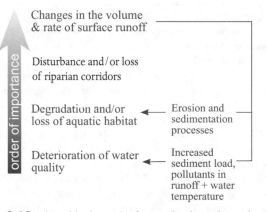

Figure 8.12. This table shows the factors that limit the ecological values of urban streams. In addition to being the most important factor in the degradation of aquatic ecosystem values, changes in the volume and rate of surface runoff also contribute significantly to the degradation of aquatic habitat and the deterioration of water quality. (Source: Booth, 2000)

50 percent of the site can, with substantial effort, be kept pervious; but these statistics suggest that such effort is for naught. Judging by this work, at 50 percent impervious levels no fish have survived.

And it is not the pollutants in the streams that kill the fish. Chemical pollution in streams becomes a serious problem at impervious levels over 50 percent of the watershed. At this level, enough chemical and particulate matter flows into streams to clog and poison the gills of the crustiest coho. But, in fact, Mr. Crusty is long gone by this point—killed years before when the disruptions caused by development in his watershed had altered water quantities, temperatures, and flow rates enough to utterly destroy his habitat. But it is not the pavement that kills the fish; it is the pipes that drain it, as discussed below.

Storm Sewers

The basic architecture of storm drain systems has not changed since the Cretan Minoans installed the first system over four thousand years ago. For all but the past seventy years of that history, the storm systems have carried both rainwater and sanitary discharge from toilets (known as black water) in the same pipe. Treating stormwater as "waste" equivalent to human waste has developed a cultural ethos and a stormwater technology focused entirely on removing this "hazard" as quickly and completely as possible, and not at all focused on understanding and working with natural processes. With stormwater and sanitary waters mixed in the same pipe, these mixed waters were indeed dangerous and needed to be kept separate from humans.[15] Only in the past seventy years have the storm and sanitary systems been separated, and thus only recently have we been able to consider these systems and the water they contain appropriately.

Methods used for sizing stormwater pipes have not changed in the hundred-plus years since the Manning formula came into common use. This formula calculates the amount of water that might fall in the various parts of a drainage area and how long it will take it to reach a discharge point. The volumes assumed are derived from an assumed extreme storm event, typically the largest storm you might expect in any five-year period, called the design storm return frequency. Storms that dump ten inches of water on a site during twenty-four hours are commonly used as a basis for this in many parts of North America. Some jurisdictions use even more conservative design requirements, applying the one-hundred-year design storm return frequency—typically a few inches per day more than the five-year return storm. It follows, of course, that systems designed solely to quickly move waters from catastrophically large storms to off-site streams will move waters from smaller, more frequent storms to receiving streams with equal or greater speed, with great damage to the receiving streams.

Four thousand years of focusing on the big storms prevents us from seeing the problem for what it is. From the point of view of the fish, it is not the big storms that matter; it's the small ones. Fish can survive the rare cataclysm; it is the day-to-day disruption caused by the way small storms are treated that kills them. In all but a few parts of North America, the vast majority of storm events are small, generally less than one inch per day. In most zones, storms under one inch in twenty-four hours (or one millimeter per hour) account for at least 70 percent of all water that falls during the year.[16] The devastating consequences

[15]A combined sewer system (CSS) is a wastewater collection system that collects and conveys sanitary wastewater (domestic sewage from homes as well as industrial and commercial wastewater) and stormwater through a single pipe (U.S. Environmental Protection Agency (EPA), 2004). During times of low or no precipitation, wastewater can be pumped to treatment facilities; however, when collection system capacity is exceeded during precipitation events, the systems are designed to overflow, discharging sanitary wastes directly to surface waters (U.S. EPA, 2004). In the United States, there are an estimated 772 communities with combined sewer systems that are responsible for the release of untreated wastewater and stormwater containing raw sewage, pathogens, solids, debris, and toxic pollutants (U.S. EPA, 2009b). To mitigate combined sewer overflows, municipalities can attempt to maximize the flow to the treatment plant. This often requires expanding their existing facilities. Other options include reducing the inflow of rainwater into the system, separating the storm and sanitary systems, or rehabilitating the sewer system components (U.S. EPA, 2004).

[16]Small rainfall events are generally described as less than half the size of the mean annual rainfall. This volume varies from region to region but in general accounts for approximately 75 percent of the total rainfall events in a given year. During large rainfall events (greater than half the size of the mean annual rainfall), runoff from impervious surfaces should be stored on-site and released at a controlled rate. Only for extreme rainfall events (those that exceed the mean annual rainfall) should it be necessary to provide escape routes for runoff with sufficient capacity to contain and convey flood flows. Generally, extreme rainfall events happen only once per year, making up a very small portion of the annual rainfall volume (summarized from Ministry of Water, Land and Air Protection, 2002).

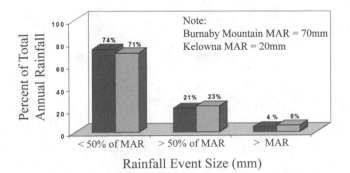

Figure 8.14. Typical volume distribution of annual rainfall. This chart shows that even though the total amount of rain differs wildly between the two examples—one from the coastal rain forest zone (Burnaby, B.C.), the other from the much drier eastern slope of the Cascade Mountains (Kelowna, B.C.), the relative distribution of small to large storms stays constant.

[17]Kunkel and Andsager (1999) studied extreme precipitation events of one to seven days duration with recurrence intervals of one or five years. They found that precipitation from seven-day, one-year events (with thresholds ranging from less than 4 millimeters per day in desert regions to more than 21 millimeters per day along the coast) accounted for only 15 percent of the total annual precipitation in the United States. The contribution of one- and three-day five-year events accounted for an even smaller percentage (Kunkel and Andsager, 1999).

[18]Pluhowski (1970) found that modifying the hydrologic environment as a result of urbanization increased the average stream temperature in summer by five to 8 degrees Celsius. Water temperature determines the distribution, growth rate, and survival of fish and other aquatic organisms through its influence on migration patterns, egg mutation, incubation success, competitive ability, and resistance to parasites, diseases, and pollutants (Armour, 1991; LeBlanc, Brown, and FitzGibbon, 1997). The highest average mean weekly temperatures for coldwater (rainbow trout, book trout, and salmon), coolwater (northern pike and yellow perch), and warmwater (catfish and bass) species are approximately twenty-two, twenty-nine, and thirty degrees Celsius, respectively (Armour, 1991).

to stream health wrought by our storm drain systems can be fairly ascribed to our fixation, understandable but still a fixation, on the cataclysmic storm, and the design of our systems centering entirely around that rare event.[17]

Retention Ponds

Some jurisdictions require that retention ponds be installed just upstream of discharge points into streams, hoping thereby to mitigate the worst effects of conventional storm drain systems on receiving waters. Retention ponds were originally required to mitigate the potential floods caused by urbanization. In this function, they are only partially successful, and in some cases they actually make floods worse by releasing waters during periods of crest when an earlier release might have been better. As for pollution benefits, their efficacy is quite limited. It is generally assumed that retention ponds remove 50 percent of pollutants that would otherwise enter streams. Removing 50 percent of pollutants is like cutting your poison dose in half: instead of dying right away, you die slowly and painfully. Research suggests that in some cases retention ponds can even add pollutants to stormwater, such that water emerging from the downstream side of the pond is more polluted than water on the upstream side (turbulence in the pond that stirs up previously settled pollutants appears to explain this mystery).

Perhaps of more importance, retention ponds do nothing to enhance infiltration and thus very little to mitigate the distortions to the stream hydrograph consequent to urbanization. This is because it is physically impossible (or if not impossible then incredibly costly and space consumptive) to have a retention pond large enough to slowly release rain water, not over forty-eight hours (which is typically the maximum residence time in retention ponds following storm events) but over the weeks and even months necessary to mimic the natural discharge rate of native soils. And even if a pond so large were constructed, it would still require a filtering mechanism that would emulate the cleaning function of soils, and a refrigerator to cool sun-baked surface water to the temperature expected by aquatic stream species.[18]

"Total Impervious Surface" versus "Effective Impervious Surface"

The recently discovered direct correlation between the amount of impervious surfaces in the watershed and the collapse of fish stocks in the streams has been important but also depressing. Unfortunately, it has commonly provoked responses among some researchers, environmentalists, and policy experts that lead to more sprawl, not less. The 10 percent total watershed impervious threshold, where fish stocks begin their steep collapse, has led many to suggest that new urban developments should not exceed a total maximum impervious surface level of 10 percent of the entire watershed. This would result in a maximum density of about one dwelling unit per two acres or less (possibly far less, depending on the presence of commercial areas and major roadways in the watershed). Some, including Tom Holz of Lacey, Washington, have even gone so far as to suggest that no single-family zones should be approved at densities higher than one dwelling unit per five acres accessed on a gravel road, with most new density absorbed by isolated tall towers linked by low-impact elevated transit lines.[19] Faced with such extreme solutions, many have despaired and concluded that healthy watersheds and walkable, affordable communities are incompatible. When a choice is made in these stark terms, certainly the fish will lose. Fortunately, this does not have to be the case.

Total Impervious Area versus Effective Impervious Area

Much of the research that led to these depressing conclusions was conducted in watersheds where streets and rooftops were directly piped into streams, with great damage to the receiving waters. But it is conceivable for pavement to have little or no impact on receiving waters. For example, if you have a backyard of one thousand square feet with a one-hundred-square-foot paved patio, the impervious area of that backyard is 10 percent. This ratio of hard space to soft space is known as total impervious area, expressed in percentage terms. Presumably, this patio, when combined with all the other roads and rooftops and driveways in the area, contributes to the destruction of the watershed.

[19]Tom Holz chaired the Salmon in the City Conference held May 20–21, 1998, in Mount Vernon, Washington, where he presented a paper with Tom Liptan and Tom Schueler, "Beyond Innovative Development: Site Design Techniques to Minimize Impacts to Salmon Habitat," available online at http://depts.washington.edu/cuwrm/research/sitc.pdf. More recently, he has presented the concept of zero-impact development to various city councils throughout Washington State, including Lacey, Sammamish, Tumwater, and Shoreline.

(a)

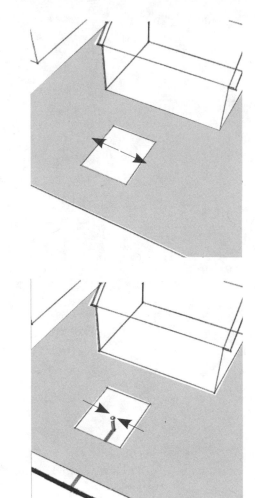

(b)

Figure 8.15. When runoff is directed into the pervious lawn (a), the EIA of the patio is 0 percent, but when runoff is directed to a pipe system (b), the EIA of the patio is 100 percent.

[20]An integrated stormwater management system seeks to maintain a site's natural water balance by capturing rainfall at the source and returning it to natural hydrologic pathways (which in the vast majority of landscapes are predominantly infiltration and evapotranspiration). This can be achieved through the adoption of low-impact development (LID) practices and source control. In addition to maintaining natural vegetation and reducing the compaction of soils, LID practices minimize the creation of impervious surfaces by building compact communities with reduced road width, building footprints, and parking requirements. Source control involves preserving natural vegetation and stormwater features, such as wetlands and riparian forests, and preserving natural infiltration and evapotranspiration capacity through absorbent landscaping, infiltration facilities, green roofs, and reusing rainwater for irrigation and indoor uses (summarized from Ministry of Water, Land and Air Protection, 2002).

But what if the water that falls on this patio runs off into the soft grass around it, and what if the soil around the patio is porous enough to always accept this discharge? In this instance, the influence of the patio on the watershed is zero. Conversely, what if the patio is equipped with a center drain and that drain is connected to the street storm drain system, either by a hard-pipe connection or via a drain that discharges at the curb or on the driveway or some other hard channel? In this instance, the patio is "hydrologically connected" to the storm system. That, it would seem, would maximize the patio's negative impact on the watershed.

How then can we distinguish the paved surfaces that are harmless, like the patio that drains into the grass, from the paved surfaces that are harmful, like the patio with the drain connected to the street drains? We can do so by distinguishing the *total impervious area* (or the TIA) from the *effective impervious area* (or the EIA) of the site. In both cases described above, the TIA of the yard is the same: 10 percent (TIA is a measure of pavement and rooftops and makes no distinction consequent to drainage method). But the patio that drained into the surrounding grass had no *effect* on the watershed. It therefore had an EIA of zero. If all of the water shed by this patio infiltrates into the ground, then as far as the fish are concerned the pavement does not exist. It is this condition that we can and should shoot for. The following four rules provide the means.

FOUR RULES FOR INFILTRATION

Rule 1: Infiltrate, Infiltrate, Infiltrate

As in the business of real estate, where the only three words are *location, location, location*, when urbanizing or retrofitting existing urban areas for low impact on streams, there are also only three words: *infiltrate, infiltrate, infiltrate*.

If all the rain or most of the water that falls on the site could go into the ground, then the predevelopment hydrograph is emulated.[20] If this can be fortified by a robust planting strategy for streets, yards, and, at certain densities, rooftops, then the predevelopment hydrograph can be nearly matched. The importance of trees in the urban landscape cannot be overemphasized; trees mitigate site water discharge in many ways, ranging from holding large amounts on leaves (evergreen trees are particularly good at this) to holding vast quantities of water within their extensive root systems.[21]

It is possible to approximate natural hydrographs no matter how much impervious surface there is. For example, it is possible to design a zero-impact landscape where 100 percent of the site is covered with sidewalks, streets, and rooftops. Such a site would have a TIA of 100 percent but could also have an EIA of zero! This would be accomplished through holding water on rooftops and then infiltrating it under foundations and street sections. It would be costly to infiltrate all this water, requiring expensive infiltration chambers under all streets and walks, and high-performance green roofs on all buildings, but it could be done. Of course, infiltrating water on sites with less than 100 percent TIA is easier. Streetcar city districts, at ten to twenty dwelling units per acre are often still 50 percent pervious, providing ample soft areas to work with. The soft portions are largely the lawn and landscaped surfaces of yards and roadside tree boulevards (Condon and Teed, 1998).

Rule 2: Design for One Inch per Day of Infiltration

But how much of the rain must we infiltrate? Obviously, infiltrating all of the rain should be the goal if we are to completely emulate predevelopment performance. Unfortunately, in some parts of North America storms may dump more than ten inches of rain on the ground in a twenty-four-hour period. These so-called one-hundred-year storms are the basis for stormwater system design, but should they be for infiltration systems? If soils are capable of infiltrating that much water in twenty-four hours, the answer is yes, but few soils can do so. Fortunately, aquatic species can manage the occasional large storm event, and for the most part so can the stream channel.

The real problem is not the big storm, which happens once in a while in natural environments too. The bigger problem is how urbanization fundamentally alters the behavior of streams under more ordinary circumstances. Since the research suggests that watersheds start to degrade when impervious surfaces reach a threshold of 10 percent TIA, what if we were to design urban landscapes with a TIA of, say, 50 percent, as if they

[21]Research suggests that establishing urban forests that mimic native forests is key to more sustainable stormwater management. Urban trees and forests tend to reduce stormwater runoff amounts and peak runoff rates. The interception of precipitation by leaves delays precipitation reaching the ground and allows for some evaporation and absorption of this precipitation from the leaves or stem of the tree. A study in Sacramento, California, found that runoff reduction from interception alone averaged 15.2 percent for small storms (less than 5 millimeters per day) but only half that for large storms (greater than 25 millimeters per day) (Xiao et al., 1998).

were only 10 percent paved? What if we design them such that the TIA is 50 percent but the EIA is 10 percent? It follows logically that if you could absorb 90 percent of all the water that falls on the site, you would be emulating the performance of sites with a TIA of 10 percent.[22] If your objective is to capture not all but most of the rain that falls on the site, then obviously your best bet is to let most of the biggest and hardest-to-capture events go, and infiltrate all the rest. But what size storms should you always capture to meet this performance threshold? For many landscapes in North America, the answer is this: *capture all storms of less than an inch and the first inch of all larger storms to capture 90 percent of all water that falls on the site.*[23]

Surprisingly, this amount does not vary much from one part of the United States and Canada to another (the exception appears to be thunderstorm- and hurricane-prone Florida).[24] A cursory analysis of midwestern, northeastern, southwestern, and Cascadia (coastal British Columbia to coastal Northern California) landscapes suggests that a range between .85 and 1.25 inches per day will achieve the 90 percent infiltration target. It may at first seem strange that a standard for the rainy Northwest is roughly the same as for the dry Southwest, but what matters here is not the total amount of rain in a year but the percentage of total annual rainfall for a particular region that is provided by small storms versus large storms. For all but one part of the continent, the small storms contribute more total rain to receiving waters than do storms over one inch per day.

The one-inch-per-day rule is the most important of the rules listed. Negotiations around stormwater performance targets can often quickly bog down in the arcane language of civil engineering, most of which reflects a view of rainwater as a nuisance to be disposed of rather than as something to be retained. No flow rate or pipe size calculations are needed for putting water back in the ground. It stays where it falls. Thus, part of the value of the one-inch-per-day rule is its simplicity. It is memorable, easy to apply, and, most importantly, correct.

Rule 3: Infiltrate Everywhere

The one-inch-per-day rule works only if you can infiltrate on every inch of the site. But any developed site will have some areas that are less appropriate than others for infiltration. In our

[22]Limiting runoff volume to 10 percent of total rainfall should be sufficient to maintain baseflows, water quality, and aquatic ecosystem health. Infiltrating rainfall feeds stream baseflow, removes many pollutants from stormwater, and maintains the timing and volume of runoff, thereby reducing the risk of flooding and stream channel instability. This can be accomplished by preserving or restoring natural vegetation along the riparian corridor and natural features, such as wetlands; maintaining instream features, such as channel complexity and spawning gravel; and controlling sources of water pollution from point and nonpoint sources (summarized from Ministry of Water, Land and Air Protection, 2002).

[23]The majority of rainfall occurs at intensities of less than one inch per day. In the Pacific Northwest, a stormwater management system designed to absorb one inch (twenty-four millimeters) per day will absorb almost 90 percent of all the rain that falls on a site (Condon et al., 2003).

[24]Most areas receive at least 50 inches of rainfall per year. Florida is one of the wettest states in the United States, although it exhibits great annual variation often resulting in a year of flood followed by a year of drought (Black, 1993). Storm events with a one-year reoccurrence and twenty-four-hour duration range from 3.5 to 5 inches per day (Hershfield, 1961), meaning that in a typical year the largest storm event could account for up to 10 percent of the total annual rainfall.

example streetcar suburb, all infiltration should occur on the soft lawn and boulevard areas, which constitute 50 percent of the site. If these lawns can infiltrate the one inch per day that falls on them, and can infiltrate the water that flows off of adjacent paved surfaces that constitute the other 50 percent of the site, then we will have met the target. Many soils can manage two inches per day without difficulty. It gets harder when you direct runoff to a more limited space. If you take the water that falls onto the impervious 50 percent of the site and for whatever reason direct it to a "rain garden" (a planted area designed to accept large amounts of water) that covers only 5 percent of the site, that rain garden will have to infiltrate the one inch that falls on it plus ten additional inches. Eleven inches is a lot of rain. Very few unamended soils are capable of infiltrating this much. For this reason, you must infiltrate everywhere—in every yard and every road verge—never ignoring any opportunity to do so.

Rule 4: Understand That Heavy Soils Are Good Soils

Different soils have different capacities to infiltrate, but almost all soils are capable of infiltration at rates higher than the requisite one millimeter per hour or one inch per day rate. This point is key. Most civil engineers know a fair amount about soil infiltration, but they have very different performance assumptions in mind when the subject is raised. For most engineers, soils with infiltration rates below 10 or even 20 millimeters per hour are considered impervious soil, or "clay" soil.[25] The engineering community considers a soil to be porous when it has infiltration rates in the range of hundreds of millimeters per hour or more.

This lack of common understanding between the value of ubiquitous slow infiltration for stream health and the engineering community's assumption that infiltration is only possible in highly porous soils creates extremely difficult implementation barriers. Long and careful discussion is required, usually in a charrette setting, to overcome these barriers. Proponents of infiltration strategies must be wary of this language difference and the difference in understanding of the minimum soil conditions necessary for infiltration. From an engineering perspective, only sandy soils are capable of stormwater infiltration. From a broader sustainability perspective, almost all soils are ca-

Figure 8.16. The Pringle Creek sustainable community in Oregon incorporates infiltration into streets, boulevards, and yards. Shown here is the installation of previous asphalt on self-mitigating streets.

Soil Type	Typical Hydraulic Conductivity Range
Sands & gravels	> 50 mm/hour
Sandy loams	10 – 50 mm/hour
Silty loams	5 – 40 mm/hour
Clay loams	2 – 6 mm/hour
Clays	< 2 mm/hour

Figure 8.17. Soil texture triangle. (Source: Hydraulic Properties Calculator, Washington State University, http://hydrolab.arsusda.gov/soilwater/Index.htm)

---

[25]True clay soils are actually quite rare. Most soils that are called clay simply have a larger than usual percentage of smaller soil particles.

pable of infiltration, even heavy soils. Watershed performance, no matter what the soil, is dependent on the soil's capacity to absorb and hold water. If a watershed soil is heavy, it leads to a very precise regimen of interflow where waters will be retained in the heavy soils far longer than in sandy ones, will be cleaned far better than in sandy ones, and will lead to a landscape more frequently incised with small productive streams than in watersheds dominated by sand. In short, the same things that make heavy soils difficult in the minds of many engineers are the very things that make watersheds biologically rich.

GREEN INFRASTRUCTURE FOR PARCELS

Parcels can be any size but are usually small, averaging far less than an acre in most regions. Occasionally, they are publicly owned, as in the case of schools or parks. For watershed protection, parcels should be designed to retain water in accordance with the four rules above. This is immensely simplified if 40 to 60 percent of the site is still soft. In residential landscapes, this is usually lawn area. At the streetcar densities of ten to twenty dwelling units per acre, this is achievable if buildings are tall (as in a three-story home with a small 25- by 35-foot footprint, for example) rather than spread out (as in a one-story ranch house with a 35- by 75-foot footprint, for example). Here, where our focus is on infiltration, the tall structure with the small footprint allows medium-density dwellings to be compatible with preserving yard space for play, for gardens, and for infiltration.

Rooftops

At streetcar densities, rooftops can cover about over 25 percent of the gross development site. Rooftops can be designed to retain water and transpirate it into the atmosphere while protecting the building from excessive heat in summer and from premature failure of roofing materials or roof membrane. Roofs with a layer of plant materials, however elaborate or simple, are called green roofs. A great deal of information exists on the topic of green roof construction, so no more technical detail is required here.[26]

[26]For more information on green roofs, see Dunnett and Kingsbury, 2008, and Luckett, 2009.

What *is* needed here is to place green roof strategies in the proper relationship with parcel and street strategies, something that is rarely, if ever, done. Water can be retained on roofs and transpired on roofs, but it cannot be infiltrated on roofs. Water in excess of amounts that can be stored and transpired must be drained to the ground. During rainy seasons, such as the Pacific Northwest winter, most of the rain that falls on a green roof will somehow run off to the ground.[27] In rainy winters, green roofs are useful to slow the transmission of water to the ground, but this is their only major benefit. In warmer climates and in climates where rain is more evenly distributed throughout the year, green roofs have greater benefit. In the United States, green roofs are probably most useful in Gulf Coast areas and Florida, where it is hot and rain is reasonably well distributed throughout the year. Consequently, in these areas irrigation is not required to maintain the cooling benefits of transpiring plants. As one moves north and west from the Gulf Coast and Florida, the inherent value of green roofs is reduced but not eliminated.

However, green roofs become more important for *stormwater* control as building coverage rates increase. In certain industrial areas, rooftops can cover over 70 percent of the gross area (with paved roads consuming the rest). Absent significant vegetated ground areas to infiltrate on, robustly functioning green roofs can be crucial—especially if they are located in sensitive watersheds.

These cautions are provided to counteract the overly enthusiastic claims of many green roof proponents. Green roofs are in and of themselves of limited value unless they are integrated into a system of green stormwater infrastructure. When integrated into a system, the relative costs and benefits of green roofs must be weighed against the costs and benefits of strategies applicable to the ground of the parcel, the street, or other public areas within the development site or neighborhood. This contextualization of the green roof strategy is seldom done. Some jurisdictions are calling for a blanket requirement for green roofs while not requiring mitigation strategies for runoff from paved areas of the parcels. This constitutes a failure at the policy level to understand how the whole urban watershed system operates and where mitigation strategies might be most cost effective.

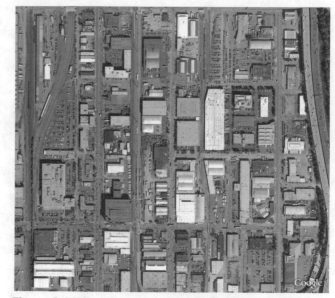

Figure 8.18. An industrial area in Seattle, Washington, where rooftops cover the vast majority of the site and paved roads consume the rest.

[27]In 2005, a study was conducted by the Centre for the Advancement of Green Roof Technology in Vancouver to "investigate the performance and practical application of extensive green roof systems in Canada's west coast climate" (Connelly, Liu, and Schaub, 2006). Green Roof 1 (GR-1) contained 75 millimeters of growing medium planted with sedums while Green Roof 2 (GR-2) contained 150 millimeters of growing medium planted with a mix of fescues and grasses. Although both green roofs delayed the start of runoff and reduced the peak flow and amount of runoff, the extent of these effects varied with the particular rainfall event and differed for the two green roof systems. In the dry season, mid-April to the end of September, GR-1 and GR-2 both performed well, retaining 86 percent and 94 percent, respectively, of the 242 millimeters of rainfall that fell during this time. During the rest of the year, however, only 18 percent and 13 percent of the 1,266 millimeters of rainfall was retained, resulting in an annual retention of 29 percent for GR-1 and 26 percent for GR-2 (Connelly, Liu, and Schaub, 2006).

The Ground

Once water comes off of roofs, it should be spread out into soft surfaces as quickly as possible. For most types of residential structures, this can be done at little or reduced cost by eliminating gutters in favor of long overhangs (cruelly, overhangs are often impeded by setback requirements that count overhangs as part of the structure's allowable site volume—usually restricted by a ratio of building square feet to site area called SFR, or surface/floor ratio)—often making the building uneconomic). A drip line of crushed stone at the fall line will help distribute the water into lawn and underlying soil.

Parcel grading is also significant. It has become traditional for lawn parcels to be graded fairly steeply out of fear of water returning to basements. Yet, grades of greater than 2 percent can send water over lawns too quickly depending on storm event or soil conditions. Grades between 1 percent and 2 percent or even flat depressions are therefore recommended. Yards should be graded to avoid channeling flow but should spread flow as much as possible across all yard space. The obvious intention is to give roof drainage as much chance as possible to come into sustained contact with lawn and landscaped areas and their underlying absorbent soils.[28]

Ordinary site development practice destroys the capacity of site soils to infiltrate water. If development sites contain good topsoil, it is often stripped and sold when ground is broken. One year later, or when construction is complete, a much smaller amount is returned to the site to be thinly spread over native subsoil severely compacted by a year of heavy equipment traversing the construction site. Severe compaction crushes the void spaces from the parent soil, making it impossible for water to penetrate and rendering these soils incapable of supporting root growth. Lawn areas over such soils will not infiltrate water and, after drenching rains, will send most rainwater into adjacent streets as runoff, performing only slightly better for infiltration than the concrete it abuts.

We suggest a simple remedy comprised of two parts. First, ensure that soils around buildings are not compacted, and then deep-till this soil when construction is done. Second, return at least as much topsoil to the site as was stripped and possibly more. As mentioned above, about 50 percent of a site will

[28]In Massachusetts, it is required that on-site infiltration measures be used to handle stormwater where suitable soils exist. The stormwater management system for the Reebok headquarters in Canton, Massachusetts, uses source control, structural and nonstructural treatment methods, proper maintenance regimes, and stormwater best management practices to maintain water quality and infiltration rates during construction and post development. The Reebok stormwater system has successfully achieved "zero net runoff," and natural drainage patterns have been retained and now act as natural stormwater management strategies on-site. The total system cost was $65,000 (in 1995 U.S. dollars), providing an effective, easy-to-install, and economically feasible choice for infiltrating stormwater on-site (summarized from UBC James Taylor Chair, 2000).

remain soft after construction is complete. If the site has six inches of decent topsoil before construction, then this stockpile should contain enough soil to return a foot of soil to all of the soft portions of the site. For many sites where subsurface soils are heavy, this is likely the most effective strategy. Such a thick layer of highly porous and organically rich soil makes an ideal sponge to absorb and slowly release water into parent soils below. At the East Clayton project in Surrey, British Columbia, for example, it was these extra-deep topsoil layers that performed far better than expected.[29] A requirement to double backfill the soft portions of the site up to a depth of twelve to sixteen inches is therefore reasonable and far more cost effective than a green roof requirement in most locales. One foot of topsoil, assuming it is reasonably dry, can absorb approximately three full inches of rain, far in excess of the two inches required (remember that the overall target is one inch per day but that the site is only 50 percent pervious so each soft part of the site must absorb two inches in twenty-four hours).

Figure 8.19. Topsoil preserved from the initial site grading is returned to residential lots at the East Clayton development in Surrey, British Columbia.

Walkways

In many parts of North America, directing roof drainage across lawns will mean squishy conditions on grassy areas for many weeks of the year. This likelihood has impeded implementing these recommendations in more than one jurisdiction. The solution is to include paved walkways where needed. Unfortunately, this can add to the TIA, and possibly to the EIA as well. Stepping stones are an effective low-impact solution for occasionally used backyard paths. Stepping stones, like the patio solution discussed earlier, are by definition surrounded by soft pervious areas. In most soils, it is likely that stepping stones will have an EIA of zero. Stepping stones flush with surrounding lawn or crushed stone beds are considered accessible under Americans with Disabilities Act (ADA) rules where and when compliance is required.

For walkways that are more frequently used, such as the walkway from the front door to the sidewalk, or from the back door to the garage or lane, a continuous paved surface is required. Pervious pavement is an effective means to reduce EIA to zero for these surfaces, but it is often equally effective to simply cross pitch (slope slightly to the side) impervious concrete or

[29]The East Clayton Neighbourhood Concept Plan is the first phase of the Headwaters Project, a real-life demonstration of sustainable development principles and performance standards in a community neighborhood environment. Initial results of the development's performance indicate that permeable areas and on-site infiltration devices are viable for stormwater management (*ACT Phase E: Final Report (Headwaters Project)*). For more information on the project, visit http://www.jtc.sala.ubc.ca/projects/Headwaters.html.

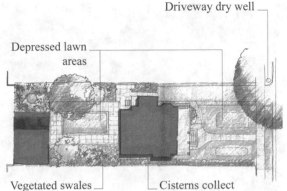

Figure 8.20. A landscape design for a single-family residence in Los Angeles, California, that works with, rather than against, natural cycles of water and waste.

Figure 8.21. This illustration shows how the filter bed and the subsurface infiltration basin work to treat and hold stormwater runoff from the large, impervious parking area. The filter beds allow space for sidewalks, trees, and shrubs near the building, while the plants contribute to the treatment of stormwater and reduce the energy use for cooling during hot summer months. (Source: Condon and Moriarty, 1999)

---

[30]In the site plan shown in figure 8.20, a single-family residence in Los Angeles uses the landscape to work with, rather than against, natural cycles of water and waste. Rain falling on the building's roof is directed to depressed lawn areas, or "sunken gardens," which retain rainwater until it can be absorbed into the ground. Only during rainfall events exceeding the one-hundred-year storm does overflow need to be directed into the existing storm drain system. Rain that is not directed into the lawn is collected and stored in two 1,800-gallon cisterns that capture rain during the wet season and gradually release it for irrigation during the wet season. A roof wash unit collects the "first flush" water and sequesters it long enough to settle out the summer-long buildup of dust and bird feces before the clean water decants into the cistern. Cisterns are also used to regulate the flow of water during storms, reducing flood risk. Vegetated/mulched swales slow the flow of stormwater, increase infiltration, and filter pollutants while also recycling greenwaste from the property. Runoff from the driveway is intercepted by a dry well, which retains and cleans rainwater (summarized from Condon and Moriarty, 1999)

asphalt into adjacent grass or hedges. These same rules apply to driveways, if and when required. Adjacent yard areas can be subtly dished with minor depressions to capture stormwater, allowing puddles to form for short periods after severe storms.[30] This ephemeral feature is an enormously effective infiltration practice and adds visual delight to the yard. Unfortunately, allowing "standing water" on lawns for even a few hours defies most current conventions and biases against retaining rainwater on-site; in other words, we are afraid of puddles. This cost-free strategy is therefore often difficult to implement.

Parking and Service Areas

At streetcar city densities of ten to twenty dwelling units per acre, parking lots should not be required. All recent city of Vancouver projects, private commercial, and residential projects over a gross dwelling units per acre of twenty-five now have underground parking. (This is sometimes required but more often is the consequence of the by now mature Vancouver area market for higher density housing, where buyers insist on enclosed parking and are put off by the appearance of parking lots.) Below this density, parking is provided on streets, on lanes, or in garages. As a consequence, there is generally no need for surface parking lots.

However, if provided, surface parking lots too can meet the 10 percent EIA target in the following ways. Pavements can be pervious concrete or asphalt, as described in the section about roadways below. Alternatively, parking lots can discharge into specially designed rain garden planters at parking lot edges or between bays. This second strategy requires highly permeable soils, as the rain garden features will probably cover less than 10 percent of the total surface area of the lot and thus will be required to infiltrate ten or more inches per day to meet the overall target of one-inch-per-day infiltration. If soil conditions are not this forgiving or if performance targets are high, then infiltration under the lot via drain tiles or infiltration chambers may be required. This last strategy is especially effective when combined with rain gardens, as they clean silts out prior to delivering stormwater to drain tiles. Unfortunately and obviously, this is the most expensive strategy of the three strategies discussed.

Rights-of-way

Rights-of-way are any publicly owned or publically accessible lands. In the United States and Canada, rights-of-way are almost all streets and highways.

A street right-of-way (ROW) usually includes a paved street with verge areas astride it. Verge areas usually include some combination of sidewalks, tree boulevards, and road shoulder. ROWs are often much wider than the paved surfaces in them. For instance, the traditional streetcar city residential street ROW is sixty feet. Of this ROW, less than half, or roughly twenty-eight feet, is consumed by the paved street, measured from curb line to curb line. The remaining thirty-two feet is most often allotted to sidewalks and tree boulevards for both sides of the street. In most urban areas, street ROWs consume between 25 percent and 40 percent of all land (depending on district street network type, existence or absence of rear lanes, and land use), making them by far the most extensive and ubiquitous of all urban public land types. With so much of the site covered in public ROWs, it follows that street ROWs generate 40 percent, 50 percent, or even more of the total districtwide impact of impervious surfaces and storm drainage on receiving waters.

Figure 8.22. On a traditional queuing street in Vancouver, British Columbia, parking is allowed on both sides of the 27-foot (8.2 m) wide paved way, which requires oncoming cars to take turns, or "queue." Sidewalks are provided on both sides of the street and are separated from the paved street by a 7.5-foot (2.3 m) grass and tree boulevard. (Source: Condon and Teed, 1998)

PERVIOUS OR IMPERVIOUS

As discussed earlier in this chapter, if we want to save watersheds the key is abandoning our dependence on pipes to take water off the roads and finding ways to get the water into the ground near or under the road instead. There are two basic ways to accomplish this: (1) make all of the pavement in the road pervious so the water goes right down through it, or (2) find a way to infiltrate the water in the soft surfaces of the verge or tree boulevard.

Pervious Pavement

Much confusion exists about pervious pavements. For applications in North America, there are really only two hard-surface options that are both affordable and effective: pervious asphalt

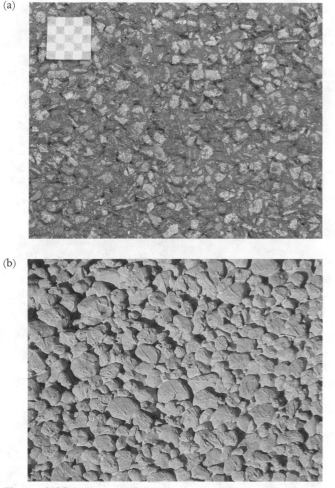

(a)

(b)

Figure 8.23. Pervious asphalt (a) and pervious concrete (b) shown at same scale (checkered square is one inch), are cheaper and more effective than pavers, allowing water to infiltrate through voids left in the paving when small aggregates and fines are eliminated from the mix. The scale here is one inch square.

and pervious concrete. These pavements are fully capable of allowing 100 percent of even the largest storms to penetrate into the structural base below. At the time of this writing, the best community-scale application of both pervious asphalt and pervious concrete is at the Pringle Creek Community project in Salem, Oregon. This project was discussed in chapter 7 for its system of linked natural areas and parks, and here it is discussed for its use of pervious pavements.

Impervious unit pavers are often sold as a pervious pavement solution, with infiltration presumably occurring in the joints. They are not recommended for most applications. They are many times more expensive than pervious asphalt or concrete, and due to the limited area between pavers available for infiltration, they tend to clog with silts (this occurs unless the units themselves are pervious or the joints between the pavers are extremely wide). Unfortunately, the unit pavers industry is well organized and markets its products extensively by making strong claims to the contrary, while no industry exists to advance the use of simpler pervious asphalt and pervious concrete.

The two surface types, pervious asphalt and pervious concrete, are very similar. Both pavements are identical to ordinary asphalt or concrete, except that the smaller aggregates ("rocks," in layman's terms) and fines (sands), which constitute a large part of mixes for impervious pavements, are absent. A typical size for aggregates in pervious pavements is three quarters of an inch. Absent the smaller aggregates and fines, the liquid asphaltic binders of asphalt pavement or the cement of concrete pavements glues the large aggregates together, leaving ample void spaces between the three-quarter-inch rocks for water flow.

Because pervious and impervious asphalt and concrete are virtually identical, costs and application techniques are similar as well. Visually, the pervious surfaces have a somewhat rougher appearance but are as smooth or smoother than unit pavers and therefore do not pose a barrier or hazard to the handicapped. In short, anywhere that you can install ordinary impervious asphalt or concrete, you can install pervious asphalt or concrete for the same, or close to the same, amount of money.

Ensuring that pervious pavements function well and last a long time is a different matter, however. Details of the road section below the paved surface must be reconsidered for enhanced infiltration, and care must be exercised during construction to ensure that infiltration is not compromised. Any roadway—or any paved surface, for that matter—has two parts: the hard surface or pavement, and the earth below that holds it up. All well-engineered and installed roadways need earth below that is stable over time and structurally capable of holding up the pavement. Not all soils are. Clayey soils are particularly prone to deforming during freeze-thaw cycles and thus are not used under pavements. "Gravel"—a mixture of fine and course sand particles and small and medium-sized stones—is usually used instead. This mixture does not deform or flow when weight is applied from above, as clay is prone to do, nor does it retain water long enough after rains for it to freeze solid, lifting and cracking the pavements above. These structural soils are more important in pervious pavement applications than in impervious applications because they have an additional requirement: they must store, infiltrate, and deliver rainwater within them.

Structural soils all have some capacity to store and infiltrate water, some more so than others. Ordinary gravel has tiny voids between the particles such that 10 to 15 percent of its total volume is available for storing water. Thus, to store 1 inch of water in the gravel would require a total cross section area of 7.5 to 10 inches. Other structurally suitable materials have even more void space. Crushed basalt aggregates of a uniform size can also be used as a structural base. Graded and washed stones commonly between 0.5 and 1.5 inches, used in place of gravel, have between 30 and 35 percent void space. Thus, to store 1 inch of water in a structural base of crushed basalt would require only 3 inches of depth.

Storing the one or more inches of water in the base may not be required if the surrounding soils are extremely porous. In such cases, water will flow immediately into parent soils, requiring no residence time and no reservoir function in the base. However, such soils are rare. More commonly, there will be a need to hold rainwater in the section for a certain amount of time, allowing it to gradually seep into surrounding parent soils. The heavier the surrounding soils, the longer this might take, and the larger the required reservoir space might become.

Flow within the Section

Highly pervious structural sections will also allow water stored in the reservoir to flow along the section under the pavements.

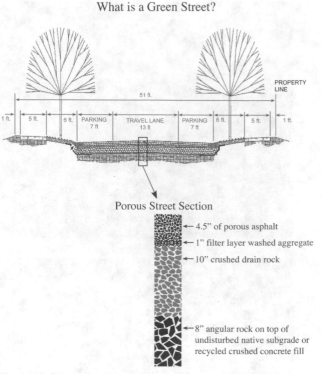

What is a Green Street?

Porous Street Section

← 4.5" of porous asphalt
← 1" filter layer washed aggregate
← 10" crushed drain rock

← 8" angular rock on top of undisturbed native subgrade or recycled crushed concrete fill

Figure 8.24. A porous street section. (Source: Pringlecreek.com)

Figure 8.25. The pervious paving used at the Pringle Creek Community in Salem, Oregon, uses crushed basalt aggregates as a structural base, which also act as water storage.

Figure 8.26. The standing water seen here is actually the high water table revealed during the winter. The finished road surface is only a few inches above this point yet stays dry as water travels through the street section and surrounding soils via interflow, emerging in the banks of Pringle Creek, almost visible in the distance beside the trees. The surface of the creek is only a foot or two lower than the water table but is sufficient to draw down the water if interflow is not impeded.

[31]Research conducted by the U.S. Environmental Protection Agency found that the risks of groundwater contamination are significantly higher with subsurface injection than with surface infiltration (Pitt, 2000). This seems to stem from the fact that most stormwater pollutants are more mobile in water than in soil. A large number of studies (for details, see *Bulletin No. 13* at http://www.jtc.sala.ubc.ca/bulletbody.html) have shown that shallow surface infiltration systems—such as bioretention swales, vegetated buffers, and permeable paving—are an effective means of removing the vast majority of residential-source stormwater pollutants, preventing their entry into groundwater sources (Condon and Jackson, 2006).

This can be a good thing, allowing rainwater to use the structural section below the pavement like an intermittent stream, facilitating the distribution of water on the site from saturated acres to acres that have better soils or more favorable water table conditions. If streets are steeply sloping, this flow can be too fast, reducing the opportunity for rainwater to infiltrate into surrounding soils. In such instances, various adjustments can be made, such as installing a somewhat less pervious structural base intermittently along the street or simply using impervious pavements for the parts of the site with steep roads, directing that water to the more shallow road gradients below.

What Is Not a Problem

As in all things pertaining to sustainable communities, while the principles are easily accepted, the specific application of these principles is controversial. No agreement yet exists in the engineering community about the practicality and durability of pervious pavements. These concerns are more extreme in the parts of the continent where winters are cold and freezes are frequent. The vast majority of these concerns are ill founded. The seminal collection of research on this topic is in Bruce Ferguson's timeless and comprehensive book *Porous Pavements* (2005). Suffice it to say here that pervious pavements, if properly installed, do not crumble and are safe. The first applications of pervious pavements are now over thirty years old and still working fine, even in wintery New England. What prevents their use is an inertia built into the industry of paving roads and a fear of assuming liability for changes from accepted norms.

Pervious pavements clean pollutants out of urban environments better than do pipe systems. The majority of pollutants found in urban environments adhere to dust particles and get trapped in the structural layers below the pavement. In pipe systems, all of these pollutants are concentrated and delivered to the fish.[31] Here, again, there is some controversy, as different jurisdictions, particularly in the United States, place pervious paved systems in the category of "injection wells." Under U.S. regulations, injection wells—typically systems that inject surface water into deep groundwater reservoirs—come under regulations governing drinking water. These regulations are far more stringent than the water quality regulations governing streams. In the hands of regulators who erroneously place all infiltration systems into the category of injection wells, this can lead to refusal to permit.

The State of Oregon and the City of Portland Department of Environmental Quality have overcome this constraint by carefully working with state and federal regulators to officially identify what types of systems are excluded from the category of injection systems. As a general rule, they have determined that any infiltration system that works from gravity alone and extends no more than twenty-four inches below the surface cannot be designated as an injection system. The street systems at the Pringle Creek Community were therefore eventually excluded from the category of injection well and were thus approved for construction.

Protection during Construction

There is, however, one very serious potential weakness with pervious pavements. They can get clogged. If massive amounts of heavy soils are dumped onto the pavements, they can fill up and block all the voids in the pavement, impeding or blocking rainwater from flowing through it. In worst-case scenarios, they can also fill in the voids in the structural base, compromising the storage and infiltration functions of the reservoir base as well. The amount of soil required to induce this catastrophic failure is so large as to constitute a relatively minor concern, except of course during one period: construction. During construction, new development sites are notoriously dirty, with silts pouring off torn-up landscapes by the ton. If this dirt makes its way to new pervious pavement sections, the storm drainage system function will be compromised. To avoid this consequence requires extra care during site construction. This extra care translates into extra staff hours and, consequently, into additional cost. At the Salem, Oregon, Pringle Creek Community, the contractors—who were contractually responsible for keeping the pervious pavement clean during construction—decided that it was safer to wrap all of the completed streets with filter fabric during the site construction phase, unwrapping them only when the dirtiest parts of the job were done—a very expensive proposition indeed.

Two factors make the added time and expense more acceptable: (1) developers are increasingly required to keep all construction-generated silts on site anyway, so the costs for silt

Figure 8.27. Construction sites are dirty places, and dirt can quickly destroy investments in pervious pavements. At the Pringle Creek project, streets were covered with filter fabric, as shown in this photograph, until the most disruptive phases of the site construction were complete.

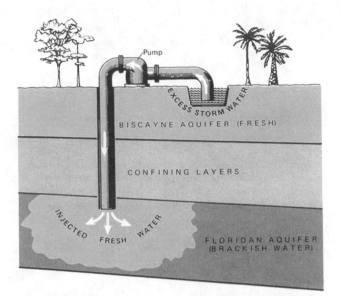

Figure 8.28. This diagram of an injection well in Florida shows how excess stormwater is injected into the groundwater. Obviously, such a device has the potential to quickly harm drinking water if regulations are not followed. The problem comes when infiltration streets are held to standards appropriate to this kind of injection system.

Figure 8.29. Amble Greene project, Surry, British Columbia. Curbless streets allow rain water to flow unimpeded along the entire length into the lowered boulevard. Infiltration for most storms occurs in the wide boulevard, enhanced by invisible infiltration galleries below.

[32]Through evaluating seventeen case studies, the U.S. Environmental Protection Agency (2007) found that in most cases significant savings were realized through low-impact development (LID) strategies (where small-scale stormwater management practices promote the use of natural systems for infiltration, evapotranspiration, and reuse of rainwater) as opposed to conventional stormwater practices (curbs, gutters, and pipes). With few exceptions, total capital cost savings ranged from 15 to 80 percent when LID methods were used.

containment are already very high; and (2) pervious pavement systems should eliminate the need for any drainage inlet basins, pipes, curbs, and other expensive elements of conventional storm systems. Savings from these items should more than off-set the cost of the extra care required.[32]

Conveyance

In most cases, pervious pavements do not eliminate the need for conveyance systems. In most parts of North America, if the infiltration target is one inch per day, there will be ten to twenty days a year when this amount is exceeded. On those days, excess water that cannot be absorbed directly through the pervious pavement section must be conveyed to a receiving location. There are two ways to do this, one expensive, one cheap. The expensive way is to include a system of drain inlets in boulevards or street edges to accept and deliver these flows. The cheaper option is to allow these occasional flows to traverse the site overland. On the thirty-acre Pringle Creek Community site, there are no stormwater pipes at all. Large flows are conveyed at the edges of pavements, then across the surface of intersections, eventually to find their way to on-site artificial wetlands and eventually, and very infrequently, overland to streams.

IMPERVIOUS PAVED INFILTRATION STREETS

You can use impervious pavement on travel ways and still have pervious streets; in these instances, rainwater is directed to street verges specifically designed to accept and infiltrate rainwater. There are many ways to perform this trick, and the following four examples illustrate the range of options.

Impervious Green Streets Example 1: Amble Greene Community, Surrey, British Columbia

Most typical residential streets trap water between vertical curbs. Trapped like this, water that should be allowed to infiltrate collects in gutters and flows downhill until it reaches an inlet, leading to a pipe, leading to a bigger pipe, and finally, dirty and hot, gets flushed into the stream. Removing curbs eliminates this problem. Without curbs to block it, rainwater can flow over the lip of pavement into grass or crushed stone verges or boulevards. Rural roads are still built this way, not to preserve watershed function but because it is by far the cheapest way to build a road. By removing the curb and gently lowering the grassy tree boulevard, broad spaces are made available for infiltrating water. If verges are broad enough and soil conditions favorable enough, the one-inch-per day infiltration target can be achieved without soil or engineering enhancements. With this system, verges need to perform double duty, infiltrating any water that falls on them as well as the watershed by the nearby roadways. As with rain gardens, this becomes increasingly challenging as the percentage of the right-of-way devoted to soft surfaces decreases. If 20 percent of the site is available for infiltration, this means that each square foot of verge area will have to infiltrate not one inch but five inches in twenty-four hours. For many soil conditions, this is not possible unless engineered infiltration devices or soil enhancements are incorporated.

The 1974 Amble Green project in Surrey, British Columbia, provides a good and durable example of this strategy. The curbless streets in this project infiltrate 100 percent of the water that falls on them. Soil conditions are forgiving but by no means ideal. Nevertheless, the project infiltrates not our target of one inch per day but four inches—the amount of rain associated with the one-hundred-year storm event in this city. Project proponents were required to infiltrate all rainwater that fell on the site because of inadequate off-site city storm drain interceptors. Broad grassy boulevards located between sidewalks and the curbless streets absorb most of the rainfall, with additional infiltration provided by hidden "French drain" infiltration chambers located below. Occasional "blue-green" infiltration depressions—large dished areas often in the middle of cul-de-sac bulbs that can hold large amounts of water long enough to eventually infiltrate into soils below—are the fail-safe backup for the plan.

As this project demonstrates, curbless streets save money and do the job, But, in the minds of many, they have one problem. Without curbs, what will prevent parking cars from migrating onto the grass? At Amble Greene, this is largely not a problem, but in the few places where it is, owners have arrived

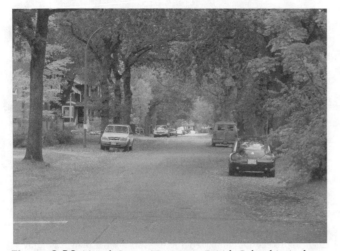

Figure 8.30. Trutch Street, Vancouver, British Columbia, is characteristic of most streets built in the city prior to 1950.

at a simple control strategy. Hand-placed rocks located at the street edge provide enough discouragement.

Impervious Green Street Example 2: Trutch Street, Vancouver, British Columbia

While not specifically designed as a green street, this road section is an even more economical and elegant solution to the problem than the one at Amble Greene. Hundreds of older streets in many streetcar cities, particularly in the Vancouver region, were built to this standard. Most still exist. Thus, hundreds of examples of this street type exist, with over seventy years of performance to assess. These extremely inexpensive streets are queuing streets (as discussed in chapter 3). Measuring roughly 28 feet from the outside edge of parking bays to the other outside edge, they are composed of two crushed-stone 6.5-foot parking bays and one 15-foot paved two-way travel section. The crushed-stone parking bays are cheap and can be highly pervious. Infiltration occurs under the cars; thus, the tree boulevards need not dish down to accept water but can rise higher than the road and parking portion of the section.

This subtle landform provides for pedestrian comfort and safety while preventing cars from migrating onto the grass. It is an extremely beautiful design that should be widely used. Sadly, all of the examples of this street type are a legacy of an earlier time. The streets at the Pringle Creek Community in Salem, Oregon, are very close to this typology, differing only in that they employ much narrower crushed-stone strips at verges, with pervious pavements doing the work of infiltration across the whole section rather than in crushed-stone beds under parked cars.

Impervious Green Street Example 3: East Clayton, Surrey, British Columbia

The East Clayton Sustainable Community plan was a product of a University of British Columbia and City of Surrey design charrette held in spring 1998. Green street sections agreed to at the charrette lacked curbs and resembled in function and form the streets of Amble Greene, also located in Surrey. Concerns raised after the charrette led to a change in the plans. Curbs were added to all streets. To allow for natural infiltration, slots were introduced into curbs to allow channeled water to escape from gutters into lowered tree boulevards. The tree boulevards allowed for infiltration and cleansing before directing excess water to drain inlets above buried infiltration chambers. These infiltration chambers were in turn tied into a subsurface system of pipes, sized in this case for the one-hundred-year storm. The hybrid system that resulted is a fairly literal combination of a green street strategy with a conventional gray street strategy. The one-inch-per-day infiltration target is achieved through ubiquitous infiltration in tree boulevards. Otherwise, with the curbs and substantial subsurface system of pipes, it operates conventionally.

In the minds of its proponents, this approach had the advantage of limiting risk. Conventional systems provided as part of the plan were robust enough, and their function well enough understood, that approving agents were comfortable they would not fail in extreme circumstances. The down side was that this "belt and suspenders" system was substantially more costly than either a curbless green street, like those at Amble Greene, or a conventional street. Contractors estimated that the system cost $5,000 per lot more than conventional street systems, or an additional $120 per foot of frontage.

Figure 8.31. First-phase yard infiltration systems for the East Clayton project. Disconnected downspouts discharge into a highly permeable crushed-stone layer. Drainage from the driveway is shed into grassy areas and then into an infiltration basin below the drain inlet shown.

Impervious Green Street Example 4: City of Seattle Public Utilities Department, Broadview Green Grid Program

The City of Seattle has long been the leader among U.S. cities on green infrastructure and green streets. They have been motivated by public concern about the loss of salmon and by increasing pressure from federal and state agencies to reduce the impact of street systems on receiving streams. The Broadview Green Grid Program is one example of many Seattle projects of its type. Patterned on the demonstration SEA Street project (for street edge alternatives), this project attempts, by its scale (four blocks and all surrounding streets), to significantly rectify the

Figure 8.32. Foreground streets are rear lanes for the future Pringle Creek development. A thirteen-foot-wide fire-access lane is paved with pervious asphalt bordered by crushed-stone infiltration verges. Filter fabric, visible at the edges, contains the crushed-stone base, preventing migration of soil fines into the reservoir.

Figure 8.33. Traditional Vancouver, British Columbia, lane paved with crushed stone. Areas outside of the tire tracks have grown over, creating healthy root zones for plant growth and associated infiltration.

---

[33]For more information, see the Seattle Public Utilities Web site at http://www.cityofseattle.net/util/Services/.

[34]For more information, see Vancouver's "Country Lane" Program online at http://vancouver.ca/engsvcs/streets/localimprovements/improvementTypes/lanes/country.htm. For more on Chicago's Green Alley program, visit the city's Web site at http://egov.cityofchicago.org/.

damage previously done to Pipers Creek, the destination for all of this urban stormwater discharge.

This project is distinguished from the other examples by the aggressive way it reconfigures street verges, creating what is in effect an entirely new street typology. The designs are also extremely rich, with a layering of engineered devices to sometimes infiltrate water, other times retain it, other times hold it for plant root uptake, and other times hold it in ephemeral ponds long enough to infiltrate into soils below. The impervious streets are curbless to allow natural flow off pavement edges into verge areas, set lower than the pavement they drain. These verge areas sometimes convey and sometimes infiltrate water, depending on verge design and the amount of stormwater received during a storm event. The critique of the Seattle Public Utilities projects are that they are far more expensive to build than conventional streets and thus do not meet the "cheaper" part of the lighter, greener, cheaper, smarter rule.[33]

Infiltration on Lanes and Alleys

All of the above strategies can be used for lanes and alleys, and since the transportation demands on lanes are usually lower than for streets, they are sometimes the easiest place to start. This is true in both Vancouver and Chicago, where there are projects to green the lanes but not yet the streets.[34]

But there is one strategy that can be used on lanes that goes even further than the four examples cited. You might simply not pave the lane at all. In Vancouver, as well as in many other North American streetcar cities, lanes were not originally paved. They were simply covered with a structurally sound granular material, usually crushed basalt or granite. Depending on the minimum size of fines and maintenance protocols, paving lanes with crushed granite or basalt is a very low cost and highly effective infiltration strategy. This is by far the most inexpensive option and one of the most effective. It is also, to the author's mind, the most beautiful. Implementation barriers in the way of this low-cost solution include fears about what children might do with the stones, and the need for new city maintenance protocols for refreshing and regrading crushed stone lanes.

At some point, our tendency to spend more and more per family on roads must surely end. Overextended infrastructure is already bankrupting some communities, and others will follow. Even at the national scale, there are problems, with estimates of the unfunded demands for upgrading U.S. highway infrastructure in the many hundreds of billions of dollars; it boggles the mind to consider what that number would be if local infrastructure were included. It must be in the trillions. Certainly, a landscape pattern that is overcommitted to the car and under-committed to transit, biking, and walking is the root of the problem. But the tendency to build infrastructure in defiance of natural system behaviors is a linked pathology. Street systems seem to have been intentionally designed to be ignorant of natural processes. Unsurprisingly, this has caused the destruction of these same systems.

Fortunately, this can be corrected. Lighter, greener, cheaper, and smarter infrastructure is certainly conceivable, and in fact already exists. While variations exist across North America, the four rules for green infrastructure are quite simple: (1) infiltrate rather than drain, (2) infiltrate everywhere, (3) infiltrate one inch per day, and (4) heavy soils are good soils. The solutions are not complex; changing behaviors, however, will be. Fundamental shifts will be required in the way the problem is approached and by the people who are at the table trying to solve it. Decision makers must think laterally about the many issues that touch on street infrastructure, not just about accommodating traffic and removing stormwater. This is even more daunting when we accept the challenge to retrofit the millions of square miles of existing street infrastructure. Fortunately, we have as much time and energy and resources at hand to fix this problem as we had to create it.

Conclusion

The last of the rules introduced in chapter 1 is *love one rule, love them all*. The essence of a sustainable community is found in its integrated systems. It does no good if there are jobs close to home but the street network still frustrates moving by any means other than a car. It does no good to be a five-minute walk from commercial services and transit unless this system is scaled up to allow for reasonable access to walkable destinations at the other end of the trip. It does no good to have a linked system of recreation areas and parks if they are devastated by uncontrolled stormwater runoff from adjacent neighborhoods. The seven rules presented in this book are an attempt to simplify what might appear complex: the overlapping and interconnected nature of the body of the world and how we might heal it.

But the most cancerous illness in the body of the world is carbon, and how we seem hell bent on taking every bit of carbon locked up in the land since the carboniferous period and launching it into the ten-mile-thin band of our atmosphere. No responsible planner, architect, landscape architect, politician, or developer can escape the moral imperative to change the way he or she does business in response.

But change what? Make buildings more efficient? Make cars operate on batteries? Erect new windmills? Yes to all of the above, but that is not enough. No amount of technological fixing can solve this problem if our per capita energy use continues to grow, if our per capita automobile use continues to climb, if the percentage of our gross national product devoted to transportation systems of all types (not just cars) continues to increase, and if our way of building new communities ignores the fundamental rules of sustainable city planning. Even absent the climate change problem, our way of building cities is unsustainable. As William Rees says, if everyone on the planet lived like North Americans, it would take six planet earths to support it—and this without even considering the carbon problem.

Equally blind are those who hypothesize wildly new forms of cities: growing food in skyscrapers, carbon-free monorails connecting every house, mining of oceans for food and materials, mega structures like concrete beehives for millions. Such proposals ignore the immense material costs of their outrageous proposals. The earth simply cannot supply the materials and absorb the waste from such a globewide urban transformation. The concrete alone would tip us into atmospheric carbon overload. We have no choice but to work from what we have, no matter where on earth we are, and rebuild it for this new emergency. I offer the streetcar city as a way to do that.

Whatever is the solution, we know for sure that the North American city will need a dramatic retrofit. According to the United Nations' Intergovernmental Panel on Climate Change, we have only fifty years to do it—but perhaps this fifty-year time frame is the most hopeful part of the message. In the fifty years between 1950 and 2000, the mechanics of the North American city changed entirely. Walking was replaced by driving, streetcars were replaced by buses and cars, community centers were transformed from key intersections in the grid where walking predominated to enclosed malls at the center of a dendritic infrastructure swarming with cars. It seems inconceivable that this transformation to every aspect of the city occurred so fast, but it did; and if we did all that in fifty years, then we can achieve a similar shift in the next fifty. But if we are to reduce our total carbon production by 80 percent, we had better start right away. New developments take ten years from proposal to occupation, city plans can take decades to realize, regional transportation plans typically have a thirty-year horizon, and natural systems can take fifty years or longer to heal.

Finally, there is a subtext to all of this, one that has been touched on here and there in this volume but was not central to the argument. These seven rules stand on their own as practical solutions to the crisis we face, but taken together they create a world that would necessarily manifest itself in experiential terms. The qualities of such a world would, I believe, show up as the very positive phenomena that Jane Jacobs isolated in her examination of New York (Jacobs, 1961): homes interface with the public realm in organic ways, the street becomes the milieu for social interaction, different demographic and cultural groups cross fertilize, moving through the city is communal, and nature is always within easy reach. Low-carbon, sustainable communities are just starting to emerge and to provide strong evidence that the qualities Jane Jacobs identified may be intrinsic to a well-built and intelligently designed sustainable community. But to explicate the qualitative phenomena of the sustainable low-carbon future would take another book, and this one ends here.

Acknowledgments

Thanks are owed to many people, but I must acknowledge a few in particular. Without them this book either would not exist or would be a much lesser work. First, to Island Press, publishers of books, such as this one, that attempt to bridge the gap between theory and practice. Special thanks to my editor, Heather Boyer, for having both the strength to insist on changes that made this work better and the wisdom to listen to alternatives when they were clearly presented—a very difficult balance to maintain.

Next I want to acknowledge all of the members of the Congress for the New Urbanism (CNU) for working so very hard for more than two decades, against terrible odds, to change policies and practices that produce sprawl—and thereby moving the everyday practice of building cities gradually toward sustainability. My conversations with CNU members, mostly over the Internet on listservs, have been tremendously important to my growth as a writer and a scholar, and in formulating what I hope is a consistent theory of sustainable urban design.

Now I turn to a very special thank you to Ms. Kari Dow, University of British Columbia (UBC) master of landscape architecture 2008. Kari has worked with me on this project for over two years, first as a student in landscape architecture at UBC and later as a staff researcher at the Design Centre for Sustainability at UBC. Her contributions are manifest in the extensive research that supports the main text and in the elegant presentation of that research in the form of research summary notes. I had intended that there be a smooth flow from main text to research notes, and a similarly smooth flow to the more in depth supporting references. I had hoped that having immediate access to this information while reading each chapter would reinforce the scientific rigor of the book while still keeping the text accessible. What sounds easy in principle became devilishly difficult in practice. Few people could have managed this task with the intelligence, determination, and seeming ease exhibited by Ms. Kari Dow. Take note of this name. You will be hearing much more from her in future years.

Finally, thanks go to the University of British Columbia for allowing me the freedom to be the best I can be, in the way I best know how. Thanks also to my UBC colleagues in the Design Centre for Sustainability, a group that is as passionate about advancing sustainable communities as I am. Heartfelt thanks also go to our U.S. partner, the Lincoln Institute of

Land Policy, and in particular to Armando Carbonell, chairman of the Department of Planning and Urban Form, for a fall 2007 Lincoln Institute research fellowship, during which many of these ideas came together.

Of course, in the end, such work requires money. Thanks to the Graham Foundation for providing the seed money to begin this effort, and to the UBC James Taylor Chair Endowment Fund for providing the money to finish it.

References

Alexander, Christopher. 1977. *A Pattern Language: Towns, Buildings, Construction*. New York: Oxford University Press.

Allen, Eliot. 1996. "Benefits of Neotraditional Development." Portland, OR: Criterion Engineers and Planners.

Amatya, Devendra M. and Carl Trettin. 2007. "Annual Evapotranspiration of a Forested Wetland Watershed, SC." Presentation at 2007 ASABE Annual International Meeting, Minneapolis, MN, June 17–20, 2007.

American Automobile Association (AAA). 2009. *Your Driving Costs 2009 Edition*. Heathrow, FL: AAA.

American Community Survey. 2005–2007. *New York–Northern New Jersey–Long Island Metropolitan Statistical Area: Commuting Characteristics by Sex*. U.S. Census Bureau. http://factfinder.census.gov/.

American Public Transportation Association. 2007. "Light Rail Transit Ridership Report, Fourth Quarter 2007." http://www.apta.com/resources/statistics/Documents/Ridership/2006_q4_ridership_APTA.pdf.

American Public Transportation Association. 2009. *2009 Public Transportation Fact Book*. Washington, DC: American Public Transportation Association.

American Society of Civil Engineers. 2009. "2009 Report Card for America's Infrastructure." ASCE (March 25). http://www.asce.org/reportcard.

American Transit Association. 1966. *Transit Factbook 1966*. Washington, DC: American Public Transportation Association. Table 2. In Randal O'Toole, "A Desire Named Streetcar: How Federal Subsidies Encourage Wasteful Local Transit Systems," *Policy Analysis*, no. 559 (January 5, 2006).

Armour, C. 1991. *Guidance for Evaluating and Recommending Temperature Regimes to Protect Fish*. Biological Report 90 (22), Instream Flow Information Paper 27, U.S. Fish and Wildlife Service.

Baker, Kermit. 2008. "As Housing Market Weakens, Homes Are Getting Smaller." *AIArchitect* 15 (June). http://info.aia.org/aiarchitect/thisweek08/0606/0606b_htdsq2.cfm.

Barnett, J. 1940. *Transition Curves for Highways*. U.S. Government Printing Office.

Barnett, J., E. Haile, and R. Moyer. 1936. "Safe Side Friction Factors and Superelevation Design." *Highway Research Board* 16:69–80.

Barnett, Jonathan. 1995. *The Fractured Metropolis: Improving the New City, Restoring the Old City, Reshaping the Region*. New York: HarperCollins.

Bauer, John. 1939. "The Street Railways Struggle against Traffic Losses." *Public Utilities Fortnightly* 23:209–17. Cited in J. Ortner and M. Wachs, "The Cost Revenue Squeeze in American Public Transit," *Journal of the American Planning Association* 45, no. 1 (1979): 10–21.

BC Stats. 2008. Quarterly Regional Statistics, Interim Report, Fourth Quarter 2008: Greater Vancouver Regional District, Ministry of Labour and Citizens Services.

Beacon Hill Online: The Neighborhood Web Site for Beacon Hill, Boston, Massachusetts. 2003. http://www.beaconhillonline.com/cgi-bin/index.cgi?cid=1.

Belzer, D., and G. Autler. 2002. "Transit Oriented Development: Moving from Rhetoric to Reality." Discussion paper prepared for the Brookings Institution Center on Urban and Metropolitan Policy and the Great American Station Foundation.

Berlin, Ryan, Andrew Ramlo, and David Baxter. 2006. "Seniors' Housing Demand in British Columbia over the Next Thirty Years." *Urban Futures Report 65* (January).

Bernstein, S., C. Makarewicz, and K. McCarty. 2005. "Driven to Spend: Pumping Dollars Out of our Households and Community." Centre for Neighbourhood Technology: Strategies for Livable Communities.

Berry, J. L., and D. C. Dahmann. 1977. "Population Redistribution in the United States in the 1970s." *Population and Development Review* 3(4):443–71.

Beschta, R. L., R. E. Bilby, G. W. Brown, L. B. Holtby, and T. D. Hofstra. 1987. "Stream Temperature and Aquatic Habitat: Fisheries and Forestry Interactions." In *Streamside Management: Forestry and Fishery Interactions*, ed. E. O. Salo and T. W. Cundy, 191–232. UW Forestry Publication no. 57. Seattle: University of Washington.

Bianco, Martha. 1998. "Kennedy, 60 Minutes, and Roger Rabbit: Understanding Conspiracy-theory Explanations of the Decline of Urban Mass Transit." Discussion paper 98-11. Center for Urban Studies, Portland State University.

Birch, E. 2005. "Who Lives Downtown?" Living Cities Census Series, the Brookings Institution. http://www.brookings.edu/metro/pubs/20051115_Birch.pdf.

Black, R. J. 1993. "Florida Climate." University of Florida, Institute of Food and Agricultural Sciences. http://edis.ifas.ufl.edu/EH105.

Blythe, Nils. 2007. "Biofuel Demand Makes Food Expensive." *BBC News*, March 23, 2007.

Bolitzer, B., and N. R. Netusil. 2000. "The Impact of Open Spaces on Property Values in Portland." *Oregon Journal of Environmental Management* 59:185–93.

Booth, D. B. 1991. "Urbanization and the Natural Drainage System: Impacts, Solutions and Prognoses." *Northwest Environmental Journal* 7, no. 1 (Spring/Summer).

———. 2000. *Forest Cover, Impervious-Surface Area and the Mitigation of Urbanization Impacts in King County, Washington*. Prepared for King County Water and Land Resources Division.

Booth, D. B., J. R. Karr, S. Schauman, C. P. Konrad, S. A. Morley, M. G. Larson, and S. J. Burges. 2004. "Reviving Urban Streams: Land Use, Hydrology, Biology, and Human Behavior." *Journal of the American Water Resources Association* 40:1351–64.

Borchert, James. 1998. *The Encyclopedia of Cleveland History: Suburbs.* http://ech.case.edu/ech-cgi/article.pl?id=S25.

Broderson, J. M. 1973. "Sizing Up Buffer Strips to Maintain Water Quality." Master's thesis, University of Washington.

Brooks, David. 2004. *On Paradise Drive: How We Live Not (and Always Have) in the Future Tense.* New York: Simon & Schuster.

———. 2008. "This Old House." New York Times, December 9.

Brown, J. 2005. "A Tale of Two Visions: Harland Bartholomew, Robert Moses, and the Development of the American Freeway." *Journal of Planning History* 4(1):2–32.

Buchanan, Kevin. 2008. "Portland Streetcar Has Record High Ridership." Fortworthology.com (October 8).

Buck, E. H., and J. R. Dandelski. 1999. *Pacific Salmon and Anadromous Trout: Management under the Endangered Species Act.* CRS report for Congress.

Buehler, Ralph, John Pucher, and Uwe Kunert. 2009. *Making Transportation Sustainable: Insights from Germany*. Brookings Institution Metropolitan Policy Program.

Buntin, Simmons. 2008. "Denver: American's Great Urban Canvas, Part I." *Next American City* (May 4). http://americancity.org/daily/entry/958/.

Burchell, Robert, Anthony Downs, Barbara McCann, and Sahan Mukherji. 2005. *Sprawl Costs*. Washington, DC.: Island Press.

Burchfield, Marcy, Henry G. Overman, Diego Puga, and Matthew A. Turner. 2006. "Causes of Sprawl: A Portrait from Space." *Quarterly Journal of Economics* 121(2):587–633.

Canada Mortgage and Housing Corporation (CMHC). 2001. *The Headwater Project–East Clayton Neighbourhood Concept Plan*. Socio-economic Series, CMHC, 78.

Canadian Facts. 2000a. "The 1999 Regional Travel Survey: South Surrey/Langley Sub-Area Travel." Translink.

———. 2000b. "The 1999 Regional Travel Survey: Vancouver Sub-Area Travel." Translink.

Canadian Home Builders' Association. 2008. "The Energy and Greenhouse Gas Performance of Canada's Residential Sector, 1990 to 2005." Report, Canadian Home Builders' Association (September).

Centre for Neighborhood Technology. 2009. *True Affordability and Location Efficiency: H+T Affordability Index*. Centre for Neighborhood Technology. http://htaindex.cnt.org/.

Cervero, R. 2003. "Road Expansion, Urban Growth and Induced Travel: A Path Analysis." *APA Journal* 69(2):145–63. http://www.uctc.net/papers/520.pdf.

———. 2007. "Transit Oriented Development in the US: Contemporary Practices, Impacts and Policy Directions." In *Incentives, Regulations and Plans: The Role of States and Nation States in Smart Growth Planning*, ed. G. Knapp, H. Haccou, K. Clifton, and J. Frece. Edward Elgar Publishing.

Cervero, R., and K. Kockelman. 1997. "Travel Demand and the 3Ds: Density, Diversity, and Design." *Transpn Res.-D.* 2(3):199–219.

Chandler, Liz, and Ted Mellnik. 2007. "New Suburbs in Fast Decay." *Charlotte Observer*, December 9.

Chen, Chao, and Pravin Varaiya. 2001. "The Freeway Congestion Paradox." PeMS Development Group. http://paleale.eecs.berkeley.edu/~varaiya/papers_ps.dir/FreewayCongestionParadox.pdf.

Chen, J. T. 1991. "Edge Effects: Microclimatic Pattern and Biological Responses in Old-growth Douglas-fir Forests." Ph.D. diss., University of Washington.

Chester, Mikhail V. 2008. "Life-cycle Environmental Inventory of Passenger Transportation in the United States." Ph.D. diss., Institute of Transportation Studies, University of Berkeley.

Chi, G. 2006. "Rethinking Highway Effects on Population Change." *Public Works Management and Policy* 11(1):18–32.

Choe, Tom. 2001. "Freeway Performance Measurement System (PeMS): An Operational Analysis Tool." Office of Freeway Operations, California Department of Transportation District 7. http://paleale.eecs.berkeley.edu/~varaiya/papers_ps.dir/PeMS_TRB2002.pdf .

City of Orlando. 2002. "Edgewater Drive Before and After Re-striping Results." City of Orlando, Transportation Planning Bureau (November 1). http://www.loupathways.org/rd_4to3_Orlando.pdf .

City of Salem. 2007. *Salem Transportation System Plan*. City of Salem, Public Works Department, Transportation Services Division. http://www.cityofsalem.net/.

City of Vancouver. 2006. *Streetcar and Local Bus Comparative*. City of Vancouver. http://www.city.vancouver.bc.ca/engsvcs/transport/streetcar/pdfs/comparativeReview.pdf.

Condon, Patrick. 2008. "Planning for Climate Change." *Land Lines*. Lincoln Institute of Land Policy (January). http://www.rpa.org/pdf/edgeless-city/2009/Planning_for_Climate_Change.pdf.

Condon, Patrick, and Jone Belausteguigoitia. 2006. "Growing a Greater Vancouver Region: Population Scenarios for a Region of 4 Million People." Design Centre for Sustainability, *Foundation Research Bulletin* 2. http://www.sxd.sala.ubc.ca/8_research/sxd_TB02_population.pdf.

Condon, Patrick, and Kari Dow. 2008. *Foundational Research Bulletin*, no. 7 (September). http://www.sxd.sala.ubc.ca/8_research/sxd_FRB07Cost_Comparisons%20Jan%209.pdf .

———. 2009. "A Cost Comparison of Transportation Modes." *Foundational Research Bulletin* 7. http://www.sxd.sala.ubc.ca/8_research/sxd_FRB07_cost.pdf.

Condon, Patrick, and Ann Jackson. 2006. *Shallow Stormwater Infiltration Devices vs. Injection Well Systems: A Comparison of Groundwater Contamination Potential*. Research Bulletin no. 13. http://www.jtc.sala.ubc.ca/bulletbody.html.

Condon, Patrick, and Stacy Moriarty, eds. 1999. *Second Nature*. Beverly Hills, CA: Andy Lipkis, Tree-People.

Condon, Patrick, Joanne Proft, Jackie Teed, and Sara Muir. 2003. *Sustainable Urban Landscapes: Site Design Manual for British Columbia*. Vancouver: University of British Columbia, James Taylor Chair in Landscape and Liveable Environments. http://www.jtc.sala.ubc.ca/projects/DesignManual.html.

Condon, P. M., J. Teed, and S. Muir. 1998. *Alternative Development Standards for Sustainable Communities: Design Workbook*. James Taylor Chair in Landscape and Liveable Environments, University of British Columbia.

Connelly, M., K. Liu, and J. Schaub. 2006. "Report to Canada Mortgage and Housing Corporation: BCIT Green Roof Research Program Phase I. Summary of Data Analysis, Observation Period: Jan. 1, 2005 to Dec. 31, 2005." http://commons.bcit.ca/greenroof/publications/CMHC%20ERP%20Final%20060910.pdf.

Cooper Marcus, Clare, and Wendy Sarkissian. 1986. *Housing as if People Mattered: Site Design Guidelines for Medium-density Family Housing*. Berkeley: University of California Press.

Dallas Area Rapid Transit. 2009. "DART Ridership Growth Trend Continues." *DART News Release* (February 5). http://www.dart.org/news/news.asp?ID=830.

Dama, Allesandro. 2005. *Solar and External Heat Gains at the Building Envelope*. Vienna: Austrian Energy Agency. http://www.keep-cool.eu/System/FileArchive/175/File_12295.pdf.

Davidoff, T. 2005. "Income Sorting: Measurement and Decomposition." *Journal of Urban Economics* 58:289–303.

Dedman, Bill. 2005. "Slower Arrival at Fires in U.S. Is Costing Lives." *Boston Globe*, January 30.

de la Rue du Can, Stephane, and Lynn Price. 2008. "Sectoral Trends in Global Energy Use and Greenhouse Gas Emissions." *Energy Policy* 36(4):1386–1403.

Demographia. 2001. "USA Urbanized Areas over 500,000: 2000 Rankings." http://www.demographia.com/db-ua2000r.htm.

———. 2005. "Major High-income World Urban Areas: Freeway Access and Capacity." *Urban Transport Fact Book* (unpublished). Wendell Cox Consultancy, Demographia.

———. 2006. "World Urban Population Density by Country and Area." http://www.demographia.com/db-intlua-area2000.htm (last updated April 1, 2006; accessed July 22, 2009).

———. 2009. "Demographia World Urban Areas and Population Projections." 5th ed. http://www.demographia.com/db-worldua.pdf (revised April 2009).

Design Centre for Sustainability. 2006. *Sustainability by Design: A Vision for a Region of 4 Million*. Vancouver, British Columbia: Design Centre for Sustainability.

Diamant, E.S., et al. 1976. *Light Rail Transit: State of the Art Review*. Chicago: DeLeuw, Cather (Spring).

Dittmar, Hank, and Gloria Ohland. 2003. *The New Transit Town: Best Practices in Transit-oriented Development*. Washington, DC: Island Press.

Doornbosch, Richard, and Ronald Steenblik. 2007. "Biofuels: Is the Cure Worse than the Disease?" Organisation for Economic Co-operation and Development.

Dougherty, Conor. 2009. "Cities Grow at Suburbs' Expense during Recession." *Wall Street Journal*, July 1.

Dunham-Jones, Ellen, and June Williamson. 2008. *Retrofitting Suburbia: Urban Design Solutions for Redesigning Suburbs*. New York: Wiley and Sons.

Dunnett, Nigel, and Noel Kingsbury. 2008. *Planting Green Roofs and Living Walls*. 2nd ed. Portland, OR: Timber Press.

The Economist. 2008. "Cars in Emerging Markets: The Art of the Possible." *The Economist*, November 13.

Edmonston, Barry, Michael A. Goldberg, and John Mercer. 1985. "Urban Form in Canada and the United States: An Examination of Urban Density Gradients." *Urban Studies* 22(3):209–17.

Electric Power Research Institute (EPRI). 2007. "Using Forest Carbon Sequestration to Create Greenhouse Gas Emissions Offsets." EPRI, Palo Alto, California. http://mydocs.epri.com/docs/public/000000000001016282.pdf.

Ellis, Cliff. 2001. "Interstate Highways, Regional Planning and the Reshaping of Metropolitan America." *Planning Practice and Research* 16(3):247–69.

Ellis, John G. 2004. "Explaining Residential Density (Research and Debate)." *Places* 16:2. http://repositories.cdlib.org/ced/places/vol16/iss2/Ellis_pg34-43.

Energy Information Administration (EIA). 2008. "Emissions of Greenhouse Gases Report." http://www.eia.doe.gov/oiaf/1605/ggrpt/.

Environment Canada. 2008. *National Inventory Report: 1990–2006, Greenhouse Gas Sources and Sinks in Canada*. No. En81-4/2006E. Greenhouse Gas Division, Environment Canada.

Erman, D. C., J. D. Newbold, and K. B. Roby. 1977. "Evaluation of Streamside Bufferstrips for Protecting Aquatic Organisms." Contribution Number 16. California Water Resources Center, University of California, Davis.

Ernst, M.. 2004. *Mean Streets 2004: How Far Have We Come? Pedestrian Safety, 1994–2003*. Washington, DC: Surface Transportation Policy Project.

Ernst, Michelle and Lilly Shoup. 2009. Dangerous by Design. Transportation for America and Surface Transportation Policy Partnership.

Ewing, R., T. Schmid, R. Killingsworth, A. Zlot, and S. Raudenbush. 2003. "Relationship between Urban Sprawl and Physical Activity, Obesity, and Morbidity. *American Journal of Health Promotion* 18, no. 1 (Sept–Oct): 47–57.

Ewing, Reid, Keith Bartholomew, Steve Winkelman, Jerry Walters, and Don Chen. 2007. *Growing Cooler: The Evidence on Urban Development and Climate Change*. Washington, DC: Urban Land Institute.

Ewing, Reid., P. Haliyur, and G. Page. 1994. "Getting around a Traditional City, a Suburban PUD, and Everything In-between." *Transportation Research Record* 1466:53–62.

Fabos, Julius Gy. 1968. *Frederick Law Olmsted, Sr.: Founder of Landscape Architecture in America*. Amherst: University of Massachusetts Press.

Fabos, Julius Gy., and Jack Ahern, eds. 1995. *Greenways: The Beginning of an International Movement*. Amsterdam: Elsevier.

Federal Highway Administration, U.S. Department of Transportation. 2007. "Highway Statistics." http://www.fhwa.dot.gov/policyinformation/statistics/2007/.

———. 2009. "Traffic Volume Trends." http://www.fhwa.dot.gov/ohim/tvtw/tvtpage.cfm (accessed July 2009).

Federal Reserve Bank of Boston. 2008. "Foreclosure Rates in Massachusetts Cities and Towns: 1990–2008. http://www.bos.frb.org/economic/.

Ferguson, Bruce. 2005. *Porous Pavements*. Boca Raton, FL: CRC Press.

Fisher, I. D., 1986. *Frederick Law Olmsted and the City Planning Movement in the United States*. Ann Arbor: University of Michigan Research Press.

Ford, L. R. 1999. "Lynch Revisited: New Urbanism and Theories of Good City Form." *Cities* 6(4):247–57.

Frank, L.D., et al. 2004. "Obesity Relationships with Community Design, Physical Activity, and Time Spent in Cars." *American Journal of Preventive Medicine* 27 (August): 87–96.

Gagnon, Luc. 2006. "Greenhouse Gas Emissions from Electricity Generation Options." Hydro-Quebec. http://www.hydroquebec.com/sustainable-development/documentation/.

Gateway Program Engineer. 2006. "Gateway Program Technical Memorandum: Final Document." June.

Gin, A., and J. Sonstelie. 1992. "The Streetcar and Residential Location in Nineteenth Century Philadelphia." *Journal of Urban Economics* 32:92–107.

Girling, C., and R. Kellett. 2005. *Skinny Streets and Green Neighbourhoods: Design for Environment and Community*. Washington, DC: Island Press.

Glassie, H. 2000. *Vernacular Architecture*. Bloomington: Indiana University Press.

Globe and Mail. 2007. "Canadian Cities New Collapse, Federation Says." CTVglobemedia Publishing. November 20, 2007.

Goldberg, M., and J. Mercer. 1980. "Canadian and US Cities: Basic Differences, Possible Explanations and Their Meaning for Public Policy." *Papers in Regional Science* 45:1. http://www.springerlink.com/content/g0881263235q4807/fulltext.pdf.

Gordon, Peter, Bumsoo Lee, James E. Moore II, and Harry W. Richardson. 2005. "Do Neighbourhood Attributes Affect Commute Times?" School of Policy, Planning and Development, University of Southern California. http://www.metrans.org/research/final/04-13_final_draft.pdf.

Gormick, Greg. 2004. "The Streetcar Renaissance: Its Background and Benefits." A research report for the St. Clair Avenue Transit Improvements Environmental Assessment Study. On Track Consulting. http://www.toronto.ca/wes/techservices/involved/transportation/st_clair_w_transit/pdf/report/streetcar_renaissance.pdf.

Greater Vancouver Regional District. 2002. "2001 Census Bulletin #3: Population by Age." GVRD Policy and Planning Department. http://www.metrovancouver.org/about/publications/Publications/Census2001-PopAge.pdf.

Greater Vancouver Transit Authority (GVTA). 2005. *Greater Vancouver Trip Diary Survey 2004*. Burnaby, British Columbia: GVTA.

Guillette, Anne. 2008. "Low Impact Development Technologies." Washington, DC: National Institute of Building Sciences. http://www.wbdg.org/resources/lidtech.php.

Gurney, Kevin, R., Daniel L. Mendoza, YuYu Zhou, Marc L. Fischer, Chris C. Miller, Sarath Geethakumar, and Stephane De La Rue Du Can. 2009. "High Resolution Fossil Fuel Combustion CO2 Emission Fluxes for the United States." *Environ. Sci. Technol.* Accepted May 23, 2009.

Gurstein, Penny. *Wired to the World, Chained to the Home: Telework in Daily Life*. Vancouver: University of British Columbia Press, 2001.

Haas, Peter M., Carrie Makarewicz, Albert Benedict, and Scott Bernstein. 2009. "Estimating Transportation Costs by Characteristics of Neighborhood and Household." *Transportation Research Record: Journal of the Transportation Research Board* (Transportation Research Board of the National Academies, Washington, DC), no. 207, 62–70.

Hahn, B. 2000. "Power Centres: A New Retail Format in the United States of America." *Journal of Retailing and Consumer Services* 7:223–31.

Haile, Solomon G., Clyde W. Fraisse, Vimala D. Nairr, and PK. Ramanchandran Nair. 2008. "Green-house Gas Mitigation in Forest and Agricultural Lands: Carbon Sequestration." University of Florida, IFAS Extension. http://edis.ifas.ufl.edu/document_ae435.

Handy, S. 1993. "A Cycle of Dependence: Automobiles, Accessibility and the Evolution of the Transportation and Retail Hierarchies." *Berkeley Planning Journal* 8 (1993): 21–43.

Havis, R. N., C. V. Alonso, J. G. King, and R. F. Thurow. 1993. "A Mathematical Model of Salmonid Spawning Habitat." *Water Resources Bulletin* 29(3):435–44.

Heisz, Andrew, and Sebastien Larochell-Cote. 2005. "Trends and Conditions in Census Metropolitan Areas: Work and Commuting in Census Metropolitan Areas, 1996–2001." Statistics Canada. http://www.statcan.gc.ca/pub/89-613-m/2005007/4054722-eng.htm#1.

Hershfield, David M. 1961. "Rainfall Frequency Atlas of the United States for Durations from 30 Minutes to 24 Hours and Return Periods from 1 to 100 Years." Technical Paper 40. U.S. Department of Commerce, Weather Bureau.

Hess, D., and P. Ong. 2002. "Traditional Neighborhoods and Automobile Ownership." *Transportation Research Record* 1805.

Hirschhorn, Joel S. 2000. "Growing Pains: Quality of Life in the New Economy." National Governors' Association Report no. 13467 (June).

Hobbs, Frank, and Nicole Stoops. 2002. *Demographic Trends in the 20th Century*. U.S. Census Bureau, Census 2000 Special Reports, Series CENSR-4. Washington, DC: U.S. Government Printing Office. http://www.census.gov/prod/2002pubs/censr-4.pdf.

Holmes, E. 1958. "Increased Safety: By Design." *Annals of the American Academy of Political and Social Sciences* 320, no. 84.

Hu, P. S. 2004. "Summary of Travel Trends 2001 National Household Travel Survey." U.S. Department of Transportation and Federal Highway Administration.

International Organization of Motor Vehicle Manufacturers (OICA). 2008. "World Motor Vehicle Production by Country: 2007–2008." OICA. http://oica.net/category/production-statistics/.

Jacobs, Jane. 1961. *The Death and Life of Great American Cities: The Failure of Town Planning*. New York: Vintage.

Johnson, D., J. Rogers, and L. Tan. 2001. "A Century of Family Budgets in the United States." *Monthly Labour Review* (May).

Kerstetter, James D. 1999. "Greenhouse Gas Emissions in Washington State: Sources and Trends." Washington State University Cooperative Extension Energy Program for Washington State Community, Trade and Economic Development, Energy, Policy Group. http://www.cted.wa.gov/energy/archive/papers/wa-ghg99.htm.

Kirkby, Gareth. 1997. "Streamkeepers: Restoring Urban Streams in the Heart of Greater Vancouver." *Georgia Straight* (May 29).

Kite, Elizabeth S. 1970. *L'Enfant and Washington 1791–1792*. New York: Arno.

Knaap, G., and Y. Song. 2004. "Measuring Urban Form: Is Portland Winning the War on Sprawl?" *Journal of American Planning Association* 70, no. 2.

Kotkin, Joel. 2008. "Suburbia's Not Dead Yet." Los Angeles Times, July 6, 2008.

Kunkel, Kenneth E., and Karen Andsager. 1999. "Long-term Trends in Extreme Precipitation Events over the Conterminous United States and Canada." *Journal of Climate* 12(8):2515–27.

Kunstler, J. H. 1993. *The Geography of Nowhere: The Rise and Decline of America's Man-made Landscape*. New York: Simon & Schuster.

———. 1996. *Home from Nowhere: Remaking Our Everyday World for the Twenty-first Century*. New York: Simon & Schuster.

———. 2005. *The Long Emergency: Surviving the Converging Catastrophes of the Twenty-first Century*. New York: Atlantic Monthly Press.

Kupfer, Joseph H. 1990. *Autonomy and Social Interaction*. Albany: State University of New York Press.

Le Corbusier, Jeanneret-Gris. 1964. *The Radiant City: Elements of a Doctrine of Urbanism to Be Used as the Basis of Our Machine-age Civilization*. Orig. 1933. New York: Orion Press.

LeBlanc, Robert T., Robert D. Brown, and John E. FitzGibbon. 1997. "Modeling the Effects of Land Use Change on the Water Temperature in Unregulated Urban Streams." *Journal of Environmental Management* 49:445–69.

Ledwith, T. 1996. "The Effects of Buffer Strip Width on Air Temperature and Relative Humidity in a Stream Riparian Zone." Watershed Management Council (Summer). http://watershed.org/news/sum_96/buffer.html.

Leinberger, Christopher. 2008. "The Next Slum?" *Atlantic Monthly* (March). http://www.theatlantic.com/doc/200803/subprime.

Levinson, H. S. 1999. "Street Spacing and Scale." Paper presented at the Urban Street Symposium, Dallas, Texas, June.

Light Rail Now. 2002. "Status of North American Light Rail Projects." http://www.lightrail.com/projects.htm.

Linklater, Andro. 2002. *Measuring America: How an Untamed Wilderness Shaped the United States and Fulfilled the Promise of Democracy*. New York: Walker.

Lipman, J. 2006. "A Heavy Load: The Combined Housing and Transportation Burdens on Working Families." Centre for Housing Policy, Washington, DC (October). http://www.nhc.org/pdf/pub_heavy_load_10_06.pdf.

Litman, T. 2006. *Rail Transit in America: A Comprehensive Evaluation of Benefits*. Victoria Transport Policy Institute. http://vtpi.org/railben.pdf.

Litman, Todd. 2001. "Land Use Impact Costs of Transportation." Victoria Transport Policy Institute.

———. 2008. "Pavement Busters Guide: Why and How to Reduce the Amount of Land Paved for Road and Parking Facilities." Victoria Transport Policy Institute (January).

Lopez, P. 2007. *Housing Facts, Figures and Trends*. Washington, DC: National Association of Home Builders. http://www.tbba.net/publisher/files/fileUpload_details.pdf

Luckett, Kelly. 2009. *Green Roof Construction and Maintenance*. New York: McGraw-Hill.

Lyle, John. 1985. *Design for Human Ecosystems: Landscape, Land Use, and Natural Resources*. New York: Van Nostrand Reinhold.

Lyndon, Henry. 2007. "Rapid Streetcar: Rescaling Design and Cost for More Affordable Light Rail Transit." Light Rail Now. http://www.lightrailnow.org/features/f_lrt_2007-02a.htm.

Main, Douglas. 2007. "Parking Spaces Outnumber Drivers 3-to-1, Drive Pollution and Warming." *Purdue University News* (September 11).

Malone, Dumas. 1948. *Jefferson and His Time*. 6 vols. Boston: Little, Brown.

Marbek Resource Consultants Ltd. 2007. "BC Hydro 2007 Conservation Potential Review: The Potential for Electricity Savings through Technology Switching, 2006–2026."

Marks, H. 1974. *Traffic Circulation Planning for Communities*. Prepared by Gruen Associates, Los Angeles, California, under commission with Motor Vehicle Manufacturers Association Inc.

Mazria, Edward. 2007. "Architects and Climate Change. American Institute of Architects AIA." http://www.aia.org/aiaucmp/groups/aia/documents/pdf/aias078740.pdf.

McGuekin, Nancy A. and Nanda Srinivasan. 2003. Journey to work in the United States and its major—1960–2000. Washington: U.S. Department of Transportation, Federal Highway Administration.

McHarg, Ian. *Design with Nature*. New York: Wiley, 1992.

McIntyre, Linda. 2008. "Treeconomics: Greg McPherson and the Center for Urban Forest Research Tell Us What a City's Tree Canopy Is Worth. It's More than You Might Think." *Landscape Architecture Magazine* (February).

McPherson, E. G., J. R. Simpson, P. J. Peper, S. E. Maco, S. L. Gardner, K. E. Vargas, S. Cozad, and Q. Xiao. 2005. "City of Minneapolis, Minnesota Municipal Tree Resource Analysis." USDA Forest Service, Pacific Southwest Research, Center for Urban Forest Research.

McPherson, E. G., J. R. Simpson, Q. Xiao, and C. Wu. 2007. *Los Angeles One Million Tree Canopy Cover Assessment—Final Report*. Albany, CA: Pacific Southwest Research Station, U.S. Department of Agriculture Forest Service.

Mehaffy, M. 2001. "Orenco Station, Hillsboro, Oregon. Unsprawl Case Study." Terrain.org, 10. http://www.terrain.org/unsprawl/10/.

Memon, Klimchuk, and LaClaire Scholefield. 2006. "Vancouver Transportation Plan, Progress Report." Prepared for Vancouver City Council.

Meredith, J. R. 2003. "Sprawl and the New Urbanist Solution." *Virginia Law Review* 89:447:447–503. http://www.jstor.org/stable/3202437?seq=8.

Metro. 2007. "Portland–Milwaukee Light Rail Project: Frequently Asked Questions." Metro (Portland, OR). http://www.metro-region.org/files/planning/faq_history.pdf.

Metro Vancouver. 2009. "Regional Growth Strategy: Metro Vancouver 2040." Draft (February). Metro Vancouver.

Meyer, J. L., M. J. Paul, and W. K. Taulbee. 2005. "Stream Ecosystem Function in Urbanizing Landscapes." *Journal of the North American Benthological Society* 24:602–12.

Mezza, Patrick, and Eben Fodor. 2000. "Taking Its Toll: The Hidden Costs of Sprawl in Washington State." Seattle: Climate Solutions.

Miles-Doan, R., and G. Thompson. 1999. "The Planning Profession and Pedestrian Safety: Lessons from Orlando." *Journal of Planning Education and Research* 18(3):211–20.

Milner, Matt. 2007. "How the Interstate System Reshaped Nation." CNHI News Service, Record-Eagle: Northern Michigan's Newspaper, January 7. http://static.record-eagle.com/2007/jan/07interstate.htm.

Ministry of Water, Land and Air Protection (MWLAP). 2002. *Stormwater Planning: A Guidebook for British Columbia*. MWLA, Provincial Government of British Columbia. http://www.env.gov.bc.ca/epd/epdpa/mpp/stormwater/guidebook/pdfs/stormwater.pdf.

National Association of Home Builders. 2007. *Housing Facts, Figures and Trends*.

National Center for Education Statistics (NCES), U.S. Department of Education. 2009. *Digest of Education Statistics, 2008*. NCES 2009-020, ch. 2.

National Highway Traffic Safety Administration (NHTSA), U.S. Department of Transportation. 2008. "National Pedestrian Crash Report." June. http://www-nrd.nhtsa.dot.gov/Pubs/810968.PDF.

National Oceanic and Atmospheric Administration (NOAA). 2004. "Alternatives for Coastal Development." http://www.csc.noaa.gov/alternatives/.

National Transit Database. 1998–2007. "Profiles for Transit Agencies in Urbanized Areas over and under 200,000 Population." http://www.ntdprogram.gov/ntdprogram/data.htm.

Neighborhood Streets Project Stakeholders. 2000. "Neighborhood Street Design Guidelines: An Oregon Guide for Reducing Street Widths." http://www.jtc.sala.ubc.ca/reports/neighstreetwidths.pdf.

Nelson, Arthur C., and Robert Lang. 2007. "The Next 100 Million." American Planning Association (January). http://www.surdna.org/usr_doc/The_Next_100_Million.pdf.

Nelson, Arthur C., Rolf Pendall, Casey J. Dawkins, and Gerrit J. Knapp. 2002. *The Link between Growth Management and Housing Affordability: The Academic Evidence*. Washington, DC: Brookings Institution.

Newman, O. 1972. *Crime Prevention through Urban Design: Defensible Space*. New York: Macmillan.

Norberg-Schulz, Christian. 1980. *Genius Loci: Towards a Phenomenology of Architecture*. New York: Rizzoli.

Norman, Jonathan, Heather L. McLean, and Christopher A. Kennedy. 2006. "Comparing high and Low Residential Density: Life-cycle Analysis of Energy Use and Greenhouse Gas Emissions." *Journal of Urban Planning and Development* (March): 10–21.

Nova Scotia Department of Energy. 2007. "Climate Change: Greenhouse Gas Emissions in Nova Scotia." Government of Nova Scotia.

Office of Energy Efficiency. 2005. "Comprehensive Energy Use Database." National Resources Canada. http://oee.nrcan.gc.ca/corporate/statistics/neud/dpa/comprehensive_tables/index.cfm.

Ohland, G. 2004. "Return of the Trolleys: In Transit, the Old Is New Again." *Journal of the American Planning Association* 70(5):12–13. http://web.ebscohost.com/ehost/pdf?vid=2&hid=106&sid=94168b44-b8f3-4aee-89a1-88b16340e411%40sessionmgr107.

Oregon Coastal Zone Management Association (OCZMA). 2008. *Land Use: Senate Bill 100*. http://www.oczma.org/items.php?category=28&topic=4.

Papas, M. A., A. J. Alberg, R. Ewing, K. J. Helzlsouer, T. L. Gary, and A. C. Klassen. 2007. "The Built Environment and Obesity." *Epidemiological Review* (May 28).

Paul, M. J., and J. L. Meyer. 2001. "Streams in the Urban Landscape." *Annual Review of Ecology and Systematics* 32:333–65.

PCO2R Partnership. 2006. "Plains CO2 Recution Partnership (Phase 1) Final Report/July–September 2005 Quarterly Report." Energy and Environmental Research Center, University of North Dakota. http://www.undeerc.org/PCOR/newsandpubs/pdf/finalreport.pdf.

Person, Mark, Jennifer McIntosh, Victor Bense, and V. H. Remenda. 2007. "Pleistocene Hydrology of North America: The Role of Ice Sheets in Reorganizing Groundwater Flow Systems." *Review of Geophysics* 45.

Phillips, J., and E. Goodstein. 2000. "Growth Management and Housing Prices: The Case of Portland, Oregon." *Contemporary Economic Policy* 18(3):334–44.

Pisarski, Alan. 2006. *Commuting in America III*. Washington, DC: Transportation Research Board.

Pitt, R. 2000. "The Risk of Groundwater Contamination from Infiltration Stormwater Runoff." In *The Practice of Water Protection*, ed. T. R. Schueler and H. K. Holland. Ellicott City, MD: Center for Watershed Protection.

Pluhowski, E. J. 1970. "Urbanization and Its Effect on the Temperature of Streams on Long Island, New York." Geological Survey Professional Paper, 627-D.

PMC Associates. 2002. "Damascus Community Design Workshop: Design Package." Prepared for the Coalition for a Livable Future, 1,000 Friends of Oregon. http://www.jtc.sala.ubc.ca/Damascus/Design%20Package_finalMay16_02.pdf.

Podobnik, Bruce. 2002. "The Social and Environmental Achievements of New Urbanism: Evidence from Orenco Station," Department of Sociology Lewis and Clark College Available online: www.lclark.edu/~podobnik/orenco02.pdf

Polzin, S. E. 2006. *The Case for Moderate Growth in Vehicle Miles of Travel: A Critical Juncture in U.S. Travel Behavior Trends*. Washington, DC: U.S. Department of Transportation, 2006.

Public Purpose. 2000. "Urban Transport Fact Books: US Public Transit New Start Projects: FY 2000 Cost per New Passenger Trip." http://www.publicpurpose.com/ut-2000rail.htm.

———. 2002. "Dallas Transit Down, Car-Pooling, Telecommuting Up: Implications for Urban Transport Policy."

Pucher, John, and John L. Renne. 2003. "Socioeconomics of Urban Travel: Evidence from 2001 NHTS." *Transportation Quarterly* 57(3):49–77.

Pushkarev, B., and Zupan, J. 1977. *Public Transportation and Land Use Policy*. Bloomington: Indiana University Press. http://www.davidpritchard.org/sustrans/PusZup77/index.html.

Putnam, Robert. 2000. *Bowling Alone: The Collapse and Revival of American Community*. New York: Simon & Schuster.

Research and Innovative Technology Administration (RITA), U.S. Department of Transportation. 2009. *National Transportation Statistics 2009*. Washington, DC: RITA.

R.L. Polk and Co. 2007. "US Motor Vehicle Longevity Increases in 2006." http://usa.polk.com/News/NewsArchive/2007/2007_0215_veh_longevity.htm.

Robinson, Ryan. 2006. "Single Family House Size Data: Trends and Existing Conditions for Austin Neighbourhoods." Department of Neighborhood Planning and Zoning, City of Austin (January). http://www.ci.austin.tx.us/zoning/downloads/house_sizes2.pdf.

Rogers, J. David. 1997. Flood Damage: evolving laws and policies for an ever-present risk. Missouri University of Science and Technology.

Rogers, Teri Karush. 2006. "Goodbye, Suburbs." *New York Times*, January 8.

Rowe, Peter. 1991. *Making a Middle Landscape*. Cambridge, MA: MIT Press.

Royal LePage Advisors Inc. 2001. "The GVRD Office Market: Supply Demand and Spatial Distribution." Royal LePage Advisors Inc., Vancouver, BC.

Rudolph, D. C., and J. G. Dickson. 1990. "Streamside Zone Width and Amphibian and Reptile Abundance." *Southwest Journal* 35(4):472–76.

Sadler, Sam. 2007. "Inventory and Forecast of Oregon's Greenhouse Gas Emissions: 2007 Revisions and Update." Oregon Department of Environment. http://www.deq.state.or.us/aq/climate/docs/inventoryReport.pdf.

Schalch, Kathleen. 2008. "Home Prices Drop Most in Areas with Long Commute." *NPR*, April 21.

Schimek, P. 1996. "Automobile and Public Transit Use in the United States and Canada: Comparison of Postwar Trends." *Transportation Research Record* 1521.

Scott, Allen John. 2001. *Global City-regions*. Oxford: Oxford University Press.

Searchinger, Timothy, Ralph Heimlich, R. A. Houghton, Fengxia Dong, Amani Elobeid, Jacinto Fabiosa, Simla Tokgoz, Dermot Hayes, and Tun-Hsiang Yu. 2008. "Use of U.S. Cropland for Bio-Fuels Increases Greenhouse Gases through Emissions from Land-use Change." *Science* 319(5867):1238–40.

Siegel, C. 2006. "The End of Economic Growth." Preservation Institute. http://www.preservenet.com/endgrowth/EndGrowth.pdf (accessed May 7, 2008).

Smith, Hubble. 2003. "Average Lot Size Shrinks." *Las Vegas Review-Journal*, July 12. http://www.reviewjournal.com/search/.

Smith, Mark. 2006. "Plan for North Las Vegas to Point City in New Direction." *View*, May 2. http://www.viewnews.com/2006/VIEW-May-02-Tue-2006/North/7044637.html.

Smithson, Robert. 1979. *Frederick Law Olmsted and the Dialectical Landscape. The Writings of Robert Smithson: Essays with Illustrations*. New York: New York University Press.

Southern Nevada Regional Planning Coalition (SNRPC). 2005. "Montgomery County, Maryland, Overview of Moderately Priced Dwelling Unit Program (MPDU)." http://www.snrpc.org/WorkforceHousing/Development/MontgomeryCounty.pdf.

Southworth, M., and E. Ben-Joseph. 1997. *Streets and the Shaping of Towns and Cities*. Washington, DC: Island Press.

Spackman, S. C., and J. W. Hughes. 1994. "Assessment of Minimum Stream Corridor Width for Biological Conservation: Species Richness and Distribution along Mid-Order Streams in Vermont, USA." *Biological Conservation* 71(3):325–32.

Spadaro, Joseph, V., Lucille Langlois, and Bruce Hamilton. 2000. "Greenhouse Gas Emissions of Electricity Generation Chains: Assessing the Difference." *IAEA Bulletin* (International Atomic Energy Agency) 42, no. 2. IAEA Planning and Economic Studies Section, Department of Nuclear Energy. http://www.iaea.org/Publications/Magazines/Bulletin/Bull422/article4.pdf.

Statistics Canada. 1992. "1992 General Social Survey." Unpublished tabulations.

———. 2001. *A Profile of the Canadian Population: Where We Live*. 2001 Census Analysis Series. Ottawa: Statistics Canada.

———. 2003. *Where Canadians Work and How They Get There*. Census Analysis Series, Catalogue No. 96F0030XIE2001010. Ottawa: Statistics Canada.

———. 2005. "2005 General Social Survey." Unpublished tabulations.

———. 2006. *Commuting Patterns and Places of Work of Canadians, 2006 Census: Portrait of the Largest Census Metropolitan Areas in the Country's Regions*. 2006 Census Analysis Series. Ottawa: Statistics Canada. http://www12.statcan.gc.ca/english/census06/analysis/pow/34_vancouver.cfm

Steinblums, I. J. 1977. "Streamside Buffer Strips: Survival, Effectiveness, and Design." Master's thesis, Oregon State University.

Strickland, James. 2008. "Energy Efficiency of Different Modes of Transportation." http://www.strickland.ca/efficiency.html.

Swift, Peter. 1998. *Residential Street Typology and Injury Accident Frequency*. Longmont, CO: Swift and Associates.

Switzer, Carl. 2003. "The Center Commons." Portland State University research presented at the Rail~volution Conference (http://www.railvolution.com), September 11–14, Atlanta.

Taylor, B. 2000. "When Finance Leads Planning: Urban Planning, Highway Planning, and Metropolitan Freeways in California." *Journal of Planning Education and Research* 20:196–214.

Texas Transportation Institute. 2009. *Urban Mobility Report*. University Transportation Center for Mobility (July). http://tti.tamu.edu/documents/mobility_report_2009_wappx.pdf.

Thomas et al. 1993. *Forest Ecosystem Management: An Ecological, Economic, and Social Assessment*. Report of the Forest Ecosystem Management Assessment Team, Washington, DC.

Toronto Star. 1999. "Streetcars Derailed: Canada Escaped Plot That Scuttled US Transit." *Toronto Star*, June 27.

Translink. 2008. "2008 Transportation and Financial Plan." Greater Vancouver Transportation Authority, Translink (June).

Toronto Transit Commission. 2007. Ridership and cost statistics for bus and streetcar routes, 2006–2007. Toronto Transit Commission.

Turcotte, Martin. 2005. "The Time It Takes to Get to Work and Back." Statistics Canada, General Social Survey on Time Use: Cycle 19, Catalogue no. 89-622-XIE.

———. 2008. "Dependence on Cars in Urban Neighbourhoods." Canadian Social Trends, Statistics Canada.

UBC James Taylor Chair in Landscape and Liveable Environments. 2000. *Technical Bulletin No. 3* (August). http://www.jtc.sala.ubc.ca/bulletbody.html.

U.S. Census Bureau. 2000a. *2000 American Community Survey Data Profile Highlights*. Washington, DC: U.S. Census Bureau.

U.S. Census Bureau. 2000b. "Means of Transportation to Work for Workers 16 Years and Over." Data set: Census 2000 Summary file 3.

U.S. Census Bureau. 2007. 2005–2007 "American Community Survey Report (ACS): Means of Transportation to Work by Selected Characteristics in the United States."

U.S. Census Bureau. 2008. "Selected Social Characteristics in the United States: 2005–2007." American Community Survey.

U.S. Census Bureau. 2009. "Lot Size of New One-family Houses Sold Excluding Condominiums." In

Characteristics of New Housing for 2008, U.S. Census Bureau. http://www.census.gov/const/www/charindex.html.

U.S. Department of Energy (DOE). 2009. *2008 Buildings Energy Data Book*. Washington, DC: DOE. http://buildingsdatabook.eren.doe.gov/.

U.S. Department of Transportation. 2003. *Transportation Statistics Annual Report 2003*. Washington, DC: Bureau of Transportation Statistics, U.S. Department of Transportation.

———. 2008. *Transportation Statistics Annual Report 2008*. Washington, DC: Research and Innovative Technology Administration, U.S. Department of Transportation.

U.S. Department of Transportation. 2009. National Transportation Statistics. Research and Innovation Technology Administration, Bureau of Transportation Statistics. http://www.bts.gov/publications/national_transportation_statistics/

U.S. Environmental Protection Agency (EPA). 2000. *State Greenhouse Gas Inventories*. http://www.epa.gov/climatechange/emissions/state_ghginventories.html.

———. 2003. "Greenhouse Gas Emissions from the US Transportation Sector 1990–2003." *US Greenhouse Gas Inventory Report*. http://www.epa.gov/oms/climate/420r06003.pdf.

———. 2004. "Report to Congress: Impacts and Control of CSOs and SSOs." http://cfpub.epa.gov/npdes/cso/cpolicy_report2004.cfm?.

———. 2005. "Emission Facts: Average Carbon Dioxide Emissions Resulting from Gasoline and Diesel Fuel." EPA420-F-05-001 (February). http://www.epa.gov/oms/climate/420f05001.htm.

U.S. Environmental Protection Agency. 2006. Carbon Sequestration in Agriculture and Forestry. U.S. Environmental Protection Agency.

———. 2007. *Reducing Stormwater Costs through Low Impact Development (LID) Strategies and Practices*. Washington, DC: EPA.

———. 2008. "Inventory of US Greenhouse Gas Emissions and Sinks: 1990–2006." U.S. Greenhouse Gas Inventory Reports (USEPA #430-R-08-005). http://www.epa.gov/climatechange/emissions/usinventoryreport.html.

———. 2009a. "2009 U.S. Greenhouse Gas Inventory Report (1990–2007)." http://epa.gov/climatechange/emissions/usinventoryreport.html (accessed July 20, 2009).

———. 2009b. "National Pollutant Discharge Elimination System." http://cfpub.epa.gov/npdes/home.cfm?program_id=5.

Urbanstreams.org. 2006. "Spanish Banks Creek Vancouver." http://www.urbanstreams.org/creek_spanishbanks.html.

Valdez, Roger. 2009. "Easing off the Gas: Northwesterners Using Less Gasoline." *Sightline Reports* (June 30). http://www.sightline.org/publications/reports/ (accessed August 2009).

Vernez Moudon, Anne, Chanam Lee, Allan D. Cheadle, Cheza Garvin, Donna Johnson, Thomas L. Schmid, Robert D. Weathers, and Lin Lin. 2006. "Operational Definitions of Walkable Neighborhoods: Theoretical and Empirical Insights." *Journal of Physical Activity and Health* 3 (supp. S99-S117).

Vronskii, B. B., and V. N. Leman. 1991. "Spawning Stations, Hydrological Regime and Survival of Progeny in Nests of Chinook Salmon, *Oncorhynchus tshawytscha*, in the Kamchatka River Basin." *Journal of Ichthyology* 31(4):91–102.

Walsh, Christopher J., Allison H. Roy, Jack W. Feminella, Peter D. Cottingham, Peter M. Groffman, and Raymond P. Morgan II. 2005. "The Urban Stream Syndrome: Current Knowledge and the Search for a Cure." *J. N. Am. Benthol. Soc* 24(3):706–23. http://www.bioone.org/doi/pdf/10.1899/04-028.1.

Wang, Michael, May Wu, and Hong Huo. 2007. "Life-cycle Energy and Greenhouse Gas Emission Impacts of Different Corn Ethanol Plant Types." *Environmental Research Letters* 2, 024001.

Ward, A. D., S. W. Trimble, and M. G. Wolman. 2004. *Environmental Hydrology.* Boca Raton, FL: CRC Press.

Warner, Sam Bass. 1962. *Streetcar Suburbs: The Process of Growth in Boston, 1870–1900.* Cambridge, MA: Harvard University Press.

Watson, Donald, Alan Plattus, and Robert Shibley. 2003. *Time-saver Standards for Urban Design.* New York: McGraw-Hill.

West Coast Environmental Law. 2002. "Cutting Green Tape: An Action Plan for Removing Regulatory Barriers to Green Innovations." http://www.wcel.org/wcelpub/2002/13724.pdf.

Weyrich, P. M., and W. S. Lind. 2002. *Bring Back the Streetcars!* Prepared by the Free Congress Research and Education Foundation. http://www.apta.com/research/info/online/weyrich.cfm#wdi.

Williamson, S. C., J. M. Bartholow, and C. B. Stalnaker. 1993. "Conceptual Model for Quantifying Presmolt Production from Flow-dependent Physical Habitat and Water Temperature." *Regulated Rivers: Research and Management* 8:15–28.

Wilson, A., and J. Boehland. 2005. "Small Is Beautiful, U.S House Size, Resource Use, and the Environment." *Journal of Industrial Ecology* 9(1–2):277–87.

Winkelman, Steve, Allison Bishins, and Chuck Kooshian. 2009. "Cost-effective GHG Reductions through Smart Growth and Improved Transportation Choices: An Economic Case for Investment of Cap-and-trade Revenues." Center for Clean Air Policy, Transportation and Climate Change Program (June). http://www.ccap.org/.

World Business Council for Sustainable Development. 2002. "The Cement Sustainability Initiative: Our Agenda for Action." July.

Worrel, E., L. Price, N. Martin, C. Hendriks, and L. Ozawa Meida. 2001. "Carbon Dioxide Emissions from the Global Cement Industry." *Annual Review of Energy and the Environment* 26:303–29.

Xiao, Qingfu, E. Gregory McPherson, James R. Simpson, and Susan L. Ustin.1998. "Rainfall Interception by Sacramento's Urban Forest." *Journal of Arboriculture* 24(4):235–43.

Yancey, W. L. 1971. "Architecture, Interaction and Social Control: The Case of a Large-scale Public Housing Project." *Environment and Behavior* 3:3–21.

Yee, Dennis. 2009. "20 and 50 Year Regional Population and Employment Range Forecasts." April 2009 draft. Metro, Research Center. http://library.oregonmetro.gov/files/2030-2060_forecast_april_09.pdf.

Index

Page numbers with "f" refer to photos and illustrations, those with "t" refer to tables.

A

Agricultural land, 11n26, 21f, 46, 119n6
Alabama. *See* Birmingham
Alberta. *See* Calgary; Edmonton
Alleys. *See* Rear lanes and alleys
Amble Greene community, Surrey, BC, 155–57, 155f
American Disabilities Act, 148
Aquifer, 132, 132n5, 135f
Arctic Circle, 1, 1f
Arizona. *See* Phoenix
Arkansas. *See* Little Rock
Arterials. *See* Streets, arterials
Ashburn, VA, 13n30
Asia, 89n11
Asphalt, pervious, 150, 151f, 152f, 159f. *See also* Pavement, pervious
Atlanta, GA, 7f, 9f, 42n6, 44f, 62n2, 90, 90n16
Austin, TX, 99n9
Automobiles. *See* Car dependence; Car manufacturing; Cars

B

Barrels. *See* Cisterns, rainwater catchment
Bias. *See* Psychology, overcoming habitual behavior
Bicycling, 20n4, 42n6, 50, 122, 125
Biomass facilities, 96n2
Birmingham, AL, 42n6
Blocks
    building configuration within, 50f, 91, 100, 100f
    definition, 48
    gross density, 51 (*See also* Housing, density)
    jobs can fit into, 91

mixed use, 97
    size, 48–54, 50f, 51f
    super blocks, 41f, 48–49, 49f, 50, 73
Boise, ID, 76f
Boston, MA
    Beacon Hill, 23, 23n8
    Boston Common, 22
    Emerald Necklace, 112, 113–14, 114f, 115f, 120–21
    fire response and street width, 57, 57n10, 58f
    five-corner intersections, 70
    Green Line, 32
    home price and household income, 5–6, 5n14
    informal web street pattern, 47
    town houses, 23f
    urban sprawl and suburbs, 3, 5–6, 6f
    walking access vs. streetcar access, 24f
British Columbia. *See* Burnaby; Coquitlam; Delta; Kelowna; Langley; North Vancouver; Pacific Northwest; Richmond; Surrey
Broadview Green Grid Program, 158–59
Brockton, MA, 82, 83–84, 83f, 84n9
Brownfields, 91
Buildings. *See also* Landscaping
    architectural character, 103, 103f, 105
    configuration within block, 50f, 91, 100, 100f
    footprint, 52, 76, 135f, 141n20, 145
    four-story or five-story, 19–20, 19f, 23
    friendly face to the street, 103, 103f, 107–10 (*See also* "Snout houses")
    GHG emissions, 95–96, 95f, 95n1, 97–101
    job-site, size, 88–89, 91
    point towers, 52, 98, 99, 103
    residential (*See* Housing)
    setback, 42n5, 133n7, 147
Burnaby, BC, 28n12, 139f

Commute. *See also* Traffic flow
  carpooling, 63, 69n2
  distance, 3, 3nn6–7, 13n30, 79
  mode of transportation used, 62n2, 73n6
  sustainability and, 29
  time, 3n7, 12n29, 23, 23n6, 29–30, 79, 83
Comprehensive Permit Law (Chapter 40B law), 84,
    85, 103, 110
Concrete/cement, 10–11n25, 32, 148–49, 150, 151f
Conduction, heat, 98n6
Congestion. *See* Traffic flow, congestion
Convection, heat, 98n6
Conversion. *See* Retrofitting
Coquitlam, BC, 28n12, 74
Corn, 11, 11n26
Costs
  bus system, 33, 37f, 38f
  energy, savings due to trees, 101, 101n13
  food, 11n26
  green stormwater management, 147n28, 155n32,
    158, 159
  housing, 4–5, 5nn12–13, 106t
  infrastructure, 4–5, 129n1, 130n2–4, 131, 160
  neck down intersection, 60
  pervious pavement, 151, 154–55
  property, 5, 36
  rail system, 32, 33, 33n17, 37f, 38f
  rear lanes and alleys, 61
  subdivision development, 4–5, 5n12, 15, 18–19,
    129n1, 130n3
  transit, 33n17, 36–37, 36n25, 37f, 38f
Council of Educational Facility Planners Intl.
    (CEFPI), 76, 77
Crime, 61, 108, 108f, 108n19
Cul-de-sacs and dead ends, 39, 40, 40n2, 45, 45f, 56,
    57f, 75
Culver City, CA, 101n14

D

Dallas, TX, 80, 81f
Damascus Area Design Workshop, 87–88, 89, 91, 91f,
    119–25, 121f
Dayton, OH, 20
Dead ends. *See* Cul-de-sacs and dead ends
Delta, BC, 69n2
Demographia, 81

Demographics. *See* Population demographics
Dendritic street system
  big box retailers are favored, 43–44, 43n7, 92f
  car-dependent, 40f, 42–43, 42n6, 100f
  cul-de-sacs and dead-ends, 39, 40, 40n2, 45, 45f, 56,
    57f, 75
  entrenchment as status quo, 41–42, 64
  fire access, 57
  gated communities, 44–45, 44f, 49
  percent of urban landscape, 63
  prone to congestion, 40, 42, 44
  transit wait time and transfers, 73
Denver, CO, 29, 110n23, 118
Design Centre for Sustainability, 35, 36n24, 41, 64n15
Detroit, MI, 7, 7f, 7n17, 12
Developers. *See* Real estate developers
Disabilities, 42n6, 76, 148, 151
Discrimination. *See* Zoning policy, segregation by
    class and income
Doughnut hole effect, 7n17, 130f
Driveways, 52, 53, 61, 61f, 109, 149n30, 158f. *See also*
    Rear lanes and alleys
Dry well, 149n30

E

Earth Day, 116
East Clayton community, Surrey, BC, 110n23, 148,
    148n29, 157–58, 158f
Ecological considerations
  capitalist ecology, 82
  city as an ecosystem, 117
  ecological footprint, 67, 127
  ecological overshoot, 67
  economic ecology, 105
  forest, 112n1
  natural areas, 124, 127
  parkways, 124
  streams, 112, 113–14, 116, 127, 137t
  trees and plants, 101n13, 131–32, 132f, 141–42,
    142n21
Ecological design, 111–12, 131
Economics. *See also* Costs
  capitalist ecology, 82
  car dependence, 9–10, 36
  economic ecology, 105
  economy of scale, 130n2

growth control, 4, 4n10, 5n13, 119, 120

increase in building size with, 88–89

Levittown, 4f

Traditional Circular Model of Sprawl, 130n4

U.S. Department of Housing and Urban Development, 86

U.S. Department of Transportation, 86

U.S. Environmental Protection Agency, 86, 153n31, 155n32

U.S. Federal Housing Administration, 40n2

U.S. Fish and Wildlife Service, 134

U.S. Senate hearings, 1–2

Utilities. *See also* Stormwater drainage system

  cost with subdivisions, 4–5, 5n12, 15, 129n1, 130n3

  greener strategies, 129n1

V

Vancouver, BC. *See also* North Vancouver, BC

  block size, 50–51, 50f, 51f, 52, 53, 53f

  car ownership and usage, 69, 69n2

  city densification, 7, 12–13, 13f, 18–20, 74, 98, 103

  commute time decrease, 12, 12n29

  historical background, 18–20, 18f, 19f, 31f

  housing, 64n15, 98, 99, 103–5, 103f, 104f

  job distribution in metro area, 28n12, 80n5

  Kitsilano District, 18, 18f, 19f, 22f, 61f, 76 (*See also* Fourth Avenue under this heading)

  Livable Region Strategic Plan, 25–28, 27f, 69n2, 93

  nodes and city planning, 25–28

  parking, 149

  salmon habitat loss, 135n11

  schools, 76, 77f

  as a streetcar city, 20, 31f

  streets and arterials

    bike streets, 50

    Broadway corridor, 34–35, 43

    Davey Street, 22

    Denman Street, 22

    Fourth Avenue, 18, 18f, 19f, 69f, 69n3

    Granville Street, 18f, 22

    green design, 157, 157f, 159, 159f

    gridiron street system, 40f, 46f

    rear lanes, 61, 159f

    re-use of historic streetcar lines, 31f

    Robson Street, 22

    Trutch Street, 157, 157f

  transit, 3n5, 72 (*See also* Skytrain)

Vaux, Calvert, 48

Vehicle-miles traveled (VMT)

  decrease, 8, 29, 90n16

  increase, 3, 5, 8, 8n18, 20n4, 79

  town houses and, 23n7

Verge, 144, 150, 155–57, 155f, 159, 159f

Villebois community, Wilsonville, OR, 118

VMT. *See* Vehicle-miles traveled

W

Walking. *See also* Trails and paths

  fatalities, 42n6, 54

  health effects due to decline in, 9, 9n21

  lack of infrastructure, 8, 9n20

  pedestrian safety (See Safety issues, pedestrians)

  pedestrian shed or catchment area, 68n1, 77f

  to and from school, 4, 14, 60, 75–77, 77f

  services within a five-minute walk

    commercial (See Commercial services, within a five-minute walk)

    neighborhood housing pattern, 100–101, 101n16

    overview, 14, 49, 64, 67–69, 67f, 77–78

    sense of place, 70–71, 71f

    as a threshold, 68, 68n1, 69

    transit (See Transit, within a five-minute walk)

  in streetcar districts, 36

  and urban form, 20n4, 22–24

Walkways, 148–49. *See also* Trails and paths

Washington, 96, 96n2. *See also* Olympia; Pacific Northwest; Seattle

Washington, DC, 13n30, 21n5, 47, 47f

Washington, Pres. George, 21n5

Wastewater treatment. See Water treatment

Water

  black, 138

  drinking, 153, 155f

  flood conditions

    effects on streams and fish, 133–35, 134n9, 136f, 136n14

    one-hundred-year storm, 5n12, 138, 142, 149n30, 156, 158

    time lag to peak stream flow, 137f

  flow within property, 147, 148–49, 149f, 149n30, 152–53

  footprint, 127–28

  groundwater, 132, 132n5, 133, 134, 134n9, 135f

  Horton overland flow, 136n13